The
Gunpowder
Gardens

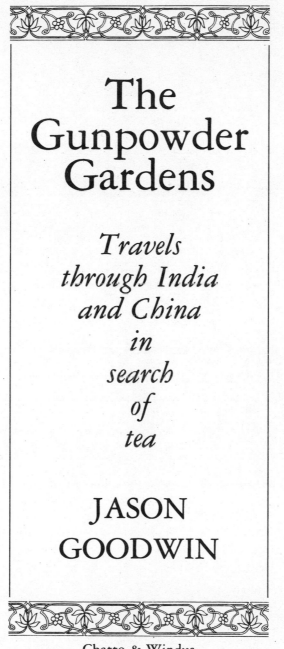

The Gunpowder Gardens

Travels through India and China in search of tea

JASON GOODWIN

Chatto & Windus
LONDON

Published in 1990 by
Chatto & Windus Limited
20 Vauxhall Bridge Road
London SW1 2SA

A CIP catalogue record of this book is
available from the British Library

ISBN 0 7011 3620 0

Photoset by Rowland Phototypesetting Limited
Bury St Edmunds, Suffolk

Printed in Great Britain by
Mackays of Chatham PLC,
Chatham, Kent

I'd like to thank Caroline Courtauld, Caroline Dawnay,
Richard Goodwin, Charles Powell, Frank Spufford,
Stewart Walton and Shane Watson; *The Spectator* and British
Airways; in China I received help from people who must
go unnamed because of the political situation, as well as from
Françoise, Tom, Mark and Ann, the history faculty at
Fuzhou University, and Peter Sutch; in India there are too
many people to name them all here but I should mention
Eleanor and Arjun Chaudhuri, Danny and Pussy Mahtab ,
Armajeet Singh, Micky Chinnoy and Duncans Ltd, Bobby
and Raj Grewal, Navim Huria.
Chinese names are given in the form most likely to be
recognised, which is not necessarily Pinyin.

for Kate

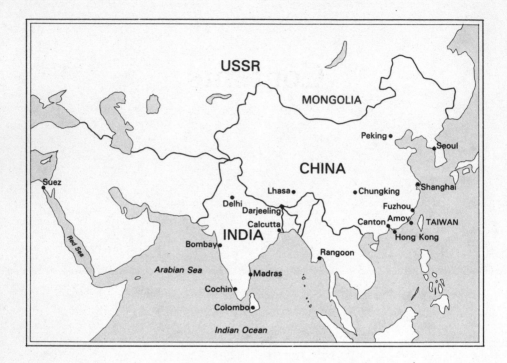

Contents

*The progress of this famous plant has been
something like the progress of truth: suspected
at first, though very palatable to those who had
courage to taste it; resisted as it encroached; abused
as its popularity seemed to spread; and
establishing its triumph at last, in cheering
the whole land from the palace to the cottage,
only by the slow and resistless effects of time and
its own virtues.*
Edinburgh Review 1828

*Thank God for tea! What would the world do
without tea? How did it exist? I am glad I
was not born before tea!*
Sydney Smith

*Who says that tu is bitter? It is as sweet as the
shepherd's purse.*
Confucius, 600 BC

Introduction

In Chinese legend it is said that when the Worm of Chaos was defeated (a hideous slimy thing that emerged from the Egg of Creation), peace reigned for many centuries and Man learned most of his useful ways from the Three Emperors. 'Cha' was revealed to the Second Emperor, Shen Nung, Divine Healer, who discovered millet and the curative herbs, the manufacture of the first plough, and tea, which he came upon in 2737 BC. Until then his people drank boiled water with the taste of flat irons, unwillingly. He brought them *cha*, tea, picked and dried on the third day of the third month. Just as his father's gifts of fire and husbandry were more essential than his own, so his gift of *cha*, in Chinese eyes, ranks above those of his son – the vine, astronomy.

Shen Nung, an emperor with the head of an ox and the body of a man, died at the end of his 120-year reign from eating a poisonous herb.

But today in China you may be offered *cha* by the very poor, and it is only boiled water, hot, with the taste of flat irons.

Tea was certainly known and drunk in the era of the Three Kingdoms (AD 222–7). Picked first in the wild, by the third century AD tea was being cultivated in the southwestern province of Szechwan; as today, every farmer probably had his patch of tea, and the habit – sanctioned by doctors, who claimed, among other things, that tea was a cure for poor eyesight, and by Taoist priests, who used it as an ingredient in their elixir of immortality – spread through the crescent of southern China, and was known to connoisseurs in the north. It was under the Tang Dynasty, however, that tea-drinking became an art. In the eighth century AD the tea merchants commissioned a book on tea, history's first commercial puff. The man they chose to write it was Lu Yu, a foundling, who had run away from a monastery to become a popular conjurer and acrobat. He devoured the works of Confucius and Lao-tzu, the Five Books regarded as the storehouse of Chinese wisdom, and before long he produced his commissioned work, the Cha Ching – the Tea Classic. It became, in his lifetime, part of the canon of Chinese literature and learning; the Emperor sought his friendship, disciples flocked to hear him. In 775 Lu Yu became a hermit; twenty-nine years later, he died.

He had written:

The best quality tea must have creases like the leathern boot of Tartar horsemen, curl like the dewlap of a mighty bullock, unfold like a mist rising out of a ravine, gleam like a lake touched by a zephyr, and be wet and soft like fine earth newly swept by rain . . .

There is ordinary and ground tea. What is called cake tea is put in a bottle or jar after being pounded, and the boiling water is poured over it. Sometimes onion, ginger, jujube, orange peel and peppermint are used, and it is left to boil for some time before the froth is skimmed. Alas! this is the slop-water of a ditch.

'Cha' was soon to be taken into the Himalayas over the passes between China and Tibet, and along the northern caravan routes, particularly the famous Silk Road through Mongolia and Turkestan. Nomads on the Chinese borders developed such a craving for *cha* that it became a useful weapon in China's diplomatic armoury, more efficient than the Great Wall. The quality of the tea the nomads received was atrocious – but as they prepared it like the slop-water of a ditch it probably made no difference. It was brick tea, made of compressed coarse leaves, twigs, adulterants and what not (in a diet that consisted mainly of meat and milk it supplied the want of green vegetables), and Tibetans churned it – as they still do – with sour yak milk, butter, salt and spice to make a nourishing tea soup. A Captain Turner drank it in Tibet in the eighteenth century: 'We found this liquor extremely unlike what we had been used to drink under the same name,' he wrote; 'it was a compound of water, flour, butter, salt, and Bohea tea, with some other astringent ingredients, all boiled, beat up, and intimately blended together. I confess the mixture was by no means to my taste . . .'

Later he changed his mind: 'Habit had not only rendered this composition agreeable to our tastes, but I was never more disposed to praise the comfortable practice of the country, having constantly observed that the first object of attention with every man at the end of a long journey is to procure himself a dish of hot tea.' The name of the drink beyond the borders of the Empire was '*chai*' in Tartar Russia and in India, '*cha*' in Afghanistan and Persia, '*cha*' throughout the Arab world, where centuries later Tommy Atkins – always scavenging for argot – picked up the word and took it home.

While the Tang dynasty had boiled tea, transported as a cake, the Sung adopted whipped tea, shaved from a hard tablet of compressed powder. Their tastes were, naturally, a great deal more refined than those of the outer barbarians. Special teas were plucked in imperial enclosures in southern China, and sent north as tribute to the emperor. Reverence for the tea arts was so great that generals were known to seek their reward in this fine tea rather than in land.

The importance of tea reached its zenith under the Sung Emperor Kiasung (1101–24), who was a great failure as an emperor but an important patron of the tea industry. He held tournaments at which courtly exquisites vied to identify different types of tea, a practice that remained common in China and Japan for centuries. Kiasung had 3912 beautiful women in his palace, but he succumbed to the charms of the famous courtesan Li Shi Shi, causing great scandal by settling a non-virgin in the palace. A while later he turned his palace into a department store and staffed it with his harem. His devotion to these amusing reforms, along with the heavy task of writing a *Treatise on Tea*, which turned out admirably, left him little time to administer his empire, and one day he and his son were surprised in the very grounds of the palace by a Tartar raiding party. He was to be given every opportunity to examine the leathern boot of a Tartar horseman, for the mounted riders took him off to their barren lands beyond the Great Wall. He died there in exile nine years later, far from good tea, leaving a sad poem. Seven hundred years earlier, in 317 AD, in a letter to his nephew, a Chinese general on a border campaign had been sad without resorting to poetry: 'A catty of dried ginger, a catty of the yellow medicinal root and a catty of cinnamon, which I have received, are the necessary things to me. Now I feel aged and depressed and want some real tea. Send it on.'

Tea-drinking arrived in Japan with Buddhist monks, generally from Korea. According to Zen myth Boddhidharma, who brought the faith from India to China in the fifth century AD, grew sleepy towards the end of a seven-year vigil. Angrily he plucked off his eyelids and threw them to the ground, whereupon two bushes sprang up whose leaves possessed the power to ward off sleep. (The same story is told of the origin of the poppy. Only much later do the stories of tea and opium intertwine.)

In his *Book of Tea* (1906) the Japanese aesthete Okakura Kakuzo describes the periods and schools of Chinese tea:

The Cake-tea which was boiled, the Powdered tea which was whipped, and the Leaf tea which was steeped, mark the distinct emotional impulses of the Tang, the Sung, and the Ming dynasties of China. If we were to borrow the much-abused terminology of art-classification, we might designate them respectively, the Classic, the Romantic, and the Naturalistic schools of Tea.

Tea drinking was in its 'romantic' phase – whipped into a green froth after the Sung practice – when Japan ended her inspiriting contact with the outside world. From 1281 until Commander Perry arrived in 1856, the island paid next to no attention to world events, and took no part in them. Developing in seclusion, Japan produced – or preserved – the elaborate ritual of *cha no yu*, the tea ceremony.

Okakura-Kakuzo describes a famous performance of the *cha no yu* by Rikiu, a great tea master, who was accused of plotting to kill a despot and sentenced to die by his own hand:

On the day destined for his self-immolation, Rikiu invited his chief disciples to a last tea ceremony. Mournfully at the appointed time the guests met at the portico. As they look into the garden path the trees seem to shudder, and in the rustling of their leaves are heard the whispers of homeless ghosts. Like solemn sentinels before the gates of Hades stand the grey stone lanterns. A wave of rare incense is wafted from the tea-room; it is the summons which bids the guests to enter. One by one they advance and take their places. In the *tokonoma* hangs a *kakemono* – a wonderful writing by an ancient monk dealing with the evanescence of all earthly things. The singing kettle, as it boils over the brazier, sounds like some cicada pouring forth his woes to departing summer. Soon the host enters the room. Each in turn is served with tea, and each in turn silently drains his cup, the host last of all. According to established etiquette, the chief guest now asks permission to examine the tea-equipage. Rikiu places the various articles before them, with the *kakemono*. After all have expressed admiration of their

4

beauty, Rikiu presents one of them to each of the assembled company as a souvenir. The bowl alone he keeps. 'Never again shall this cup, polluted by the lips of misfortune, be used by man.' He speaks, and breaks the cup into fragments.

The ceremony is over; the guests, with difficulty restraining their tears, take their last farewell and leave the room. One only, the nearest and dearest, is requested to remain and witness the end. Rikiu then removes his tea-gown and carefully folds it upon the mat, thereby disclosing the immaculate white death robe which it had hitherto concealed. Tenderly he gazes on the shining blade of the fatal dagger, and in exquisite verse addresses it:

> Welcome to thee,
> O sword of eternity!
> Through Buddha
> And through Dharuma alike
> Thou hast cleft thy way.

With a smile upon his face Rikiu passed forth into the unknown.

In China the Sung collapsed in 1280, and after a brief interregnum in which the provinces of China sought to go their separate ways and the empire was ruled by Mongol lords (Marco Polo visited Genghis Khan at this time), the Ming succeeded to the Dragon Throne.

The Ming struggled to rebind the nation and to revive the glories of the Sung imperial past, but Sung culture had all but disappeared. A Ming commentator is at a loss to recall the shape of the tea-whisk mentioned in one of the Sung classics. They took to steeping tea-leaves in water, as we do now. The change is reflected in the ceramic style of the Ming; the Sung admired blue-black and dark brown glazes which set off the depth of whisked tea, but the pale infused liquid of the Ming required a light background, and a white, or off-white, ceramic emerged that became the hallmark of Ming pottery.

It was the dying dynasty of the Mings, the tea-steepers, that received the first sea-traders to come at China from the West.

1

Hong Kong

Of course I had two grandmothers, but I never saw them meet. I never tried to find out why not: children don't assume that people of about the same age are bound to hit it off. Perhaps they met at the wedding and decided right there to become sparring partners, with the oblique venom of old ladies conserving energy. At any rate, they weren't friends.

At the age of four I was sent to live with Granny Goodwin. She lived in a cottage with a splendid garden planned to change with the seasons, a garden with lawns and dewy roses that had been dreamt about for a long time. There were ivory elephants in the cottage, sandalwood boxes, deep mahogany furniture (the mahogany, she said, felled under a full moon to keep it truly dark); there was a folding table inlaid with an ivory fat man riding on an elephant; I despised the table because it was too frail to set upright. There were silver trophies for polo and yachting, and a bronze Shiva which had breasts and didn't fudge the interesting question of how his many arms emerged from his body.

My grandfather appeared all over the cottage – scrawled inside fly-leaves, etched on all the trophies, faintly pencilled on yellowing delivery notes gummed to the rough underside of polished desks. Fairly often he appeared with a trill of pride on my granny's lips. I knew a little about him. His father had put his fortune into carriage building at the turn of the century and saw no future in the motor car until he was overtaken by one during the Great War; before long my grandfather had to abandon hopes of becoming a classics don and enter trade, first in London, later in Bombay. There he arranged for his bride to follow, travelling P & O alone. They stayed on for a while after Independence, but his health was already poor and in the 1950s they came home. She had appreciated having servants, and she loved the smell of India.

Granny Eileen's house, on the other hand, was distinguished by a trapped smell of lino, miry wellingtons, and damp. From an English family in the Argentine she had come to Cambridge, where she met Paul – Celtic and superbly dashing. He took a job with Standard Oil and his first tour, in China, had to be unaccompanied; for five years they wrote to each other every day, preparing for a reunion, and marriage. In Paris they met again, but the conventional romance of the city stilted them, and the meeting was not a success; they decided to break off the engagement. They met again at the offices of *The Times* to make the announcement. In these rather more prosaic surroundings, among people who didn't care a hoot either way, they felt much better, and, married after all, they sailed for Amoy.

They lived as well-paid members of the fast set, riding to cocktails in huge American cars. Then she had children and began to learn Chinese while he grew appalled at the corruption he found at work and took to arguing with the managers. After the War he took a posting Home; but he was marked and remembered, and he finally quit. He started a pig farm.

When Paul died Eileen sorted out the house, rummaging through silk brocades, scrolls and jade carvings, giving things away. Among her keepings was a tea-caddy of old-fashioned design – a lidded box containing two glass jars and a spoon, identical to one belonging to Granny Goodwin, though hers was of sandalwood rather than black lacquer. Both women had possessed them for years, instruments of a ritual they conducted at the same hour of the day every day of their lives in far-flung corners of the globe. But Granny Goodwin's caddy always held Assam and Darjeeling, and Granny Eileen's Keemun and Lapsang Souchong.

Out of the memsahib memories and the paraphernalia of Empire I developed a persona for myself called Captain Hawkeye who liked to swing in trees and peer keenly towards the horizon wearing an old riding hat. Captain Hawkeye had a pretty dashing time until I was prescribed spectacles. He owed a lot to a cherished line of English traders and pirates like Sir Francis Drake and Captain Blood which was carried on, I confusedly felt, by Sir Francis Chichester – not realising that Chichester's circumnavigation of the globe was really the last word on the decline of flag-planting, privateering, trading Englishmen. Chichester hadn't sailed for gain; he did not belong to the romance of trade and discovery. Somewhere the romance had split in two. Trade, after all, is pretty humdrum in an age of business trips and container ships.

With this exception, perhaps. The tea trade deals in a luxury that depends, as ever, on a particular constellation of natural conditions and human skill, where the markets have altered little over centuries, shaping their own traditions. Here and there the trade has left its mark, a scattered trail across the atlases and the history books. Those two imperial ladies with their caddies had kept history lingering a little: and it was a trail I wanted to explore.

By the 16th century, devoted to the arts of trade and gain, Venice was in her wily dotage. For centuries her position on the trading routes overland from Arabia, India and the Extreme Orient had allowed her to dominate Europe's supply of Eastern commodities like spice and silk. But as young Atlantic nations began to feel their way to the East around the Cape, the Venetians were left to search anxiously for opportunities missed in the high old days, like prospectors sifting carelessly discarded slag for gold.

Giambattista Ramusio, secretary to Venice's governing Council of Ten, gathered hard information and suggestive rumour which was published in his *Navigatione e Viaggi* of 1559. In it he transcribed the report of Hajji Mahommed, a Persian traveller, who had learned of a common Chinese drink. 'One or two cups of this decoction removes fever, headache, stomach-ache, pain in the side or in the joints, and it should be taken as hot as you can bear it. He said besides that it was good for no end of other ailments which he could not remember, but gout was one of them.' If the first mention of tea in Europe was Venetian commercial intelligence, it came too late to help Venice.

The second mention came in a letter written by a Jesuit Father, Gaspar da Cruz, the first European Christian missionary in China. The date was 1560. Da Cruz was Portuguese.

The rise of the Portuguese, who had discovered the Cape route to the Indies, was already beginning to cloud the greatness of Venice with the publication there in 1589 of Giovanni Botero's work *On the Causes of Greatness in Cities*. Botero considered the health and character of an urban population, and wrote: 'The Chinese have an herb from which they press

9

a delicate juice which serves them instead of wine. It also preserves the health and frees them from all the evils that the immoderate use of wine doth breed in us.' Venice herself would never make a trade in tea; but all her Atlantic rivals – Lisbon, Amsterdam, London – would become tea cities in their turn.

A British prize ship, late of the Portuguese East Indian Fleet, astounded Dartmouth Harbour in the summer of 1593: a leviathan with a mast 121 feet high, 600 (imprisoned) crew, 32 brass guns; and a displacement, as calculated, of 1600 tons. Her cargo was accounted for in the supercargo's ledger, with dates and prices entered for each transaction – and needed to be anchored to the ledger's meticulous script, too, for it could boggle the imagination, lying priceless in an English port: bales of silk and bushels of spice, drugs, ivory, carpets and calicoes, camphor, jewels and hides; lacquerware and painted fans; quicksilver for the alchemist, vermilion for the dyer, copper, porcelain and sugar candy. As it was the rumours burst and in the City the hum of a new El Dorado trembled like coming thunder.

A monopoly was formed under royal charter by some 250 shareholders, merchants of London. It was an East India Company with capital to raise a fleet of four ships and send out £27,000 in bullion. The leading ships rounded the Capa Bon Esperanza in the winter of 1601 with a brief to buy at their discretion. The Dutch already had a small settlement in Sumatra, and they helped the English gather a cargo of pepper which sold in London at a 95 per cent profit. Capital was subscribed for further voyages, and on the fourth, in 1608, a young man called Richard Wickham shipped as a factor, a trading agent appointed to work from one of the Dutch or Portuguese 'factories' in the East where local rulers permitted foreigners to settle and trade. On a landing party in Zanzibar Wickham was captured by natives and trussed up on the white beach, ready for sale. He was bought by a Portuguese merchant heading for Portugal's factory at Goa on the Malabar Coast, and a year later released with other prisoners in Portugal. He made his way back to England in time to be engaged on the East India Company's eighth voyage.

This time he was left with Richard Cocks at the Anglo-Dutch factory in Japan. Cocks was trying to get round the Portuguese monopoly on trade with China conducted from Macao, and to open dealings with the Japanese. Neither enterprise was enjoying much success. English factors of the East India Company now resided in Macao, Goa, and at Bantam in Java; they corresponded with one another on trade, cuckoldry, slave girls, food. Wickham's letters are preserved in the India Office Library in Southwark, in a strange seahorse hand that meanders across the parchment. And in 1615 Wickham wrote to the Macao factor: 'Mr Eaton I pray you buy for me a pot of the best sort of chaw in Meaco, 2 Fairebowes and Arrows, some half a dozen Meaco guilt boxes square for to put into bark and whatever they cost you I will alsoe be willinge accoumptable unto for them.'

Chaw: fate had plotted a tortuous route to the first recorded reference by an Englishman to tea, but it started a considerable hare.

George III, who bungled in Boston over a matter of tea, wrote a letter in 1792 to the Emperor of China asking for a more open trade and diplomatic relations.

The British merchants in Canton gave advice on how it should be delivered: they weren't paying the postage. The letter was carried to the Summer Palace by an Irish peer, Lord Macartney; also a Secretary, Sir George Staunton, with his son Tom as page, and two under-secretaries, as well as two interpreters, two artists, a botanist, a metallurgist, an experimental scientist, a surgeon, a physician-cum-natural philosopher, a watchmaker, a mathematical instrument maker, a German band, a military escort and twenty artillerymen with six brass cannon.

There is still something fantastic in sending a letter to China. The pillarbox grins and days pass. It will need translating, of course. Weeks pass. The letter has not gone straight to Mr Wu but will have been passed upwards, from the lowest clerk, through ever-widening circles of competence – perhaps past Mr Wu himself to the very *taotai* of tea, a Minister in Peking, who will receive both the letter and a suggested course of action for his approval. There is no Emperor to scrawl his marginal comments in vermilion pencil – Tremble and Obey – but the principle must be much the same. These things naturally take time. A month, then two months disappear while the letter writer gloomily recasts himself in the proper role of humble petitioner, drinks tea and watches the English rain.

And then one day the flimsiest of flimsy airmail letters settles on the mat. It is an invitation from the Tea Association of Fujian Province promising tea experts and an interpreter. I had done better than George III. 'You, O King, should simply act in conformity with our wishes by strengthening your loyalty and swearing perpetual obedience so as to ensure that your country may share the blessings of peace', the Chinese Emperor had written back.

The plane banked hard over London and headed for the South China Seas by way of Potter's Bar. In the cockpit I met the crew playing rummy while the plane nosed its way from beacon to beacon in the dark. Somewhere in the desert (DUB? KWT? BAH?) we paused at a marble airport where, in a niche between the gold and glass boutiques, oblivious to the slim hostessy shop-girls, a man in a djellaba served green mint tea in small glasses.

In the early morning the plane reached Hong Kong, making the awkward approach to the landing strip through the tenements and the office blocks.

Hong Kong was snatched up, primed and set in motion by tea men and opium traders. 'Hong Kong, deep water, and a free port for ever!' the Canton Register declared in 1836: ten years later came the notorious Opium Wars and the first Anglo-Chinese Treaty, by which foreigners were to have access to five 'treaty' ports along the coast. The Royal Horticultural Society in London promptly sent out a young Edinburgh botanist to explore the flora of the Celestial Empire. Although the treaty ports were now technically open, the agreement had yet to be tested. Maybe, along with £500 and a revolver from the Society, Robert Fortune received a commission from the secret service.

Fortune eventually made several trips to China. The first was to examine plants in general, with a slight bias towards finding out about tea; the second was specifically to procure 'the finest varieties of the Tea-plant, as well as native manufacturers and implements, for the Government Tea plantations in the Himalayas'. It was straightforward agricultural espionage; it was also a soft imperialism, probing the boundaries of British influence.

Within days of Fortune's arrival in Hong Kong two of his shipmates were dead. He blamed the fierce rays of the sun, reflecting off the treeless landscape. 'Viewed as a place of trade,' he remarked, 'I fear Hong Kong will be a failure.'

He had good reason to be sceptical. The British government had accepted Hong Kong grudgingly, fearing the expense. Hong Kong was meant to be a colossal clearing-house for the China trade, run on sound commercial principles with the least government interference, where merchants were expected to 'send down junks laden with tea, rhubarb, camphor, silk and cassia, and to send back those junks to Canton freighted with India cotton or yarn or English piece goods'. But when the artificial war-boom went bust, trade routes soon reasserted the old precedence of Canton and struck up at the Treaty Ports until the colony seemed little more than a distribution point for opium that had previously been stored for next to nothing on hulks moored in the estuary of the Pearl River.

The merchants were dismayed to find themselves marooned, and they quickly grew as crabby as penned rats, comparing the famous Peak to a decayed Stilton cheese and its surroundings 'to the back of a negro streaked with leprosy'. In 1844 a British official wrote on 'Hong Kong: its position, prospects, character and utter worthlessness in every point of view to England', while in the London music halls they sang 'You may go to Hong Kong for me', because the island was soon perceived to be a 'vaporous' death trap.

The Chinese population, which outnumbered the European six to one, was composed of every undesirable and fugitive from the mainland. Honest men kept away and people put revolvers under their pillows at night. Government House was burgled several times, which alone may have cheered up the merchants, for instead of drawing together in isolation, the British were engulfed in petty snobbery. The governor felt the dignity of his office was being pawed by the filthy hands of commerce, the traders felt snubbed, and the two sides were soon reduced to communicating through the papers. The dream Tea City looked like an expensive flop.

Then Sir George Bonham arrived as governor, to be assisted by an upturn in the region's fortunes. The unrest and rebellion that swept southern China in the late 1840s and 1850s doubled the island's Chinese population. The Pacific trade began to open up, particularly after gold was discovered in Sacramento, and the American whaling fleet started to put in for supplies and repairs. As prospectors with billy-cans drove further into the outback, more tea was shipped out to Australia. Barracked troops dropped like flies, from those fevers which arose from too much electricity in the air and the disturbance of virgin soil, but civilians busy with the revived trade were spared. New roads and drains were built, and schools and churches founded; the Victoria Theatre presented *Still Waters Run*

Deep (over a godown in Wanchai that smelled strongly of 'Singapore Goods' – bad rice and fish), and you could put up at Lane's Hotel, the Wellington or the Commercial Inn, if not at the Club. Fortune, visiting again in 1848, found that 'a great change had taken place since 1845', and he was deeply impressed with the mansions of the British merchant-princes and their gardens.

When Bonham retired in 1854 the merchants presented him with a flattering address. 'Nevertheless,' observes a historian at the turn of the century, 'this model governor, the first really popular and successful one of the Colony's rulers, was soon forgotten.'

And that is, of course, in the great tradition of the city.

Hong Kong springs forever from the drawing board, like some rubberoid cartoon optimist. Young California's first order from the new city of Hong Kong was for 'slop clothes and wooden houses (shipped in frame)'. Little has changed, really; when the bathrooms for Foster's Hong Kong Bank were winched into position the soap was found already sellotaped to the trays.

In Hong Kong the inanimate do business along with the quick. Each ramp on a concrete flight of steps proclaims the merit of a product; dustbins call your attention to the Hong Kong Bank; an enormous Marlboro cowboy hangs tough on the flank of a high-rise – as you come close he shyly disintegrates into a swirl of meaningless squiggles but recomposes himself, as moody as ever, as you walk away. At night, across the city, house-high neon takes his place: SONY, PHILIPS, HITACHI. We love you! they cry. We want you! Look at us! Even in the hotel room you are not inviolate, for at night repellent colours do soft corporate battle across the ceiling. Remember me? HONDA. CLUB VOLVO. *The Real Thing*.

Hong Kong has a non-Hong Kong Chinese population of about 100,000 residents: a town the size of Cheltenham or Dubuque. While I was there the papers announced that the British were no longer the largest foreign community, overtaken at last by the Americans.

Its dinner parties could have been used by a quiz master: what is the smallest number required to make up five parties of eight people in such a way that half the people at any party are previous acquaintances, but not the same people on consecutive nights? I met very few Chinese this way. On my birthday I went to hear a Requiem, and was surprised to recognise three people in the chorus.

One morning I woke to a dreary English voice on a phone-in programme complaining about the amount of flyposting in the city. 'There are about a dozen in Pedder Street, two in Queen's Road, one in Elgin Road, no, I'm sorry, two I think, yes . . .' I dozed off. When I reawoke he was still there, climbing the Peak road by road, irritably pointing out posters from memory. Or perhaps he was phoning from his car. He was allowed to stumble half across Hong Kong, pointing out things he didn't like, before the radio presenter said: 'Yes, I think you've got a great point there, and if anybody's got something to say on the subject of illegal flyposting, bill-sticking, or indeed anything at all for that matter . . .'

Almost every evening I found myself sharing a dinner-table with Jeremy, an amateur wine buff, salting away a fortune from supplying veneer to clients around the Far East. He spent much of his time on the phone explaining to distraught hotel managers why their lobbies had started to peel, or how it was hardly his fault if sheets of best Korean veneer had arrived corrugated at the dockside. At his dinner-party a woman burst into loud sobs at the word 'spider' and disappeared in a cab. After an hour her husband left, too.

It is small town – but a big city, with all the big city rewards. People pass through – you are an old Hong Kong hand after a year, and settlers, who have been here for three, talk of the speed with which you make friends in the city and lose them again. There is a lack of connection between the Chinese and the Westerners, who seem to move through each other's territory in gloves, leaving no prints.

I hadn't been in the city long before I began hearing about a Professor Tea. He had a real name, which nobody could quite remember; everybody seemed to have met him, but nobody could think where. I was advised to seek him out by a Dutch journalist, a German illustrator, a magazine proprietor, an art dealer and an English lady of leisure.

'Professor' was a courtesy title which in Chinese could be applied to anyone with learning and wisdom. The Professor came from a long line of tea merchants who had followed the Kuomintang to Taiwan but continued to buy from China. In his shop, people said, he sold no Indian, Ceylon or African tea at all. The gallery owner described him as a wild man, a sort of beatnik of the tea world; but the gallery owner was Chinese-American, and an Englishwoman at the Club raised her eyebrows.

'Hardly,' she said, when I repeated the description. 'He's very serious, you know, and a real connoisseur. Tea is his work, of course, but it's really his life, too. He sits in his shop all evening with his friends comparing and appreciating teas from his cellars. Well, I don't know if there are any cellars, exactly, but that's how it feels. He strikes me as a gentleman, pretty old-fashioned but an absolute buff.' I pictured the Professor as an elderly eccentric who charmed attractive women and spoke in riddles. Sometimes I was given a phone number, but not always the same one: all of them rang without an answer.

His elusiveness began to obsess me. I borrowed telephones in shops and bars. It was like scratching a bite – a moment's relief as the ringing began, followed by an inflamed desire to pin this character down.

The *taipans* still have their offices on the waterfront, from where they can watch the bustle of the harbour and stare across at Kowloon and the blue hills of China beyond. They sit high in their skyscrapers and speak as generals of free enterprise, eminent in every way, elevated above trivia to the commanding heights. So I would ask them about the tea trade and very often, after thought and maybe consultation, they would suppose that their last shipments left, oh, ten, twelve years ago, following years of dwindling returns, competition from smaller firms, or the retirement of the chap who ran that side.

Perhaps there has never been a city that owes so much to dramatic, recent history, and pays it such scant attention. Old civilisations are revealed by the turn of a plough; Hong Kong goes on ploughing, because there's money in it. Even the tea trade had been razed to make way for something brighter: concreted over and replaced by a bank and a fast food franchise.

Strange that a city built by traditionalists, the British and the Chinese, should be so mercilessly for the moment. Hong Kong's founders were agents, and Hong Kong is just an agent – financial agent, commercial agent, travel agent, secret agent – always doing, never creating, Janus-faced between client and supplier, between East and West, the mainland and the ocean.

I was looking for Professor Tea. I finally caught up with him in an underground garage hung with paintings of anguished baby-people and elongated women.

Across the tiling, with his arm around a sleek young woman, stood a surprisingly young man;

'You should have written in Sung dynasty,' he complained. 'In Sung dynasty everyone knows about tea. Young men and young women met for tea and music. They made poems, talked about tea, painted pictures. It was, uh, tea jamming?' He snickered. 'They have famous tea competitions – to taste different teas. Beautiful life. Every art most refined. In mountains, in gardens, they were Beautiful People, jamming all day.

'Beautiful scenes, you know, they believe in nature. It was perfect life. Very difficult in city life. No poetry. If you wear Issey Miyake or Chanel, I know all about you, where you go, who you see. And in China, perfect life is finished.

'It was life of feeling, for anyone with right feeling, who understand tea. You see, my best customer in the shop is a roadsweeper. Every week he buys the best tea, a little amount. He gambles on the lottery. Sometimes he must have credit, but he always pays. He has strong feeling.'

We agreed to go for dinner with a company from the gallery, but our numbers swelled by the minute and when we reached the restaurant I found myself sitting too far away to talk. Finally, in the scrum on the steps, I missed him by a few moments as I was bundled into a taxi heading my way.

In the taxi was a young Chinese who had been sitting near the Professor.

'Tonight, very quiet. Usually he is more drinking, and many songs,' he remarked.

And he gave me the Professor's phone number.

The Assistant Curator of the Hong Kong Museum of Tea Ware was called Rose Lee. 'Rose is only my English name,' she said seriously.

The Museum stood on a promontory of the Peak, possibly the lowest building in Hong Kong, a colonnaded villa in sparkling white which sailed upon a lawn of dull tropical grass with blades like dandelion. The traffic snarled about, invisible through trees, like a pride of hungry lions – and there must have been lions out there who coveted this unusual spot. Barely fifty yards from its low and tree-lined balustrade, across a network of carriageways, Hong Kong's newest Hong, the Bank of China, was rising to its 70th floor. With pressure on land so intense, and buildings so high, each rhododendron in the garden had thwarted the activity of at least thirty offices. They must be the most valuable shrubs in the world.

Every few minutes a car turns up the drive and releases a bride and groom in full fig and plastic bouquets, accompanied by a photographer. He adjusts his tripod, brushes a veil one way or another, waves the couple to and fro, calls for a smile which neither seems able to manage, and finally snaps them against the one backdrop in the city which has nothing whatever to do with it: no lights, no mirrored glass, no press of people, and which has survived, by outrageous chance, as a place for wedding snaps and teapots.

Rose Lee loved Yixing. Yixing 'purple' clay is unglazed and absorbs flavour, so that they say you may one day pour hot water into your pot and brew tea without leaves. Yixing pots should be judged, like any teapot, on their balance and the cleanness of the spout. In general they are no larger than a fist, and their shapes reflect a Taoist notion of harmony, the square and the circle reconciled, the straight line and the curve. They have practical advantages which Taoism, being the middle way, does not despise. Chinese teas can be brewed four or five times without spoiling the flavour, but in a porcelain teapot the leaves, if left too long between brews, will begin to rot. Tea can be left in a Yixing pot overnight because the lid fits so tightly. After Liberation in 1949 the price of antique Yixing had soared away from the new examples, whose quality declined. Now, Miss Lee was happy to say, the apprentice system was restored, the masters were free to create again, and collectors had returned. It was a good time to buy, really.

Clutching my Yixing teapot from the museum shop (Rose Lee had examined the chop and pronounced it very good, the mark of a rising woman potter; but later I found that the pot dribbled) I sauntered into the garden. A man in a shirt and tie stood in the flower-beds hooking frangipani blooms from a tree with a long stick. He gave the stick a twist and caught the flower as it fell to add to a small pile at his feet. 'Very smell,' he said, offering me one. I sniffed. We both inhaled deeply. He lifted his nose and said: 'Inside every, small insect.' A minute ant crawled out obediently and started to run across my fingers. Another bride in a veil and too much make-up was preceding her groom up the drive; he held grey gloves. The frangipani man held up his bloom. 'Smell for one day only,' he warned, and I thanked him for the present, and walked back to the city.

Around 10.30 one evening the phone rang.

'Is there Mr Jason Goodwin?' I recognised the voice of Professor Tea. 'Can you come over now?'

'It's quite late.'

'I know, it's very good. It would be a time to drink tea. After, we can hit some spots.'

The address brought me to a stubby apartment block. Struggling to the top I met his wife emerging through the barred outer door, the Professor standing behind her in a vest and a pair of blue shorts like a skinny schoolboy. 'My wife goes to work now. A nurse.'

The Professor wore flip-flops. 'Would you mind?' He gestured politely to a little pile of shoes by the door, and with bare feet I padded into the living room. There was a goldfish swimming in a bowl on top of the TV set. The set was on; a Chinese princess was tied to a tree and two clowns with kung-fu swords were approaching her crabwise through the undergrowth. 'Chinese Bertolucci,' said Professor Tea, starting to watch it over my shoulder. With an effort he switched it off and put on the fan instead. 'I had it on for the kid. He has fever.'

Something about the Professor put me in mind of those mysterious queries answered in the margin of *The Boy's Own Paper* before the First World War. 'The oil you need is Mulligan's at 2s 6d a jar. There is nothing to be done about the other thing.' 'You are right, nor will the Merchant Navy.' Professor Tea would have been advised: 'Try to grow straight, try to grow strong.' He was almost six foot, thin and slightly hunched. The stoop was the only real indication of his age: he had a childlike face, a nose that curled like the scroll of a violin and a grille grin like Charlie Chaplin. His teeth were dark, the lower row unattractively brown. 'Gift Horse of HK: Yes, at least twice a day with paste. If true, that is certainly too much. One cup after a cold dip and another after work should suffice.'

But Professor Tea wasn't worried. He was really proud of his teeth, which he could flash like a membership card to the exclusive world of tea connoisseurs. That tannin stain had taken years to create, like a proper English lawn. It was heavier upon his lower teeth because, like all serious tea drinkers, he would pour the liquor into his pouched lip before swilling it back over his gums and teeth.

The amah went past with a cold flannel she had taken from the fridge. When she had gone the Professor said: 'She makes me feel, you know,

19

shame, working so hard.' He had begun almost with a laugh. 'I don't work at all.'

'I thought you had a shop,' I pointed out.

'Yuh . . . Yuh.' He paused, and his expression became abstracted like a child's, as if quiet cogs were whirring in his head and he had to strain to hear them. It was an expression he adopted often, pulling himself short to consider the effect of his words, as if only by a conscious effort could he keep control over them. English tended to overpower him, leaving him speechless and irritated, and he would begin anew, explaining his explanations, in rapid assaults from various angles.

'But I just go to the shop,' he said at length. 'I don't know what work is.' He stared into his secret pond as if a sudden movement had attracted him.

'Tell me something about tea,' I suggested.

'What,' he enquired seraphically, 'would you like to know?'

In the shop he had just discovered a chest of Yunnan pressed green tea. The tea, he explained, was pressed into irregular patties while the leaves were still slightly moist before the final firing. It looked like clods of earth. Yunnan Province borders on Burma, where the Shan tribes of the hill forests still eat pickled tea called *leppet* and where the tea bush probably originated. Yunnan is not pickled but it does 'ferment', blooming and darkening over the years, so that the very thought of the well-aged chest, some fifteen years old, which had been held over by accident, was enough to turn the Professor's mood. Economics is not generally kind to this tea. The cultivator sells his pickings to a factory for hard cash; the factory, to recoup, will not store the tea even in the expectation of a better price later, but sells to the dealers, who lack storage space. The tea is not well known; the dealers are unwilling to hold onto it without the certainty of getting the right price later. 'It would be very, very expensive. So old tea like this is – rare.

'Perhaps we can have some sips,' he added.

There is an account by Goslan of drinking tea with Balzac in an atmosphere of fervent connoisseurship:

As fine as tobacco from Ladakh, as yellow as Venetian gold, the tea responded, without doubt, to the praise with which Balzac perfumed it before letting you taste; but you had to submit to a kind of initiation to enjoy the *droit de dégustation*. He never gave any to the profane; and we did not drink it every day ourselves. Only on feast days would he take it from the kamchatka box in which, like a relic, it was enclosed, and slowly unwrap it from the envelope of silk paper covered in hieroglyphic characters.

Ever with fresh pleasure for him and for us, Balzac would relate the story of this precious golden tea. The sun, he would say, ripened it only for the emperor of China; mandarins of the first rank were charged, as a privilege of birth, with watering and tending it on the stem. It was picked before sunrise by young virgins who carried it singing to the emperor's feet. China produced this enchanted tea in only one of her provinces, and this sacred province furnished but a few pounds destined for His Imperial Majesty and the eldest son of his august house. By special grace, the emperor of China, in his days of bounty, had a few handfuls sent by the caravans to the emperor of Russia. From the minister of that autocrat Balzac possessed the tea with which he, in his turn, favoured us.

The yellow tea of gold given to Balzac by M. de Humboldt was sprinkled with human blood. Kirguise and Nogais Tartars had attacked the Russian caravan and it was only after a long and murderous combat that it had reached Moscow, its destination. You could say it was a sort of Argonaut tea. The story of the expedition, which I have cut very short, didn't quite finish there: added to it, astonishing properties: too astonishing! If you took this golden tea three times, Balzac claimed, you became *borgne*, dumb; six times, you became blind.

But now, far from performing an intricate ceremonial, Professor Tea reappeared with two shallow white bowls and saucers and a thermos, from which he poured something that looked like coffee. I said so. The Professor looked upset.

He took a pouched sip from his bowl, and found the inspiration.

'The flask is not the best. But coffee is coffee and water –' he eyed the ceiling '– the coffee floats in the water. It just comes through the mouth, leaves a dry taste, like bitterness.' He swivelled towards me, grappling with an observation. 'Coffee – is – cold to taste,' he spelled out slowly.

We had taken some sips, as the Professor had suggested. The tea was light.

'Tea and water give each other life,' the Professor was saying. 'The tea is still alive. This tea has tea and water vitality,' he added, pronouncing the phrase like the surprised mum in a washing-powder commercial. 'Afterwards, the taste still happens. It is like, like, like . . . it is this stuff, uh, with hairs upwards, silk upwards, uh . . .' We contemplated the nature of this stuff together, very far apart. 'It comes up after your foot,' he said lamely.

I thought of crocodiles, then dog turds.

'You push it one way, it rises again.'

21

'Grass?' I suggested.

'No, not grass. A clothing thing. For chairs.'

'Velvet?'

'It rises like velvet. Good tea – you move your tongue and it rises afterwards. It starts here in one strength' – he dabbed his lower lip – 'and moves all the way. It changes. Then like – what? – velvet. These are its, its . . .' We were stuck again. 'Not a drink. Not like coffee, cold. It is like the way to tell a story, or – it acts.' He was very serious now, pondering the structure of the tea. 'It is a performance.'

We struggled. At last the Professor said: 'The Chinese don't have deep verbal knowledge. They have ways to understand without speaking. Lao-tzu says, if you understand you won't say.

'Whisky as a chaser?' He had an alarming command of English in many respects.

The Professor went to visit his son, whose small coughs penetrated through the partition. It was fever weather – weather like a fever, hot and clammy. Plain tiredness easily mimics fever, and Hong Kong at night is a chequerboard of lights stacked one on top of another, hard and gritty and deliriously clear-cut. The boy's relief came in the flannels fetched from the icebox by his patient amah, and perhaps from his father's visits. The Professor would wait until three, and if the fever showed no signs of breaking they would go to the hospital.

The Professor said: 'We understand each other.' I looked at him warily. Lao-tzu seemed forgotten.

'You know who I think will dominate the next century?' He enquired, with that queer expression of childlike innocence. 'Jews.'

I felt tired and woozy of a sudden. I didn't want this lover of tea and civilisation to mouth the ancient prejudices of my European world. I told him I thought the people dominating the next century would probably be Chinese. And then, half an hour too late, I left.

The next day I telephoned the Hong Kong branch of the Fujian Tea Association. '*Wei*!' bellowed the receptionist. *Wei* is Cantonese for hello, so I said: '*Wei*! may I speak to –'

'*Wei*!' she shrieked. I tried again: 'CAN I SPEAK TO MR WU?'

'*Wei*,' she replied, matter-of-factly. Unable to make much headway, or to retreat intelligibly, I put the receiver down.

The next attempt was made through a friendly interpreter at Jardine

Matheson. She put her hand over the mouthpiece. 'They say they haven't heard of you. Shall I try to make an appointment?' And so one puzzled tea-time, prudently armed with my invitation from Mr Wu, I arrived at the Association's headquarters.

Mr Hu sat on a stuffed bench, shoehorned into a baby blue Mao suit made of thick cotton, his eyes buttoned into the puckered fat of his face. He smiled continually, a bland, uncomprehending smile. His interpreter was slight and wore big smoked glasses and a skinny brown nylon suit somewhere between Mao and demob. We sat around a low table and drank tea, Mr Hu saying through his interpreter that he was pleased to meet me. I replied that I was pleased to meet him, too, and wondered about the tea. Fujian jasmine? They laughed indulgently and said I' was quite right, and Mr Hu mentioned that it came from his native county. I would very much like to go there, I said. The interpreter smiled, but did not translate.

'Mr Wu very kindly offered me help in visiting tea gardens in Fujian,' I explained. After a brief confabulation the interpreter said Mr Hu was very sorry, but Wu Lao Sheng had left the Association.

'I don't think it was a personal offer. I understood that your Association could help me.'

'Mr Hu would like to know whether you have an invitation from our embassy in England.'

'I have a letter of invitation from your association, signed by Mr Wu.'

'I am afraid there is no recommendation from our embassy.'

I produced the letter. The interpreter interpreted it, and they discussed.

'Mr Hu is very sorry, but there is no record of this action.'

Could Mr Hu make the invitation himself? 'I am sorry, but we need authorisation from our head office.'

'All right, perhaps we could ask them now?' Mr Hu and his interpreter looked very doubtful, but eventually the interpreter left Mr Hu and me to smile at each other and drink our tea. He was gone for three cups.

He came back holding a telex. 'REGRET UNABLE TO ASSIST. NO HANDS AVAILABLE.'

'You see,' he explained, 'everybody is working on the harvest. Very sorry.'

Mr Hu spoke and turned a crocodile smile on me.

'He says it is better you come after tea season. You can talk to our China Travel Service.'

I took this to be the face-saver. The telex had come through very promptly, written in English, and for all I knew it had been composed by the interpreter himself. They could be fairly sure that I wasn't about to hang around for six months, but we could now part all smiles. I felt exactly what the Canton merchants of the 1830s felt – that their reasonable requests would be given a fair hearing by the highest powers, if lower officials were only willing to pass them on. It is in official nature to avoid troublesome communications with superiors, as it is natural for officials to use what powers they do possess to the full. Unable safely to say 'yes', Mr Hu had at least the satisfaction of saying no.

I stomped onto the bus, fuming. Later on I discovered Robert Fortune had met the same men. 'I had had too much to do with the Chinese authorities,' he wrote, 'to place any reliance in what they said, more particularly when their object was to procrastinate matters from day to day until I should be obliged to leave the district. When the Chinese have an end to gain, the only question with them is, whether they are most likely to succeed by telling the truth or telling lies; either method is resorted to as may best suit their purpose, with a slight preference, perhaps, for the latter.'

Fortune had a solution to the problem of delay. He just went, regardless.

2

China

Most Hong Kong belongers accept that they get their head for business from the mother city. Just 90 miles up-river from Hong Kong, mainland Canton does in many ways seem more fit for the business role. The air that blows there reeks of trade, and beyond doubt the Canton tradition is for turning a deal.

It is a tradition so profound that the Chinese have a saying: everything new comes from Canton. It is not, strictly speaking, a compliment: rather the peasant's mistrust of the city slicker and his portable craftiness and pretension. New always meant Trouble: foreigners and money, hustling and independence; it meant secret societies, money again, revolution and crookedness. Cantonese is double-dutch to most of China. Canton, almost a thousand miles from Peking, has the world on its doorstep. China is a nation of peasant farmers living off the land, but Canton lives on the movement of people and things. Nestorian Christians got a toe-hold here in the seventh century; Arabs built themselves a mosque. When the Emperor decided to confine all foreign trade to a single port he placed it here at arm's length like a stink.

A drum of ink has flowed on the iniquities of the Canton system – the confinement of foreign trade – whose usefulness did diminish over the years. But that indignation belongs to a later period, the late nineteenth century, characterised by what became known as the 'Shanghai Mind' –

the foreigners' impatience with things Chinese, disillusionment with the pace of Progress. When the tea trade flourished at Canton, Shanghai was still only a clutch of fishermen's huts, and if the system of pettifogging rules and regulations that governed the Canton trade was exasperating enough, at times, it was also rather like being at school again, and with their pranks and antics the younger barbarians found it almost larky.

China resembled a stately home, open – *noblesse oblige* – for a certain period each year, carefully cordoned, guided tours only. Like the owners it peered out to see the char-à-banc draw up on Open Day, and thought gloomily about those dreadful people who were about to disbus with their big feet and crass remarks, their faces all red and beery and covered in fuzz, asking how much everything cost. But what could you expect? China was the Middle Kingdom and her people were the Han who didn't smell and had all the advantages civilisation could bestow, while the *fanqui*, the barbarians, who only grunted and scrawled, needed rhubarb and cassia for constipation and tea for their health, and would inevitably want to honour their divine ruler in their simple oafish fashion. The main thing was to keep a lid on it and not let in too many at a time.

I came off the Hong Kong–Canton hydrofoil at a jetty where a certain revolutionary chic allows visitors their first glimpse of China inside a concrete shed with an opaque green roof of corrugated plastic, and a relaxed guard of juvenile militia in baggy green fatigues. Rain stained the walls. My visa was stamped, and when the customs officer unzipped my bag, tucked her hands down to sock level and came up with an old pair, she waved me through. The Chinese yuan had not been suddenly revalued, and I received a wad of Foreign Exchange Certificates, 'funny money', which have to be used in hotels. Only when I stood outside the building in the rain did I realise that I had no idea where to go next; no guidebook, only the name and address of a single hotel in Canton, Marwick's. A tea merchant, Dr Downing, put up there in 1836. It was destroyed by an anti-foreign mob twenty years later.

Musing, wet, I noticed two young men in dark glasses and open jackets encircling me. 'Taxi?' they whispered. The word is a concentrated whiff of destinations: salts for the traveller. I considered. 'Canton Hotel?' There was bound to be a Canton Hotel. 'Twenty yuan,' one said.

I shook my head, and they prowled away, disgusted. An elderly woman in a square-rigged trouser suit trod carefully by, stooped over an empty string bag. Shades returned. 'Sixteen,' he said.

At least we were haggling. The car sat in a yard round the back of the customs shed, an old Chinese limo upholstered in a sort of greyish-beige fabric, like nicotine and dust, which you can see everywhere from train windows to girls' legs. We settled at twelve yuan, a good day's wage. The hotel was five minutes away. They didn't smile but I could tell they were pleased.

I deserved to be duped, and I might have been gulled as easily wherever taxis ply with broken meters. Only in Canton it recalled the impression the city seemed to have given travellers and tea men years ago, when all the tea in China came through the port. The port of Canton is approached from the sea through a maze of watery alleys, creeks and defiles, a welter of false perspectives and confounding distances, where the Pearl delta itself loops sluggishly across paddy and embankments. It mingles with earth, with salt. The Pearl is not flushed straight into the sea, but idles in backwash and salt tides, twisting and looping so much that the Whampoa anchorage is at hand when the ship still has half a day's sailing to reach it. In the Bogue the river defiles between mountains, but even in the shelter of the high hills there are curious sidewinds, coming from nowhere. A bumboat starting down a short cut might find itself treacherously beached by a receding tide (a sitting duck for hostile locals). A motionless reed would suddenly shoot forward and emerge into the river as the pinnace of a mandarin boat: in the game between smuggler and customs, it was local knowledge that counted.

On the delta the visitors found mists and miasmas, honest men and outlaws; innocent children running along the bank who swerved to the foreigner of a sudden and sliced the air with their outstretched hand. Dr Downing found babies fastened by their necks to the river bank, rising and lifelessly falling with the tides. It was shifting and uncertain territory, and it breathed the muddle of rooted sin.

By the mid-eighteenth century, the East India Company, John Company, had established itself as the most important foreign trader in China. As well as governing large parts of India it had the monopoly on the carrying trade between Britain and all countries east of the Cape, and could effectively fix the price of tea. Its operations were conceived on a magnificent and lavish scale with the cost passed on to the home market. Its hospitality was legendary, and it dealt liberally with its friends. In China it haggled but didn't quibble, and it put the trade on a regular, predictable footing.

The Chinese approved, because they, too, ran a monopoly through the Hong, a body of about a dozen merchants who alone were allowed to treat directly with foreigners. In return for the privilege, which cost them up to £55,000, they had to bear responsibility for anything that went wrong: a swingeing fine would usually settle the matter. The Hongists lived in a state of perpetual anxiety that they would be bled dry. It was seldom allowed to happen, of course, and they were left to enjoy their huge mansions, their 'curiously laid-out gardens, with grottoes and lakes, crossed by carved stone bridges, pathways neatly paved with small stones of various colours forming designs of birds, or fish, or flowers', as long as they submitted to an irregular 'squeeze'.

The position of Hong merchant descended in a fairly erratic manner from one generation to another, and many of the Hong families had roots in the tea trade. Howqua, Pwankeiqua and Pwan Suy Lan's forebears had been planters in the Bohea Hills in Fujian Province; the fortunes of the families had risen, particularly in connection with the foreign trade, and they had gravitated towards Canton after the restriction of foreign trade there in 1755. Ancestor-worship and business practice coinciding, they had maintained their contacts with the tea-growers. Now the Hong merchants worked from the Hongs, a series of long godowns on the Pearl River next door to the foreign factories, from where the teas and silks could be loaded directly into lighters.

The teas came down from July onwards; plucking began in March and continued into autumn. The up-country merchant or agent would assemble a chop or batch of chests from a single region and period, made up of about 500 chests of black or 200 chests of green, each chest weighing 100 catties – 133 pounds – until the size was reduced to make stowage on the ships more flexible. The chop came down to Canton by river and coolie to be examined by the Chinese Hong before being offered for sale. The tea might arrive in a finished condition, but otherwise facilities existed in Canton 'pack houses' for rolling and refiring the leaf; for bulking – mixing the teas of one or more chop to ensure even quality – and repacking.

Packing alone provided employment for thousands, because tea is bulky and easily damaged. The original Useful Box was sent out of the country by the million, an effort in mass production which must rank the tea-chest with the Bic Biro and the Coca-Cola bottle. Just before its abolition in the 1830s the English East India Company, which had the lion's share of the tea trade, shifted 31½ million pounds of tea a year. The new chests held about 100 pounds each. So 315,000 tea-chests had to be made for each season, since they were non-returnable. That's a lot of tea-chests. Every attempt since to find a replacement for the wooden tea-chest, which gobbles forest at an alarming rate, has come to nothing: and 31½ million pounds a year is chickenfeed compared to the 530,000,000 pounds that India alone produces today. Over the years, tea-chests by the billion must have gone to keep homes warm. Millions must have been used, as they still are, to move the household to a new address. The attics of England creak beneath their collective weight.

In Canton carpenters were employed to build them of wood that was relatively odourless. Skilled plumbers fashioned lead canisters to hold the very best sorts of tea, and their apprentices worked to produce the thin lead sheeting that lined every chest to keep the tea free of damp and foreign odours. The sheeting was made by pouring molten lead over a tablet wrapped in heavy paper and dropping its mate on top. Then there were paperers, who made and fitted paper linings – European masons used the paper to rough out their ideas. Plain chests were for second-quality teas; better stuff came in painted chests, so an army of painters was required to 'adorn the exterior with grotesque flowers and fanciful devices'. Every chest received a paper label on which was printed, in English, the name of the vessel that would carry it. Finally the chests were sewn up in rough matting and secured with rattan, after which another label had to be stuck on.

Much of the work had to be done at top speed, for once the teas had been tasted and paid for the ships would be eager to sail.

Foreign ships would be waiting at Whampoa, 13 miles down-river from Canton. Only shallow-bottomed craft, including sea-going junks, could proceed higher. Foreign ships in the China trade were leviathan for their time, and the Company ships, the famous East Indiamen, were more magnificent than any. Few institutions could venture the capital locked into the 'tea waggons', as sailors called them, and few shipyards could have handled their construction. They were generally Thames-built, at a cost in 1800 of £50–70,000, and displaced anything up to 1400 tons. They were not Company property but chartered for members of a gentlemanly ring known as the Shipping Interest. Members who could afford it might own a ship themselves, but usually they formed syndicates to share expenses and risks, spoken for by one appointed 'ship's husband', or manager. The Interest was of course a closed shop, connected dynastically and socially with the Company directors, and hugger-mugger with the shipwrights, who usually owed them money and would have found it unwise to accept orders from anybody outside the ring. One cosy monopoly, the Company, thus spawned another, the Interest, and everyone was happy.

Size was valued over speed. In common with all ships of the time, and unlike the later clippers, an East Indiaman could do little into a wind; she had to work her passage with the trades and monsoons which brought her over on the round trip in a year. The English Channel was always dicey, but thereafter it was a plain run to Madeira, and the Atlantic was taken on a wide loop that often brought the ship within sight of the Brazilian coast to cross the Equator. After dawdling again in the Variables the idea was to pick up the southeast Trade which took her down to a latitude where westerly gales could be expected, driving almost to the Australian coast beneath the Cape, to the Roaring Forties, where the China-bound ship would catch the southwest monsoon up through the Straits of Malacca to the China coast. India-bound ships, or those doing the 'double voyage' – to India, then to China – would have a choice of routes at the Cape, depending on the state of winds and whether their destination was Bombay-side or Bengal.

As long as the monopoly held, the Company's teas feared no legal competition at home. Speed was unimportant. All that mattered was maintaining a year's supply of tea in storage in Britain at all times, as the Company was legally required to do. The ships moved slowly, occasionally anchoring at night, and aimed to be quite self-contained for six months. Since pirates, then as now, infested the China Seas, and French and Dutch privateers were often hostile, each ship carried enough powder and shot to fight at least two engagements.

Only men-of-war could match the tea waggons for size, but had larger and inferior crews. The Company always took first pick of the sailors, who were then exempt from the Navy press gangs. Company crews were first-rate and well paid (which amounts, literally, to the same thing), and were permitted a certain amount of 'private trade' which, apart from giving them a large bonus (larger if the goods escaped customs and excise and sold directly to smugglers operating in the English Channel), linked the interests of the company and its employees, making traders of them all.

'Traders' isn't quite the word. Foreigners were buyers rather than sellers, and for most of the Company's time the trade was one-way. There was miserably little that the Chinese could be induced to buy from the West's stock-in-trade, as the Emperor wisely observed in his letter to George III. Woollens, England's mainstay, were sluggish sellers in sultry Canton, though the Company dumped them at a loss to make up a bit of a cargo and to please the wool lobby in Parliament. The Hong merchants were prepared to underwrite the trade to an extent since they sold tea rather over the going market rate. Automata, called 'singsongs' in pidgin, sold better, things like 'snuff boxes concealing a jewelled bird which sang when the lid was opened', and clocks, too, the only Western product that ever much impressed the Celestials. But shawls and singsongs weren't much set against millions of pounds of tea, and the balance had to be paid in cash (pidgin word, from the Portuguese *caixa*). An American, W. C. Hunter, recalled arriving in Canton in 1830 aboard the *Oriental*, which had left Boston carrying a cargo of lead, furs, quicksilver, bar and scrap iron, and 350,000 Spanish dollars in kegs. (From Boston, too, the *Oriental* carried an evangelical cook. He read loudly from a Bible while he stirred his pots, and missed no opportunity of gloomily haranguing his captain and the crew, who gave him a wide berth. Twenty-five days out of Boston he sprang suddenly to the rail and leaped overboard, crying: 'You're all going to Hell, but I'm going to Guadaloupe!').

A China-bound ship put in at the Malacca Straits, and picked up a cargo of rice, tin, pepper and rattans, which sold well in Canton. Then it would cross the South China Sea. Before the look-out sighted land, the ship would swarm with dragonflies. She arrived in Canton, all being well, in late summer.

As soon as the sail could be seen from the Ladrones, the outside pilot would come up to direct the ship through the islands to the Macao roads. His boat would forge ahead with mail and passengers for Macao, where it would pick up permission in the form of a chop, or stamp of the presiding mandarin, for the ship to proceed higher up the estuary to Whampoa under the guidance of the inside pilot.

The Bocca Tigris, the Tiger's Mouth, marked the neck of the estuary, where the famous Bogue Forts guarded the approach to Canton with fixed cannon, and where another chop-house guarded it with paper permissions to enter the Pearl River. The river itself meandered through paddy, and you saw Whampoa over several reaches long before you arrived: tall masts, flying pennants, some sixty or so great ships drawn up in a crescent formation as if for battle, and flags of nations drooping from the sterns.

The ship's band, when there was one, struck up an anthem, and everyone gazed for familiar acquaintances – maybe an American vessel, moored at the top of the reach by custom, or lower down, among the yellow flags of Spain, the tricolours of the Dutch or French, or under the Company flag itself, very like the Stars and Stripes, but with a Jack for its field. Nations foreign to one another were united here in utter foreignness to the Chinese. 'Commerce herself must rejoice to see so many of her votaries collected together,' wrote Dr Toogood Downing, who came here to buy teas in 1836, 'and must feel proud of their station and importance, and that it is through her means that nations are enabled to send so large a fleet yearly to China, and to return almost wholly laden with one single article of luxury.'

Everywhere is colour and clamour. Half a dozen washboats have attached themselves to the ship, and the wash-girls are bawling for custom: 'Ah, you missee chiefee matee, how you dooa? I saavez you long tim, when you catchee Whampo last tim. You saavez my? How missee captainee? I saavez him werry wen. I makee mendee all same you shirtee last tim!' – and she will, too, mend and patch and darn and wash, and bring all your laundry safely back – and if your ship should leave of a sudden she'll keep your clothes in her covered sampan, under the floorboards, until your next visit. William Hickey, who had a nice ear for these things, heard them say: 'I washy washy your three piece', which he thought 'implied bawdy, which they are fond of talking'.

There are the egg boats, which carry passengers under egg-shaped awnings of reeds. Dr Downing found his manned by 'two good-natured pretty-looking young women . . . One of them seemed to have taken a good deal of pains in adorning herself, and had arranged some artificial flowers in her hair.' The Doctor had been five months at sea. 'As I sat close to her, in trying to make myself understood, I happened to catch hold of her arm.' The girl jumped to the very conclusion Dr Downing wishes us to avoid. 'Na! Na!' she cried, shrinking away with a worried glance towards the shore. 'Mandarin see; he squeegee mee! he squeegee mee! Mandarin see!' By squeegee she meant that money would be extorted from her. Dr Downing would have us know that he then enquired, in a spirit of abstract curiosity, whether the mandarins were always so strict. 'Na! na! nightee time come, no man see!' she replied feelingly.

These were the egg boats, then, which carried people; there were duck boats with ducks, flower boats, the most colourful sight on the river, which were floating brothels, and snake boats, which carried water-borne highwaymen. Perhaps the most beautiful of all were the mandarin boats, painted ultramarine and white, with red ports pierced by long white oars, an awning raised on slender pillars, fringed with scallops of vermilion and golden leather, fluttering with pennants and a white ensign splashed with characters in red; these carried customs officials, and patrolled the creeks with a complement of sixty soldiers on the lookout for 'smug boats', vessels like them in build, but varnished brown, and not half as smart, in the contraband trade. They looked like insects skimming the water's surface.

The ship drops anchor in the first convenient space once the tide which brought her up begins to ebb. Down then come the upper standing gear, sails and running rigging, the topgallant and even the top masts, lest in unloading she become top-heavy and risk overturning in a breeze; it will be a long wait for the teas. Now the pilot claims his *cumshaw* from the captain, a bottle of rum maybe, and scrounges what he can from the other officers — a piece of rope, some oil of peppermint, some salt beef. It is as well to hide wine-glasses, which please him altogether too much.

Landfall means fresh food and the comprador visits next, a bulwark of the control system whom it is best to befriend because your provisions for the next three months depend on him. You have a choice of compradors, but not an extensive one; it is another monopoly, and compradors rank second only to Hong merchants for wealth. Olo Acow compradored many Company ships, and Boston Jack, who had visited that city, and liked to talk about the horrors of the journey, served most Americans. 'Too muchee strong gale,' he would say of the Horn. 'Sea all same masthead — no can see sky, no can see water.' The comprador would take a glass of wine with the officers, gossip a little, and talk over old times. He was busy running between ships and he generally left his deputy to cover the day-to-day wants of the crew, a man called Sampan Sam, who came down by sampan in the morning and left by sampan in the evening, a favourite of the crew. He was, after all, responsible for the huge sides of beef which hung from the mainstay.

A yellow houseboat with neat brown doors and window frames hangs from the ship's stern: Hoppo Jack is in it. He is the customs officer who performs the ceremony of measurement and *cumshaw*; each ship pays port duties calculated on the size of her deck, regardless of her cargo, which usually comes to about £1000, and the *cumshaw* is a traditional something for the Hoppo. Hoppo Jack stays to ensure that nothing is smuggled over the side, but as Dr Downing observes, 'there seems to be some little defect in the management of these officers by their superiors, as the Hoppo is generally privy to these transactions, and is in fact, the best person to effect the business.'

A couple of days after the ship's arrival the hatches can be opened. The linguist comes down from Canton, a functionary so named, as the joke goes, because he speaks no language but his own. He fastens his houseboat to the ship, and two clerks fasten theirs to his. They are little boats of Dickensian snugness, with a high, railed stern and a gangway encircling the square house built amidships. There is a door at the front, so that the two rowers sit on the threshold, and along the side are sliding shutters painted green. The whole is carved and ornamented and tipped in white and gold, and a smaller ladder by the front door ascends to the roof garden, which is painted black, with blooms and evergreens arranged in pots. Inside you find a bedroom, parlour and altar, as well as the kitchen, where the boatman and his family stretch out at night. There is a small mast, but the sail is only set when the wind is blowing directly astern.

The clerks set up on deck small folding tables with abacus and writing implements, in order to note everything that comes out of the hatches. Their accounts will have to square when everything is again unloaded from lighters in Canton, because temptation exists among lightermen to pilfer from the cargoes. The lighters here are known by that useful pidgin word, 'chop', though known in Chinese as watermelons because of their oval shape and circular sides; the origin of the name must be their capacity to hold 500 chests of tea, otherwise a chop. They are heavy and built of wood, with a great matting sail and a long steering oar.

Under an awning the clerks sit scribbling down the particulars of the load as it swings by, and making out, with the lingo's help, a request to proceed to Canton which must be granted by the Whampoa chophouse. 'Their servants hand round to them and the strangers little cups of tea made weak, and which is drank without milk or sugar.' When the ship has been unloaded, 'the whole apparatus of tables, chairs, clerks, tea pots and linguists, vanishes with great speed, and all is left again in its former quietude'.

It will be a fairly unruffled quietude in the anchorage and a good three months before the teas come down – six, if a large cargo of silks is wanted. A few Company ships will sail early in November with a selection of teas ordered in advance at the close of the last season, so-called winter teas which go to make up the stocks held in London at all times. The other ships will be gone by the New Year, barring the odd out-of-season ship which carries off the season's leftovers and late arrivals at knockdown prices. But these ships are rare, for the winds are turning against them.

In the meantime there is Whampoa life, and things to watch, not much to do. 'No finer sight of the kind can be seen in any part of the world than the Company's fleet collected at Whampoa, with their inland cargoes discharged, and every ship in beautiful order, waiting for teas,' declared the American, Hunter. The Company captains keep splendid tables, and send a boat up to Canton every day by rote. There are walks to be had on French and Danes Islands, slightly melancholy, one supposes, because the islands are also the European graveyards, and frequent visits have to be made there to bury a shipmate who has succumbed to idleness, boredom and the vaporous exhalations of the place. A cortège of boats rows to the beat of a funeral drum, each ship sending a boat out to fall in behind as the procession passes to the top of the reach.

There is some light relief, too: paddling a sampan, for instance, which seems easy enough when the paddle is in the hands of a little girl, but which sends Jack Tar into a whirling confusion as the light craft whips round and round at every stroke, to the hoots of his shipmates. There is the barber's boat paddled from ship to ship, and the barber himself peeping up from under a wide-brimmed hat; he shaves eyelids and carries a selection of metal picks for cleaning out ears as well – which explains why the Cantonese are half deaf and always shouting, for their ear-drums have been perforated. Boys come scavenging, ready to dive for a bottle lobbed overboard, and in fact everything is scavenged, and nothing wasted, by the boat people. On a dark night, with everyone asleep, and the clustering sampans silent, Dr Downing mooning about on deck with a cigar drops a ball of paper from the poop, which falls without a sound on the water, and is carried away by the stream. And before it has quite vanished, a hand reaches out from beneath some mat covering, and fishes it hopefully in.

So the Whampoa billet is pretty quiet. The winds outside will not carry them home; and the wind that brought them up has to carry the monsoon to the tea country; they can only wait here for the right winds and the last chop down.

Meanwhile the sailors, when they are not dying of river fevers, or keeping the ship smart, or negotiating with the barber to smuggle a bottle of the local firewater, *samshoo*, aboard (success in this respect, Dr Downing thinks, is a preamble to the river fever), get their chance to visit Canton. It goes by rote, and most get in a couple of day-trips before they sail. They set out as early as possible to row the longboat 13 miles upstream under the nervous eye of a junior officer, whose anxieties they intend to justify in full before daylight or their money runs out. The journey up is a scramble through a city where everyone has keels for legs, and every stroke brings a fresh obstacle. Nets are stretched across the stream from pole to pole to entangle fish and sweep unwary barbarians from their seats; the girls whisper and giggle from their balconies on the flower boats which are barred to foreigners by law and prudence; once inside it is certain that the lusty lone barbarian would be robbed and murdered. The unfettered memoirs of William Hickey, though, recall a small inlet halfway up to Canton, known as Lob Lob Creek, where covered boats are invited to pause, and met by girls in sampans who 'lob-lob' happily until a mandarin boat sweeps past.

Sea-going junks are moored side by side forming watery alleys running across the river, their painted eyes staring towards the Bogue – 'have eye, can see; no have eye, no can see', as the explanation goes; sampans bustling to and fro through the alleys, trading fruit, bellowing for trade, paddled by anyone, homes for families; log rafts manoeuvred by punters, moored by the boatyards and guarded by someone who builds a shack on top and lets space to all comers to make a floating shanty town, which further blurs the already confused distinction between land and water, with ships drawn up on the banks, and houses on the river, and balconies out on stilts over the mud, and the shoreline obscured by masts and sails and the difficulty of distinguishing between a bamboo house ashore and a bamboo boat afloat. Everything is in perpetual exchange. Rice boats, egg boats, duck boats, salt junks, plying and shouting, and laden chops running down the tide with a wind behind – unstoppable watermelons scattering everyone before them. And where the press is thickest, and the black water is scarcely visible between the jostling craft, rise flagpoles between the masts. Among them, looking very small indeed, the Union Jack proclaims the Factory.

There are thirteen factories in all. They run barely 1000 feet along the bank, bounded to the west by a fetid creek; at the eastern end the Danes are separated from the Spanish by an alley of curio shops, New China Street; then French, which is all but empty during the Napoleonic Wars but which gets going again when the French decide that tea is a cure for cholera; then a building used by Chunqua, one of the Hongists; Old China Street; the American factory; the Imperial factory, which is actually a convenient device for Englishmen to evade the Company monopoly rather than for bona fide Austrians; the Swedish factory; the Old English Factory; the chow-chow (mixed) factory; then Hog Lane and the New English, the Dutch, and Creek.

Smack opposite Hog Lane is a sloping stage for sailors and Chinese, handily placed because Hog Lane is where the sailors plan to spend the day. It runs the depth of the factories – 400 feet – and offers every vice but women.

Women – foreign or native – are strictly forbidden in the Factories, where foreigners may conduct their business for the six months of the season. The rest of the year they should spend on the voyage home or in Macao, and the no-women rule is one way to ensure their departure. The joke goes that the mandarins doubt their own ability to resist the charms of European women; but secretly some factory men cherish the clubby atmosphere. W. C. Hunter recalls an unauthorised visit by some American ladies to the factories in 1830. 'The second day after they arrived several old codgers were seen in immense coats, which had been stowed away in camphor trunks for ten or fifteen years, and with huge cravats on, and with what once were gloves, on their way to make visits!' The locals were overwhelmingly curious, but not hostile, and an evening stroll down New China Street had to be curtailed when at a shout of 'Foreign Devil Women!' a huge crowd pressed round with lanterns. When the ladies finally left, 'an inveterate bachelor said, "I hope we shall not be *bothered* with ladies in Canton again", but he was a notoriously crusty old fellow.'

The Company Factory, known simply as the Factory, has the atmosphere of an old-fashioned college, and is in fact built as a series of small courts. A garden, more gravel paths than grass, leads up from the river gate. There is a chapel with Canton's only public clock, by which everybody regulates their watch, and behind it Thames eights and sixes hang on a wall. The narrow façade of the factory is colonnaded, crowned by a pediment bearing the arms of England and the Company motto *Pro Regis et Senatus Angliae*; beneath this, beyond the verandah, lie the billiard rooms, the library and the great dining room with the full-length portrait of George IV that the Emperor refused to receive from Lord Amherst, and bedazzling chandeliers, and candelabra on the table, where thirty guests may eat off silver plate with footmen behind each chair. The first floor is given over to sitting rooms and supper rooms, each approached from the courts by separate staircases, while the top floor contains comfortable sets for visitors and the two dozen gentlemen who make up the permanent Factory settlement. These are the Chief Superintendent and his two deputies, who form the all-powerful Select Committee; a chaplain; two surgeons; an interpreter, when one exists; about twenty writers or clerks; sometimes a silk inspector called 'grubs'; and always an inspector of teas, entitled the Expectorator. He is paid well not only for his skill but also for 'the abstemious life which preserved it'. The whole investment – the factory, the ships, the men – rolls across his palate, so it had better be clean.

Factories of this sort make nothing, of course, unless it is money, which they seem to make almost literally, for the air rings with the sound of coin poured out of copper scuttles, dancing on the floor, in the corridors and the counting room and in front of the fortified treasury. Every coin coming in or out has to be passed by a shroff who has learned, from shroffing school or bitter experience, the difference between all pieces, native or foreign, by their weight and their feel, the purity of their silver, and the sound they make when rung on stone. The shroffs can spot a fake among thousands; perhaps a coin shaved very lightly, or hollowed out and filled with lead, or a straightforward counterfeit.

The Chinese, who invented paper money in the eleventh century and lost it again in the thirteenth, did not recognise coins as tokens of value, except the small copper cash, which had a hole in the middle, and was used for common transactions. The rest was bullion, carried in small blocks called shoes from their resemblance to the shoes worn by women with bound feet, which could be cut into exact weights with a dexterity that never failed to astonish foreigners. Their coin, Spanish, Mexican, or US silver dollars, was accepted for its silver content, and as the purity of each piece was verified by the shroff it was stamped with his mark, or chop, for which he stood security. He seldom made mistakes. There was one, though, which derived from his exaggerated respect for tradition.

Though all coin was accepted for its weight, the Chinese had a curious regard for the Spanish dollar of Charles IV, called an 'Old Head', which had been in circulation for a long time and commanded a premium over its silver value of about 15 per cent. It was inexplicable – the American firm of Russell and Co. once traded 60,000 dollars' worth of Old Heads for 78,000 New Heads, realising for their purposes a clear profit of 18,000 dollars.

At the season's end the shroff sells his floor to a speculator, who combs it for specks of silver, and replaces it with new wooden boards at his own expense.

Technically the shroffs do not work for the foreigners: nobody does, for imperial subjects cannot be subject to the whim of a barbarian. The Hong merchants appoint a comprador, and the comprador appoints the servants. Like his Whampoa equivalent, the factory comprador is in charge of provisions, domestic accounts and discipline among the servants; he is also responsible for examining the coin, for which he receives 20 cents in 1000 dollars. A busy man, he farms out the work to shroffs, whom he pays 10 cents per thousand dollars.

As at Whampoa each factory is appointed a linguist by the Hoppo, or customs, to manage all communication between the authorities and the merchants, and to act as a fixer. He takes messages and petitions, via the Hongists, to the provincial governors; their reply comes to the Hongs, who pass it on to the linguist, who explains it to the Chief of the nation concerned, 'that he might reverently inform himself of it and be duly obedient'. The lingo tells foreigners of any change in regulations, or of new edicts, and arranges permissions for an outing sanctioned by 'oula custom' (old custom) to the flower gardens of Fattee, or the Honan temple, or a visit to Macao. Foreigners are strictly forbidden to enter the walled city of Canton itself, as they are forbidden to learn the Chinese language. In season the lingo organises the loading, checking that goods are ready and that the chop-boats are standing by with permissions to go down to Whampoa.

The teas were released in October, chop after chop, putting everyone's nose to the grindstone. The Hongs advertised their stock. All teas, other than those which had been contracted for at the end of the last season, were traditionally offered first to the English East India Company. This may be why the Americans, also known as 'Flowery Flag Devils', were often referred to as the 'second-chop Englishmen'. China's experience

suggested that culture and language were the basis of political unity, and all Han people, speaking Chinese, were the Emperor's subjects (to this day, 'overseas Chinese' are included in the official census of the People's Republic of China, as if Australians and Marylanders were to be returned in figures issued in London). Political independence, even over a matter of tea tax, was not a concept furnished by Confucian thinking. It was easier to fall back on the evident distinction, that one lot got a crack at the teas before the other lot did.

The Company divided its purchases between the Hong merchants on a system of shares; Howqua, for example, had fourteen and sold the Company twice as much as Pankweiqua, who had seven. The allotment could, of course, vary. That was the point: in the absence of a free market it discouraged the tendency of Hongists to combine through threats and the promise of rewards.

On the whole, though, the atmosphere was one of trust, and relations between foreign and Chinese traders were cordial. They understood each other, and had nothing to gain from playing tricks, and they were at least united in their impatience with the Hoppo, on whose goodwill the trade rested. W. C. Hunter records a typical chat with Howqua, up at his Hong, in the 1830s:

'Well Howqua, have got news today?'

'Have too muchee bad news,' he would reply. 'Hwang Ho [Yellow River] hav spillum too muchee.'

That sounded ominously. 'Mantalee [Mandarin] have come see you?'

'He no come see my. He sendee come one piece chop. He come to-mollo. He wantchee my two lac dollar [200,000 dollars].'

'You pay he how muchee?'

'My pay he fitty, sicky tousand so.'

'But s'pose he no contentee?'

'S'pose he, Number One, no contentee, my pay he one lac.'

The Tartar Hoppo didn't exactly hobnob. Dr Downing was fortunate enough to be present at the only known visit of a Hoppo to the factories. He had been sworn in the day before, and it was thought that he wanted to have something to tell the Emperor in a forthcoming interview, should he be asked about the foreigners.

The barbarians in the English Factory had prepared him 'a first-rate breakfast after the English fashion'. Blancmange, jellies, fruits and seasonal 'viands' had been laid out on a snow-white linen tablecloth. The foreigners stood behind a rail at a little distance, to see and be seen. The Hoppo ensconced himself at the head of the table, 'an old man of about sixty years of age, and of rather a prepossessing countenance'. He wore a small beard, and a peacock's feather in his cap to signify the Emperor's personal favour; a ruby there indicated his rank and he was dressed in court robes of red and blue embroidered silks. He sat on a small throne, surrounded by secretaries, linguists, friends and servants, while downstairs the Hong merchants waited anxiously in armchairs set out in the reception room.

The old man eyed the good things upon the table, and, as he had the whole of them to himself, no one presuming to take a seat, he whispered to his attendants to fetch them for him. As each dish was brought successively, and held up to his eye, he examined it very carefully all around as an object of great curiosity, and then languishingly shook his head, as a sign for it to be taken away. Thus he proceeded for a considerable time, until he had looked at everything on the table, without finding a single article suitable to his delicate stomach.
The foreigners all this while were looked on with very different feelings. Their appetites were wonderfully sharpened by viewing so many good things, especially as it was now the usual time for luncheon. Many of them, were witty in their abuse of the old gentleman for his want of taste; and some called him an old fool, and were sorry that they were so situated that they could not show him *how to eat*. However, the Hoppo understood none of these sayings, but quietly proceeded with his examination of the exotic dainties, and when the table had been entirely ransacked, he shook his head once more in sign of disapproval, and then called for a *cup of tea*. The Fanquis could not bear this; but the greater number left the room, leaving the prejudiced old Tartar to drink his national beverage by himself.

Perhaps the Hoppo at least enjoyed his tea, which must have been selected by the Expectorator.
The trust that existed between Hongist and foreign merchants allowed for whole cargoes of tea to be bought on the evidence of a 'muster', or small sample, drawn from each chop. The overall weight of a chop was calculated from a random selection of chests, measured against weights held in the guild offices of the Chinese tea merchants. By the beginning of the nineteenth century the Company dealt in five broad classes of black tea and three green; the Americans, retarded perhaps by their experiences in 1776, began to buy black teas only in 1828. These, in order of quality, were Souchong, Campoi, Pekoe, Congou and Bohea, which the Chinese called *da cha*, big leaf, coarse and cheap and common. The best green tea was imperial, or bloom, tea, made from the smallest leaves; Singlo, from

the Singlo Hills; and Hyson. Gunpowder was a better quality of Hyson. There were varieties and qualities of each – Canton Bohea, for example, which grew locally, was particularly poor, while Padre Souchong was almost priceless, and never offered for sale.

Padre Souchong came from the Bohea, or Wuyi, hills of Fujian Province. Bohea tea had once meant teas of Bohea origin, but over the years the name was extended to mean any black tea the *fanqui* supposed to have been made in the Bohea style, which included just about every bad black tea in China. Canton bohea sounded something like Bolivian Champagne. Padre Souchong, though, must have been the tea Balzac was thinking of when he gave his friends the spiel about virgin pluckers and the Emperor of China, for Padre was made for the Emperor's sole use. It came with a paper, on which was written:

In a deep recess of the Wuyi Hills, surrounded by shrubbery and trees, almost impenetrable to the human eye, stands the Temple of the Silver Moon. Its antiquity is so great that all traces of its origin are lost. The temple has been inhabited from time immemorial by a family of the Tea Sect which, at the period of the year coinciding with the maturity of the leaves, makes offerings of fine tea to its patron saint. Close by the temple stand three small tea trees, which are tended by the family. They produce but one catty each. These trees were originally planted thousands of years ago by divine hands, and they have never been known to yield more nor less than three catties.

The foreigners understood that it was produced by monks; hence the name. Padre Souchong appeared from time to time in Canton as a gift, in fractional amounts – possibly the same tea described by J. Ovington in 1689 when he was in India on Company business. Brought to India by a Chinese ambassador, the tea was 'so valuable in China, that a single Catte of it was reputed a noble Present for the chief Ministers, however he brought with him a Taste of it for our President . . .' In Canton, a Hong merchant who received some down a line of favours would find it made more sense to advertise the fact than to drink the tea, so he divided it up and passed it on at New Year, when the Chinese traditionally distribute presents. Like any work of art, it had come to possess a value beyond profit and cost, beyond even pricing the pleasure it gave as a taste, since it was scarcely ever touched.

Foreigners were stumped for suitable presents to give in return. 'Smellum water' – lavender water and *eau-de-Cologne* – was appreciated. Tea itself wasn't a bad idea. 'The natives rarely use even the black tea immediately after it has been manufactured, but keep it by them for a twelvemonth. You cannot, in fact, make a more welcome present to a Chinaman, than a chest of his own tea which has been a voyage to England, as they consider it by that time very much improved', said Dr Downing. Another author explains: 'Well-to-do Chinese drink black tea, but not usually new tea. They keep it closely shut in earthen jars for a couple of years before using it. This moderates the acrid or pungent quality which new tea possesses more or less, and renders it softer and more acceptable to the palate.' Nothing wrong with that, either: no more than you expect from a good wine. But good teas, like good wines, commanded a premium – and the temptation always existed to help their development along.

Mr Barrow, who accompanied the great postman Lord Macartney to Peking in the 1790s, wrote:

Having one day observed my Chinese servant busily employed in drying a quantity of tea-leaves, that had already been used for breakfast, and of which he had collected several pounds, I inquired what he meant to do with them; he replied, to mix them with other tea and sell them.

'And is this the way,' said I, 'in which you cheat your own countrymen?'

'No,' replied he, 'my own countrymen are too wise to be so easily cheated, but yours are stupid enough to let us serve you such like tricks; and indeed,' continued he, with the greatest *sang froid* imaginable, 'anything you get from us is quite good enough for you.'

Affecting to be angry with him, he said he 'meant for the second-chop Englishmen', which is a distinction they give to the Americans.

Perhaps the Americans were more easily gulled. After all, the Company had a longer experience of buying teas in China, and its tasters saw more musters than anyone else. The Americans, for example, caused a crisis in the 1820s by looking for more Young Hyson 'than could be properly manufactured. The natives supplied them according to their wish, but with a vile substitute. The imposition, however, was immediately detected by the inspectors, when it was offered to the English.'

Nonetheless the Company ran a monopoly, and was itself prey to the obvious temptations. Perhaps the Company was not too nice in its examination, having nothing to lose by accepting the Hongists' merchandise without a fuss. In Britain itself a whole industry was devoted to the adulteration of tea, which even had a name, smouch, and was widespread enough to dilute the Company's contribution. Only after the abolition of the monopoly did free trade bring the Chinese end of the business into the public eye, and, after a shaky start in which inexperienced free traders were palmed off with the worst sort of Chinese smouch, competition began to improve the quality of tea drunk. But by then, arguably, it was too late to restore the reputation of Chinese tea.

Meanwhile the Company employees took every care of the tea once it had been paid for. Writers and linguists worked into the small hours to draw up the manifests, check accounts, and ensure that everything due to be shipped next morning was ready at the Hongs, with the necessary clearances. Down at Whampoa Chinese stevedores (another pidgin word, from the Portuguese *estivar*, to pack close) would be laying down the ballast; sometimes it was shingle, laid in the ship's bottom with a smoothness that would delight the most pea-shy princess, but more often, in the eighteenth century at least, a cargo in its own right, mercury, copper, and porcelain, because anything that could be packed tight and heavy and remain unaffected by a rinse in bilge water would do, and a cargo was better than deadweight.

With the hatches down, an East Indiaman carried not only the tea, but also the cups and saucers and pots to drink it with. Chinese porcelain had no peer in Europe before the end of the eighteenth century, when it was replaced (rather than matched) by cheap pottery developed in Europe in response to Chinese competition. Henry Hobhouse calculates that between 1684 and 1791, when porcelain imports were dropped, some 24,000 tons of fine porcelain – perhaps 215 million pieces – were brought to Britain in Company vessels. Every sort of European commission was undertaken by the Chinese manufacturers, with the sole caveat that the shapes should stack tight and that the cargo should present a completely flat surface on which to start stowing the tea chests.

The porcelain was ludicrously cheap. William Hickey recalls breakfasts with his friend Bob Potts in Canton in 1767, in a story which testifies either to the value of porcelain, or to the liberality of the Company establishment, or to the iconoclasm of Hickey's friends. Or to all three:

If he [Potts] took it into his head that Maclintock was too long at the meal, or drank too much tea, he without the least ceremony overset the table. The first time he practised this, I was very angry at such a quantity of handsome China being thus mischievously demolished, and expressed my displeasure thereat, which only excited the mirth of young pickle. 'Why, zounds!' said he, 'you surely forget where you are. I never suffer the servants to have the trouble of removing

44

a tea equipage, always throwing the whole apparatus out of the window or downstairs. They easily procure another batch from the steward's warehouse.'

In 1730 a tea service for 200 people, made to your design and bearing your coat of arms, cost just over £7.

The sailors cheer the arrival of the first chop-boat at Whampoa. The tea chests disappear down the hatches. Any gaps will be stuffed with dunnage – cassia probably, a laxative. Reeking camphor, a profitable export, is forbidden on tea ships. Finally the chow-chow chop comes down with all the last-minute muck and truck (paper lanterns, umbrellas, lacquerware). The clerks pack up their tables and teapots and the comprador gives *cumshaw* to the officers and crew – baskets of oranges and pots of sweetmeats for which nobody has enough room in their cramped quarters. 'I chin chin you werry fine voyage,' he says, shaking hands as the capstan bars are manned and the anchor is raised to the sound of a shanty; and as the ship heels to the ebbing tide, and sail after sail unfurls to the wind, the comprador's floating house drops astern, until only the light of joss papers can be seen, and the sound of firecrackers and a gong is heard, imploring the gods of wind and water to grant the barbarians a safe voyage home.

Up at the Factories, now that the market is cleared of teas, the ships gone and the business done, contracts are negotiated with the Hongs for the next season. With this dealing goes the chin-chinning, and 'chopstick dinners' at the Hong merchants' mansions, and reciprocal dinners at the factories. The *fanqui* have a schoolboyish desire to tease, and they linger in the Factories while the authorities want to get them out for the winter. The annual ceremony begins when the Emperor sends an order to the Viceroy of Canton to wind up business and send the *fanqui* away until the next season. The Governor, Lieutenant-Governor and Hoppo of Canton publish an edict and the Hongs transmit it via linguists to the Factories, who promptly make their excuses. After a while the Emperor sends to find out if they have gone, and the *fanqui*'s excuses are forwarded to Peking, in the company of excuses from the Governor, the Lieutenant-Governor and the Hoppo. The edicts grow more alarming: 'Say not that you have not been forewarned . . . tremblingly obey it – take warning by it – a special edict.' The barbarians have reasons to doubt the vaunted power of the Empire and its dragons, but when, almost cringing and very much afraid now, the Hong merchants suggest 'more better you go Macao', they order up the chop-boats, converted nicely into sleeping apartments and sitting rooms, and set off, to a cacophony of Chinese crackers.

3

Modern Canton

The hotel the taxi hustlers had selected for me was called the Love the Masses Mansion and it had enough entrances for them all. I skittered up and down looking for the right one in the shelter of an arcade with rain spurting up my legs from cracked paving stones, and I knew I'd found it when nobody in the hall would speak to me. Inside were all the years of Sino-Soviet friendship, from the patchy red pile to the heavy stained wood on the walls, a pastiche of tawdry European glamour dependent on stuffed plush and chandeliers, antimacassars on the armchairs and doilies under every ashtray. Stalin probably loved it, but it looked out of place in the tropics.

The hotel faced the Pearl River, with sweeping views across to the industrial suburbs of Honan. My room was on the other side of the corridor. It was the size of a bathroom, wedge-shaped, lit by a low-watt bulb; the window commanded views over a brick wall I could reach out and touch. The bed, which looked hard, enfolded me in a clammy hug. When the floor attendant brought me a thermos of hot water I brewed up with a little envelope of jasmine tea I found on the side table, since you don't have to make green tea with boiling water. The stuff in my mug tasted dusty.

On the top floor of the hotel, in a circular restaurant with panoramic views, I chose a table overlooking the river, where two ferryboats crossed from one bank to the other in counterpoint, describing a gentle figure-of-

eight which brought them both in to moor head up to the current. On
either bank the black heads of passengers slowly massed on the pontoon
until the boats came and drained them all away, at exactly the same
moment. Oddly, a bridge crossed the river about a hundred and fifty yards
away. Now and again the loop was pierced by a string of flat-walled barges
made of wood like the old chops. They were going downstream with an
outward cargo, probably for Whampoa, but whatever they carried looked
more like coal than tea.

I craned my neck for a better look, but a tenement roof had suddenly
obscured the view, with a dripping clutter of antennae and some garments
put out to dry a few years before.

Slowly, to the strains of international muzak, the restaurant revolved,
a stylish gift of the Russians, probably, revolving and tinkling like a sort
of gigantic latter-day singsong. Democratic socialism will give everybody
a view of the river. I supposed that the river was the object, because the
rest of the city curving into view was not pretty, just a shabby rack of
small windows and fire-escapes and dingy blocks on blocks. Guilleman's
French cathedral poked two towers into the skyline, back in business.
Fifty yards away some chefs in aprons and round caps leant their elbows
on the window-sill and smoked, while the top of an oven behind them
shot flame. The distant hills were clouded; from them comes the best
tea water in the province, brought to connoisseurs in crockery jars. A
lamentation of violins stirred up the loudspeakers. *Please release me . . .*
we were back on the river, and two punt barges slid downstream side by
side, with a clutch of skiffs hanging from the stern. Then the antennae
started to nudge into the picture again and I left.

Outside it had stopped raining but the broken pavement still sucked
under my feet. By the river bank, under the trees, fruit-sellers squatted
on their hams, and near them a tea man had set up a little folding table
with tumblers of tepid tea, each one covered with a square of glass as
protection against soot and the flies. Here and there the river was screened
from the road by brick sheds, loos, ticket booths, and the offices of riverine
officialdom: depth gaugers and traffic manipulators and cargo agents. In
England they would be sitting in tiny cubby-holes under strip lighting,
with a mug of tea to keep warm. Here they lounged at ease behind iron
bars, fanning themselves with official papers.

Around me lay Sun Yat-sen's city, laid out with the modernising fervour
of the New China, which in the 1920s had cleared the crooked alleys and

47

hovels of old Canton for proper sanitation and brick houses, wider streets and an automatic telephone exchange to replace the 'Hello Girl' system. A great fire on the river had sorted out the problem of how to clean up the City of Boats. The ancient city walls, upon which two pairs could gallop abreast, were demolished to provide building materials. It was Dr Sun's bequest to the city where the 1911 Revolution began.

The Cantonese are very independent – of Peking, of foreigners, of employers, of one another and of most rules. Nobody much likes them. The Emperor said that 'for bad practices of every kind there is no place so bad as Canton'. The Nationalist Generalissimo Chiang Kai-shek slaughtered thousands of them as Communist rebels in the 1920s. But the city was one of the last to fall to the Communists in October 1949, and the Cantonese gave up their wickedness grudgingly. Foreigners always mistrusted them, with some cause. One hundred and twenty thousand foreigners, mainly Arabs, were said to have been massacred by the rebel Huang Chao in 879; a thousand years later the Victorians were mobbed; these days the backpackers call Canton a major rip-off, and most of them try not to stop here at all on their way into China. Only Dr Sun liked them, and he was a born Cantonese rebel himself, from his scorn for the Manchus to the crown of his brushed top-hat – and a Cantonese businessman too, one of the first able international fund-raisers, tapping the wealth of Chinese living overseas.

A lot has been buried under Sun's new Canton. At the back of the Love the Masses was Shisanhang Lu – Thirteen Factories Street. Dr Downing's Marwick Hotel had taken over a part of the former East India Company factory after the company was abolished, so I wouldn't have been far off if I'd looked up the old address. Without the street-name there would be no sign, for the river-bank has been reclaimed and the Company's garden is under a building well back from the Pearl.

The factory ledgers, were they to be dug up from the foundations of the Love the Masses, would show tea exports rising in volume from about a million pounds a year at the beginning of the eighteenth century to 40 million and more in the 1830s. Something had to come into China to flush the tea out. For most of the eighteenth century it was bullion, a limited commodity. Then it was opium, tea's *alter ego*.

Some say that Boddhidharma's eyelids made the poppy, some say the tea bush. Each was introduced as a medicine – tea as a stimulant, opium as a painkiller. The one induced wakefulness, the other drowsiness. Opium went up in smoke and tea went down the drain. Tea won devotees, but opium enslaved. De Quincey pictured them together, beauty and the beast.

Paint me, then, a room . . . near the fire paint me a tea table; and (as it is clear that no creature can come to see one on such a stormy night) place only two cups and saucers on the tea-tray; and, symbolically or otherwise, paint me an eternal tea-pot . . . The next article to be brought forward should naturally be myself – a picture of the Opium-eater, with his 'little golden receptacle of the pernicious drug' lying beside him on the table.

Opium was originally smoked, by dipping tobacco into an opiate solution, but in the eighteenth century its strength was raised from about 0.2 per cent morphine to 10 per cent by a new method of preparation. Crude opium was simmered with water in copper pans until it formed a paste which could be pressed into thin sheets. The sheets were soaked in water overnight and the filtrate was boiled and stirred for half the next day until it became treacly. In this state it was stored in jars. The smoker would work a piece on the end of a wire held over a small flame until it swelled and softened, ready for the pipe. The stem went between his lips and the bowl over the flame, so that he inhaled opium-laden steam.

At the end of the eighteenth century opium was being manufactured in Bengal and in some of the native states on the Bombay side. 'Patna' bore the Company stamp and was sold in chests containing forty four-pound balls at the Calcutta auctions to British and Parsee country traders. 'Malwa' opium in loosely packed lumps came through Bombay. Opium sales and taxes were increasingly valuable to the Company's Indian revenue; in China the drug trade grew to be almost as large as the tea trade itself. The irony of it was that the legitimate tea trade was conducted entirely at Canton in the most formal and controlled way imaginable, while the illegal opium trade flourished beyond control all up the South China coast. Clipper ships ran the opium from India to the Pearl Estuary, where, in the lee of Lintin Island, it was received by permanently moored hulks manned by Lascars, Malays and Chinese. Smug boats, known as scrambling dragons, shot back and forth between the hulks and the innumerable creeks along the coast, delivering the chests to receiving agents for hard cash. Sometimes clippers would make direct for ports like Amoy or Ningpo further up the coast. 'Transactions seemed to partake of the nature of the

49

drug,' W. C. Hunter recalled. 'They imparted a soothing frame of mind with 3 per cent commission on sales, 1 per cent on returns, and no bad debts!' Local officials were squared, and if a new appointee, in his eagerness, proved 'too muchee foolo', it was only a matter of raising the sum until he saw wisdom. 'So perfect a system of bribery existed (with which foreigners had nothing whatever to do) that the business was carried on with ease and regularity.'

From time to time the authorities had to be seen to be doing something. A few small-time pushers were executed. Vague proclamations were posted at the factories ordering 'vessels loitering in the outer anchorage' to come in (declaring their cargo) or go away. When the opium clipper fleet left Lintin for India they would be pursued just over the horizon by bristling war junks keeping slightly out of range. Thousands of crackers would be fired off, making the sound of a full-scale battle carry to the shore; and news of a victory over barbarian pirates would eventually reach Peking.

The Company itself had nothing to do with smuggling the drug into China. It simply sold opium at the Calcutta auctions. Later on the country traders banked their profits in silver with the Company in Canton, in return for a bill on London. The Company used the cash to buy silk and tea. The country traders grew rich, England got her tea, the Indian revenue was supported, and the Chinese got what they paid for.

Further along the riverbank the Pearl was joined by a canal, stolid and unruffled, the colour of a workman's cuppa. The canal was crossed by a small bridge where I was approached by a fat lady with an umbrella over her head and a straw boater fastened under her chin: she was remarkably well-provided for the vagaries of the Canton weather.

'Changee?' She asked, rolling her finger through the air and almost blinding me with an umbrella spoke. 'Eff Ee See, *renminbi?*'

She was referring to Foreign Exchange Certificates, which I bought for dollars, officially equivalent to *renminbi*, the People's money, the common currency.

'How much?' I ventured in my best Mandarin.

She raised one finger, then three, not taking her eyes off me. The exchange rate was 10:13.

'A hundred for 140,' I countered in a low voice. She crossed the bridge and stood in the shade of a tree, leaving me to pull two fifties from my pocket with studied nonchalance. When I sauntered up to her she gave a hasty double chin left and right and passed me a roll of tens. I counted quickly and handed over my Foreign Exchange Certificates.

All exchanges are mysterious, concerned with private notions of value, where both parties are left satisfied with the swap because each values the other's property above his own. Trade is founded on basic disagreement, and no wonder the Cantonese, who have for so long overseen the exchange between China and the outside world, have such a reputation for being disagreeable. Even language can be bartered here. Thanks to the imperial prohibition on teaching foreigners the Chinese script or language, the Cantonese made contact with a new language of exchange: pidgin (from 'business') English.

Pidgin is not uniquely Chinese. The Mediterranean coast was once covered from Portugal to the Holy Land by a sort of pig Latin called *sabar*. West Indian pidgin evolved in time into a creole, no longer hunting in other languages for its vocabulary and syntax but developing into a full-blooded language of its own. Long-haul sailing ships took on crewmen of all nationalities and evolved pidgins in little, spliced together from odds and ends and sailors' jargon. Chinese pidgin contained innumerable nautical terms, and it was the most widespread pidgin of all. It gave us the term, after all.

Pidgin was a tool of exchange limited to a few hundred terms at most, but fairly expressive on the right subjects. It combined Chinese syntax and pronunciation with words from Portuguese, English and Cantonese, and its use extended to communications between Chinese on the South Coast whose dialects were mutually incomprehensible – the officers of the army of the 1911 revolution were obliged to use it between themselves. Crow's Guide Book for 1930 explains:

'He belongee too muchee boilum tea' means 'He has boiled the tea too long.' *Can do* is used for yes. The Chinese servant will seldom use the word yes, and when he does use it, he often means no. *Maskee* is a very useful word which means all right, correct, never mind, however, but, anyhow, and nevertheless. *Chop chop* is equivalent to hurry – seldom done in China. *Finish* is complete, or exhausted. When your boy tells you 'Ice have finish', he means there is no more ice. *How fashion?* is a familiar form of interrogation meaning Why? or What is the matter? When the boy tells you 'Ice have finish', you should ask 'How fashion?' to which he will almost invariably reply 'My no savvey', meaning that he knows nothing of the reason for its finishing and disclaims all responsibility therefor.

As Crow was writing, pidgin was dying out. The Communist takeover in 1949 killed it off. Thereafter there were not enough ignorant foreigners on the coast to warrant its survival. Odd phrases linger on, and several are retained in the modern jargon of tea.

The constant translation between one civilisation and another has been, and still is, a strain on Canton. It was in Canton in 1839 that the imperial Commissioner Lin, instructed to stamp out the illegal trade in drugs, blockaded the British in their factory until they had surrendered their opium stocks. Captain Elliott, the British official responsible for the Canton trade, saw no way out of the impasse and told the merchants that the British Government would compensate them for their loss. The opium was destroyed and Lin declared that he didn't fear a war.

The British Government, however, was exasperated. The Chinese, for one thing, refused to deal with British officials as representatives of a sovereign and equal state; the Chinese emperor's assumption of universal sovereignty turned men like Captain Elliott into presumptuous rebels. This naturally made a dialogue between the two states impossible. Of course, it was only the British who wanted a dialogue; the Chinese simply wanted obedience, especially over the opium question.

Lin's action in Canton represented the type of quixotic high-handedness which so exasperated British merchants, and it provided the excuse for British troops and gunboats to force their point. The war begun in 1840 was fairly ludicrous, as the inexperienced and antiquated Chinese army lost battle after battle against a well-disciplined expeditionary force equipped with modern weapons. For two years, though, Peking refused to bow to the inevitable, waiting until a British fleet had moved some way up the Yangtse River in 1842 before suing for peace. The result was the Nanking Treaty, which opened five ports to foreign trade and established the right of foreign nations to maintain consuls on Chinese soil.

The war failed to interrupt or seriously damage the trade in tea or opium. The merchants were delighted to receive full compensation for their destroyed opium stocks; the price of opium naturally rose, and fortunes were made the next season. In London the imagined threat to tea supplies led to considerable speculation. When Lin issued his ultimatum to the British factory the price of congou jumped sixpence in London, and every fresh piece of news raised the price. At one point, congou stood at 3s 6d a pound. The price was unjustifiable, since tea continued to be shipped out of China throughout the war; the Nanking Treaty brought on a collapse. Says Martin: 'Probably at no period since the celebrated Mississippi scheme was there ever greater and more prolonged speculation in one article. The steady pursuit of trade was abandoned for the wildest gambling, men who rose wealthy in the morning were beggars at night; and suicide, bankruptcy and ruin to many a hearth and home closed the sum.'

The realisation of that peculiarly Victorian nightmare would have been cold comfort to the Chinese. When war between Britain, France and China broke out again fifteen years after the Opium Wars, the Cantonese, who had no love for Peking but still less for the bullying ways of contemptible *fanqui*, tried to kill the issue by torching the factories. It was an attempt to return to a prelapsarian age before foreigners, before complexity, before all the strain of translation.

Of course there was no possibility of opting out. For a few hours the mob possessed the foreign ground, watched it burn to ashes, and sensed relief. Then the barbarians came back.

This time they took lessons from Chinese practice. Foreigners had once been corralled; now they would build their own stockade. They took a sandbank on a bend in the Pearl, enclosed it behind a massive granite embankment and extended the Creek into a canal that encircled it to the north and east to make a slender island a mile and a half in circumference, which they called Shamian, sandbank. They built two bridges over the canal, with gates that were shut at ten at night, and although there were no signs to say that dogs and Chinese were not allowed, they forbade any Chinese but the compradors of foreign firms to buy land or reside on their island. The French took a fifth of the land, which they had paid for, and the rest was put under a British Municipal Council elected by about two hundred ratepayers. The ratepayers built their premises in 'the Italian style of architecture', quite well, as most are still standing today.

Even after the ectomorphic banalities of Hong Kong and the dreary arcades of Canton proper, the villas are not beautiful. Engineer-classical, two-storeyed, with gloomy loggias and pantiled roofs, they owed something to Italy, seen through a London fog; more, perhaps, to an image of Queen Victoria, plumply comfortable and whaleboned in widow's weeds. A Mrs Gray, who came out in 1877 to live with her husband, the Shamian chaplain, wrote delightedly to Mother of her new home, with a verandah on the river, a decently-sized hall and a drawing room with French windows. Beyond the dining room lay a subsidence of sheds which she supposed to contain the kitchens – supposed, that is, because she never actually went there and never, to her surprise, met the cook. Her servants were all men – Harold thought it wiser not to employ local women, though it made his wife feel as if she were living in a hotel – and she simply told one of them how many were expected to dine, and whether Chinese cooking, or 'the English style of cuisine' was wanted.

Down by the Creek the French Empire had left a settlement of greater charm and colour; more stucco, slender pilasters, a host of flippant mouldings ordered from Marseille by catalogue, and green exterior shutters. In the 1860s, when these houses were built, Napoleon III was Emperor, a very small man and a gay dog; not as young as he was, and a little creaky in the joints. (He also enjoyed a cup of tea, a habit he learned from his days as a policeman in Leamington Spa.)

Despite the permanent presence of four British gunboats in the Pearl, the island had been effectively dominated by Parisian women. Silk for the milliners of France was the chief export, though some second-rate local tea was always shipped to Australia, the South Seas, Hong Kong and the Straits; and even to the Dutch East Indies, where tea was cultivated but not to the taste of the Chinese community. Generally the tea trade had moved elsewhere after the opening of the Treaty Ports further up the coast.

Behind the green shutters, clerks were taking their afternoon nap, their trousers rolled up to the knee, open-shirted, their heads cradled in their arms, while gatekeepers dozed in little cabins, drowsily swatting flies or blinking grumpily at a snouted truck that ground past, grossly overloaded with building sand, its flatbed tilted precariously to the pavement. There were few people about and it took me a few minutes to realise that those few breaking the rule of siesta were all foreigners like myself.

I hadn't seen any foreigners in the old city, but here in the former concession we exchanged smiles, polite and reservedly curious, as if we were sizing up the new neighbours, and had our dogs and a house on the same street in common, and might strike up an acquaintance on the strength of it by and by. But mostly the street was empty, rather to my relief after I sank to my knees in a pile of wet cement I mistook for sand. I smeared what I could from my socks with a banyan twig and hobbled out of the foliage to a dazzling surprise: twenty-five gleaming storeys of White Swan Hotel, and a pink neon sign saying Croissant Shop at its foot. Naturally I sprinted in.

Between reclamation and demolition the Chinese had made room for this new hotel, the first five-star hotel in China; though it looked less like an elegant waterfowl than a giant fridge for crisping foreigners like lettuce, it dabbled its webs in the water.

There was no sign to say that dogs and Chinese were not allowed here either, but no Chinese would be able to stay: no money, no permissions, no good reason. But there were locals who had rolled down their trouser-legs to come and stand by the gallery rail and watch.

I had checked out of the Love the Masses without spending a night. Along with foreign houses, foreign food and foreign population levels, Shamian Island had a plethora of hotels for foreigners. In all Canton there were two; on tiny Shamian, five. The White Swan was the biggest and most expensive; smack opposite was the smallest and cheapest, and there I shared a dorm with a gorilla from Brooklyn, a Bavarian maths professor, an icily beautiful Swiss banker and a deeply mysterious lady traveller who had so fortified her corner with a rampart of nets, bags, rucksacks, boxes, heaps of books and clothes that you could never be sure whether she was at home or not.

They slept in late, and went early to bed. They had no reason to be in Canton except to get away again, either inward or on their way out: they were forever sloping off to railway stations and booking offices, and discussing woes and triumphs over aeroplanes and long-distance buses. The hostel was where the needs of arrivals and the outward-bound met, and brought out the trader in us all. Literature was weighed by the pound, so a bad fat book was worth perhaps two slim classics; a novel could be swapped for a nearly new *Newsweek* and details of cheap flights to Bangkok; a cheap set of Chinese draughts for an explanation of the game and *Newsweek*; I belatedly secured a guidebook in return for a pocketful of loose HK change. A young man with dangling moustaches appeared again and again at the door, doggedly enquiring whether we'd seen a man with a book in Norwegian to exchange. Finally the Brooklyn gorilla remembered a guy who'd checked out the day before. The Nordic moustaches drooped with disappointment.

The Brooklyn gorilla was called Jerrold. He was bespectacled and hairy. He had worked his way over on a courier flight. He'd done Europe two or three times that way, Japan, South America, and now he was in China with a fortnight and little money to spend. He sat on his bed rubbing his fingers between his toes and playing tapes, and he quizzed every passer-by

55

with avid naïvety. 'That was good, huh? So where's this place? Cheap, right? Where'd ya stay? That's cheap?' It was conversational voodoo: he listened to the flesh of their tales with impatience; he wanted their bones. He wanted the stories to work for him, to strip out the storyteller and replace him with himself. 'So, what, I'll see these minorities real easy? Like they'll be wearing different clothes? What do I do at the station?'

He had been in Canton three days, picking it all up. He'd learned about the tiered prices on the railways: for locals, for overseas Chinese, and for foreigners, payable in FEC only. He wanted the best price, but was too hairy to pass as an overseas Chinese. Then he met a Cantonese called Charlie, who offered to get him the local price.

Jerrold was supposed to collect the ticket early next morning for the lunchtime train.

His Maker had meant him to crash like a log and snore, but he was sensitive. Jerrold couldn't sleep. The mosquitoes bit him. He dropped the net and squeaked about in the dark, tucking it under the mattress with ham-fisted delicacy. It got stuffy, and he listened desperately to his own laboured breathing. He untucked the net and draped it this way and that, head in, head out, feet in the sheet, feet in the air, sheet on the floor, grunting and cursing until I fell asleep.

I opened my eyes next morning and stared across the gap at a bloated white face, practically featureless but for a terrible self-satisfied leer. After a horrible moment I sprang up and covered Jerrold's bottom with his towel; it stirred cosily beneath. Jerrold himself lay half-garrotted by his net. The lady of the barricades was already out, and everyone else was asleep. I nudged Jerrold's form. He told me to go away.

'You've got to get your ticket off Charlie,' I reminded him in a stage whisper.

'Fuck off,' he croaked.

I prodded him with savage abandon after that but he sank deeper and never said another word. After tea and noodles at a street stall nearby I went back to get my things. Jerrold still led the universal sleep-in. I had given him up when the lady traveller stuck her head up over the parapet of her rucksack and brushed a pair of thick socks from her brow.

'He's meant to get a ticket off someone called Charlie,' I explained.

The lady traveller trembled on the brink of conversation. 'You can get him through the money change people,' she said at last. 'Ask on the bridge.'

I didn't much like Jerrold but the idea of his snoring two weeks away in a Canton dormitory when he could be riding the iron rooster and spotting minorities was dispiriting. I had nothing better to do; so I went out after Charlie.

After twenty minutes on the bridge I had despaired of Canton vice, when a woman with an umbrella walked slowly by.

'Charlie?' I asked.

'Changee?'

'Charlie?'

She said OK and I trailed her at a distance. We cut across Shamian, skirting the central gardens where tennis and croquet were once played, and ladies with parasols had leaned against the balustrade, close to the shade, and clapped their gloved hands politely for a good ball. It was deserted, but somebody was looking after it, coming to mow the lawn and trim the hedges. Across the northern bridge we turned east and dived into the free market, a street of country produce crammed with buyers.

We emerged in the western suburbs, and where the Pearl forked we went down an alley onto scrubland. Locos steamed at a marshalling yard, and low godowns descended to the river's edge. Against a back wall was a tent made up of bamboo and blankets and a polythene sheet, with a new Japanese motorbike outside, for getaways, I thought.

Later I changed my mind. Whatever Charlie did, it was conspicuous enough. When I put my wrists together like a handcuffed criminal Charlie laughed hard, exposing for a moment his neck, and silver molars. 'No probrem,' he giggled, 'no probrem.' He had a good Voice of America accent although his English was patchy: he picked up both on a glittering radio tape-deck wired up somewhere outside the tent, and I wondered how he syphoned off power, and whether the gadget was safe to touch.

He wore snazzy clothes: Aertex, green army trousers and Nike gym shoes, with almost collar-length hair. There was nothing to suggest that he had been doing anything at all when I arrived. A small folding table was bare. The tent had the childish atmosphere of a den, or a treehouse, as sinister and sinful as Roger and Titty.

'Hello, my fren',' he greeted me. 'My name is Charlie. You got some probrem? I can help.'

A locomotive let out a surprised whoop, as if its bottom had been pinched.

'No problem,' I explained. 'You bought a train ticket for an American called Jerrold. Today's train.'

'You wan' ticket? Very difficul today. Tomollow okay.'

'I don't want a ticket. Do you have Jerrold's ticket?'

He looked impassive.

'Jerrold is asleep, in my hotel. I can take the ticket to him. Otherwise it will be too late.'

Charlie and I stared at each other for a moment: I suspected him of suspecting me.

'Jerrold is my friend,' I began, as he said: 'So sorry. You my fren', he also very good fren'. I fink he come later. Now, wha' you wan'? You wan' some ticket?'

'No, thank you,' I said.

'Tomollow, where you go? Guilin? You wan' very cheap ticket, OK.'

'I've got my ticket.'

'No probrem, you wan' change money?'

Out of curiosity I asked how much for a hundred FEC yuan.

'No hundred! No! No!' Suddenly he was dancing with fury, pulling wads of *renminbi* from his pocket. 'Five, seven hundred okay! One, two fousand okay.' It was quite a lot of money.

'No change,' I said. 'Can I take Jerrold's ticket?'

'You want meet girl? I have very beautiful girl. She my sister.'

He was an old-fashioned hustler, and I don't think sisters are offered any more. I fled from Charlie and his services.

Coming through the alleyway I met Jerrold himself.

'Hey, whaddya doing down here?' He shouted.

I opened my mouth to reply and suddenly decided against it. Trust seemed to be at a premium today. 'I was seeing Charlie about tickets,' I answered carefully.

Charlie was like the vice merchants who once settled in their thousands on the fringes of the tea trade like bluebottles clustering on the lip of a jar. The linguists, I could see, had been Charlies appointed and refined. Real Charlies had once swarmed on the now empty river. Was Charlie the tail-end of old crookedness, or was he a beginning, an early product of slackening controls, and mass tourism, and all too convertible currency? He had made a strongbox of his mouth, like a sailor, and laundered his profits through his teeth. He had somebody's protection, and I suppose he divided his little portion, like Padre Souchong, among the change women who worked for him. Thus a net of patronage and corruption was trawled through the port, something like a resumption of old habits of factory days: the old underhand exchanges, the urge to parity that Jerrold and I and thousands like us, travelling fairly freely, had once more brought to life.

During China's virtual isolation through the 1960s and early 1970s, Canton remained the place for necessary if distasteful exchanges with the outside world. Perhaps for the old reason: that Canton was far away from the seat of government in Peking; perhaps because of the insurmountable weight of tradition, even in revolution, or the whisperings of Cantonese cadres in the ear of the Bureau of Economic Affairs. This trade, like the tea trade of a century before, was hemmed in by regulations. Foreign buyers were invited to visit the annual trade fair. They were escorted from the airport or the docks to foreigners-only hotels, and assigned interpreters. They were discouraged from friendly contact with locals. They were not allowed to wander at will — to enter the city proper, in other words, without a guide. They did their business with state concerns at fixed prices, in hard currency, and as soon as it was done they had to leave.

Under the concrete arcades I put in at a glittering red restaurant for 'tea-house snacks'. Each vast dining hall seemed more crammed and jolly than the last, and my appearance produced a thunder of jokes and laughter. I didn't mind at all but the waiters disapproved and steered me into a side room to sit alone, like Arthur betrayed, at a round table laid for sixteen. Perhaps their instincts were good: nobody's dignity was spared by my attempt at ordering pork dumplings, which descended to the basest pantomime in lieu of Cantonese. I made bad work of the dumplings, too, when they arrived, for they were pink and unseasoned. The tea though, was hot and clean and an antidote to the greasy rawness of the dumplings.

The cause of greatness in cities, Botero might have said, was disease, at least the dread of it. The first fleet of the East India Company suffered the conventional tribulations of a sea voyage (pirates, scurvy, tempests, giant squids) and lost twelve men, but it returned to a city wasted by a plague that had expunged or expelled a third of its inhabitants. It was an average plague, too. The thought that Death was as likely to meet you at your front door as to follow you to the ends of the earth goes some way to explain men's willingness to venture into the unknown. It explains, too, the eagerness with which they sought ways of combating disease: in the search for life-preservers the West was glad to pilfer the wisdom of the East.

European quacks had their cure-alls and specifics – Universal Pills and chimney smoke, healing soups, spells, arrowroot and pomanders of sweet herbs. Almost anything that could be swallowed was pressed into the service of the apothecary, and so it was with tea, which was sold by apothecaries almost as soon as it was introduced at the coffee-houses.

The East India Company's first cargo to England had been pepper; tea started to be imported only seven years after a coffee-house proprietor called Thomas Garraway had offered it for sale: in 1664 a present had had to be found for Charles II, and a few 'tubbs of thea' went down well enough for the gift to be repeated. A few years later the company directors were making cautious small orders to their factors in Bantam and Macao. These teas were trans-shipped from China by Chinese merchants, the first direct import ('extraordinary good, being for England', cautioned the Directors) came from Amoy in 1673.

Garraway's encomium, with a list of twenty-four disabilities tea might be expected to cure, had been issued in 1658.

The leaf is of such known vertues, that those very Nations famous for Antiquity, Knowledge and Wisdom, do frequently sell it amongst themselves for twice its weight in silver, and the high estimation of the drink made therewith hath occasioned an enquiry into the nature thereof amongst the most intelligent persons of all Nations that have travelled in those parts, who after exact Tryal and Experience by all ways imaginable, have commended it to the use of their several countries, for its Vertues and Operations, particularly as followeth, viz: The Quality is moderately hot, proper for Winter or Summer. The Drink is declared most wholesome, preserving in perfect health until extreme Old Age.

This was the first lengthy description of tea to appear in Britain. Today, high on the wall in the blank crevasse of Change Alley in the City, Garraway's is commemorated by a plaque.

In London I had written to the Chinese embassy and received a sheaf of pamphlets. On the cover of one a girl in chequered slacks and a frilly blouse glared over a steaming cup. Inside, across several pages, a Professor Sheng made very much the same puff for tea as Garraway, couched in more scientific language.

Tea contains many kinds of vitamins, such as: vitamin A, vitamin B1, vitamin B2, vitamin C, vitamin P, vitamin K, especially very rich in C and P. If one takes a few cups of tea a day, one can get enough quantities of vitamin C and vitamin P needed for the body. Tea is important to prevent the accumulation of the neutral fat in the blood, reduce cholesterol and increase the elasticity of the wall of blood vessel. It plays a certain role in the prevention of atherosclerosis and cerebral apoplexy, and has some effect on chronic nephritis, acute hepatitis, diabetes, and leukaemia; it can also help inhibit rheumatic arthritis.

Certainly when the world was dirtier than it is now, less soaped, and vacuum-packed and cold-stored, tea had particular advantages. The Emperor Shen Nung said:

Tea is better than wine for it leadeth not to intoxication, neither does it cause a man to say foolish things and repent thereof in his sober moments. It is better than water for it does not carry disease; neither does it act like poison as water does when it contains foul and rotten matter.

The water was definitely boiled, and it stood three times before it was drunk: first in the kettle, lastly in the cup, and longest in the pot itself where the leaves worked like a filter to retain and strain impurities.

I left the restaurant when the tea had darkened to the point when I could no longer see the leaves at the bottom of my cup. I mooned along idly, pottering about in shops selling alarm-clocks and electrical fitments made of that dark brown plastic that once was used everywhere; stationery shops which sold exercise books ruled in squares, French fashion, and Seagull brand ink, and Shanghai Fountain Pens alongside ink blocks and sable brushes, and great white paper for calligraphy. Between a department store and an office was an arcade of carp and goldfish, tiled throughout and brilliantly lit by cheerful paper lanterns. I had been a goldfish fanatic as a small boy, beginning with something like a piece of old carrot that I won in a fair. It lived in a bowl for a while, and died suddenly. My enthusiasm grew. I asked for a tank for Christmas, and a book all about them which became my bible. 'White spot: a few drops of iodine in the tank . . .' It never worked. White spot got them all in the end, or constipation. But the goldfish – dull companions, but the best to be had in pet-denying household – fuelled my first dreams of China, dreams of a place that was not just a backdrop to my grandmother's snaps: a country where everyone loved goldfish – which had in fact invented the breed. I went so far as to visit the Chinese Embassy in Portland Place, where a charming man in a square blue suit loaded me with course books in Mandarin, a booklet on goldfish and back numbers of *China Pictorial*. My donor prudently spoke no English; it was during the Cultural Revolution, and the literature dwelt on harmony and spontaneous outpourings of love from the masses.

Meanwhile there was aggro in the tank along class lines, when a common goldfish, which had been placid and uninteresting, started to eat the fantail's fantail and had to be quarantined behind a sheet of glass. Eventually they united, belly up in death: white spot. Half a dozen feeble sicknesses like this, and my interest died. Now I walked up and down the alley of healthy specimens with respect: here fathers showed sons fat-bellied fantails and shubunkins with mob caps, bubble-eyed goldfish wearing a ludicrous cartoon air of surprise, and velvet black swallowtails whose sooty bodies glinted with scales that seemed like real gold: the hubble-bubble of filters and the murmur of admiration blended comfortably. There were clothes shops, too, hung with egg-blue shirts and flowery blouses, pleated nylon skirts and brown bell-bottoms with plastic zips. Each shop had its old-fashioned cashier in a cage who took three copies of your bill and returned one, stamped, with change, while the shop-girl wrapped your purchase in brown paper and string.

I bought a retractable umbrella, and walked past a church on a boulevard. A small notice on the gate announced that as it was Sunday, a service was about to begin.

Several hundred rather jolly old ladies with spade haircuts and gold teeth were crammed into the pews and the three-sided gallery overhead. There was an inlay of youngsters in the congregation, including a girl in front of me who would have won every Sunday school prize available. Everything about her was exemplary. She was almost loudly clean, with a glossy chignon and rather small ears, a neat bow of white lace, a white sleeveless top, pleated skirt, bobby socks and pumps. My neighbour was a beautiful old lady whose cheekbones spread like butterfly wings, and when she coughed the girl half turned with a look of bland reproach; later, albeit with an air of dutiful severity, she found her own neighbour's place in the hymn book. But I watched, fascinated, as she leaned slightly forward and pulled a tissue from a place of modest concealment, smoothed it out, folded it up, tucked it like a cone into her balled fist and tenderly put it to her lips. When she had spat she folded up the little package and slipped it away.

As the piano struck up a hymn, doors opened at either side of the proscenium and two Chinese ministers entered, a man and a woman with

62

the same black gowns invisibly buttoned and white shirts done up at the collar. They stood behind a pair of lecterns; both in their sixties, I judged, he almost bald, she with hair in a knot, gazing mildly at us all like the firm and distant parents of the Confucian ideal. A procession of children filed up the aisle, singing, and took their places behind the ministers on stage: as soon as they faced us I saw that they were, in fact, tiny women in angelic surplices. Our hymning swelled, a soaring tremolo of female voices, and the fans twirled overhead, sending a breeze like the Blessed Spirit to stir the curtains and caress the vestments of the reverend couple.

The male minister addressed us by microphone while his companion sat in profile on a throne, staring into a far distance somewhere over his head. The breeze, which had begun to explore the thin hairs of the minister's head, died suddenly; his face began to glisten and a member of the angelic choir rummaged through the shrubbery which hid her feet from the congregation to check the electrical connection. At last the fan picked up with a soft clatter, and the minister stood down.

When the female minister rose and put on a pair of spectacles she preached, I was told, on duty and obedience, on our need to serve the community, attend the wise and respect our leaders: pieties as Confucian as Christian, as communist as Confucian. I glowed with sentimentality.

When the reverend pair left the podium the old ladies began grinning and chatting, doing *petit point* in a crowd down the aisle while the choir apparently sang:

> Tea for auntie!
> Do you, do you!

Outside in the little compound the ministers were shaking hands with the congregation. 'Goodbye! Thank you for coming!' they called in English.

A young man detached himself from the crowd by the gate. 'Hullo,' he said. 'Do you speak English? Would you like to talk with me? We can go to my home,' he suggested; and I asked him to lead the way.

With a short detour to buy cigarettes from a street stall (he smoked an expensive Chinese brand: they took all his money, he said), we reached his block through a back lane hung with washing, reeking of kitchens, full of small children, stacked with baskets and barrels and crates, all the evidence of cramped thrift. A few passers-by hailed us: Where are you taking the foreigner?

To drink tea, he replied.

He worked for a state oil concern, tracking the flow of petrodollars and mega-yen around China's offshore oil fields, probably the same fields which, in foreign hands, once paid my grandfather's salary. He lived on the top floor of a tenement with an open concrete staircase rising seven or eight storeys; at the top I felt giddy, all my vertigo focused on the cracked and rain-soaked concrete steps that seemed somehow to support themselves. His oil firm had built the place two years earlier and already it assumed the air of a permanent fixture of Canton, grey and grimy and decayed. He shared with three young oil workers like himself; his own room was spartan – a concrete floor, a truckle bed, a table and an electric ring – but not cheerless, since it took in light from two sides, and had a balcony, that indispensable adjunct to Chinese tenement life, being garden and dining room, attic and spare room, laundry, larder and playpen.

For all his familiarity with the passage of huge sums of money, he was eaten up with the problems of his own trifling stipend. It was anxiety that had taken him to church, in a roundabout way which might not have gratified the ministers themselves.

'Do you believe in Supreme Being?' he asked. 'We Chinese do not. But my English teacher says it is important to understand the culture of the West to speak the language better. It is very interesting for me to go sometimes. I study English. My standard is not very excellent.'

'It's very good.'

'Not good. But I must study to get a good job.'

My friend was a sophisticated version of the converts once made by over-zealous missionaries who wanted them in bulk to overawe each other and the home subscribers; 'rice Christians', cynics used to call them. The missionaries swarmed into China armed with the Word, rights of extra-territoriality, and subscribers' money for clothes and food and schools and churches, and believed that they had stumbled, if not any longer on the kingdom of Prester John, then at least on a race of natural Protestants, or natural Catholics, or natural Seventh-Day Adventists.

My friend took comfort in English, not the after-life. Good English might mean dealing with foreigners; by establishing contact with foreign firms he would be ripe for head-hunting: his dream was to be poached by a foreign firm, like a friend of his who worked in Canton's Special Economic

Zone for 200 Hong Kong dollars a month; he might even be given the chance to study abroad. Bad news for China – he wouldn't come back.

He supposed that for writing a book I got a good salary. I explained the business end, and he said it was unthinkable in China: I could see that the irregularity made him nervous. In China, every artist or writer was on a salary. But not always, surely: how could you identify the writer to pay a salary to unless he had already done some writing? He wasn't sure; perhaps writers erupted like Athena, at school one moment and writing away on full board and wages the next. It was a very good job if you got it, he said. The system in the West must be difficult.

He couldn't afford to marry at the moment; the housing quotas were full anyway. He pinned his immediate hopes on a coming law which would throw jobs open to competition: less security, but higher wages for the good workers. Yes, he was one of the good workers. He had very much enjoyed practising his English. It was still poor. No, no, very poor.

He insisted on seeing me to the bus stop and helping me aboard. Strap-hanging in the afternoon blaze I felt horribly conscious of sensitive Chinese noses burrowing unwillingly into my armpits; nobody sat immediately on vacated seats but waited fastidiously for the plastic to cool down and, who knows, to dry. A lot of strap-hangers looked down at my feet; whether I was simply too embarrassing to look at, or whether my feet themselves held a grotesque fascination, I couldn't decide. When the park stop arrived I managed to slither and clomp off the bus.

The Museum in the park was dotty, the exhibition equivalent of a wino pushing a pram full of scraps and diggings. The third-floor inventory included a photograph of an iron anchor found in Canton in 1958; some local pottery; two lutes; local opposition to the Ch'ing; an English–Chinese dictionary; clocks; a model of a loom; a 19th-century medical treatise; a socialist realist painting of the firing of the factories in which a crowd of stern young sansculottes with operatic eyebrows and gleaming teeth torch a chapel; another by the same anonymous hand of cheerful Chinese with high-tone muscles tossing opium into a fire as a knot of top-hatted capitalist imperialists stand by looking pinched. There was a stilted little picture of a woman on a divan; her stiff embroidered coat stuck upwards and she looked out to the photographer, expressionless through a thin haze of opium smoke. On the top floor I was offered a cup of green tea and a seat on a balcony that overlooked the park and Canton

65

beyond. The Museum was housed in a tower that had once been part of the city wall: this was its highest point which had been seized by an Anglo-French force in 1863. Downstairs, Krupps cannon blindly eyed the city.

Jerrold had left the hotel and the occupancy had turned over. I was sorry not to have witnessed the departure of the international bag-lady; I wanted to know how she had demolished her mysterious mountainous corner, that dormitory Tibet. I went out to walk the northern embankment of the island to the western end, where pipes ran into the water and a small flat barge twinkled with fairy lights under a stripy awning. Tables and chairs had been set up on the deck, and a kitchen with its brazier and buckets of meat and vegetables was sunk into the hollow of the prow. 'Shamian was a little England,' said the proprietor of the floating restaurant, bringing me fried noodles. I sat and ate while sunset turned the muddy water to smoky grey like Lapsang Souchong; mosquitoes rose, and the settling dusk threw purples between the water and the sky. The noise of traffic dulled and then separated into its parts, and as the tide ebbed there rose a gentle flood of conversation as the strollers on the road above stopped and hunched themselves over the rail, blackening like bats against the dim street lights.

The gangway was steep; the night on land was gathering Canton up, gentling the people towards the ferries. Couples swinging children between them, men rolling bicycles towards the pier. Turning a corner I saw the cupola of a Roman church silhouetted against bright back light; and behind it, in a pit-prop forest, beneath arc lights, half-naked men wove to and fro like eager demons, raising some new tower in haste.

4
Treaty Ports I
Amoy

The sun was rising quickly to lift the river mist, and the city followed close, clearing its throat with the first bus which, in sudden sympathy after hours of quiet, coaxed engine revs from unseen streets, singly at first, but gradually blending to that roaring monotone a city-dweller barely hears. I walked to the tinkling of bicycle bells, the rattle of a boneshaker on a potted road, the *slap-slap* of sandalled feet and a murmur of conversation warmed by the early sun. Along the Bund the tai-chi practitioners had begun carving soft shapes in the air. The tea-seller was brewing up in a big kettle between the trees, surrounded by thermos flasks, and his upright table glinting with empty glasses – his first customer, in a vest and an open cotton jacket, stood by to perform his ablutions, evacuating first one nostril then the other onto the ground, and rounding off with a hawk so violent his jawbone seemed to pierce his skin. A young woman, conscious of the emissions of factory and citizen alike, cycled past in a white surgical mask. The sky wavered, plumped for blue, and colours in the streets became ordinary.

It got hot, too. The sun slanted beneath the trees as I tramped to the boat terminus, where the gates of the compound were choked with farewells. Under the fluorescent lights of a waiting hall we all took on a greased green pallor. Everybody carried sacks of shopping, from televisions to a gross of instant noodles. Canton's abundant imports were moving up-country.

67

Amoy, the port where I was headed, was no backwater. Imperial policy had always been to maintain balance between the provinces, but after the Opium Wars foreigners had weighted the coastline with money, machines, and new ideas; the Treaty Ports grew rich and powerful while the interior decayed under population shifts, weak government, famine and bloodshed. As a result of the Nanking Treaty the tea trade had spread up the coast from Canton in the wake of the drug runners, to Amoy, Fuzhou and Shanghai. Amoy itself had thrived, a port popular with foreign firms, who set up head offices there. Foreign residents liked the place. My grandparents moved there after the Second World War; my grandmother organised classes for the English children and my grandfather ran the Standard Oil agency. In 1949 they left for Hong Kong.

Afterwards China under Mao had pulled itself inwards like a frightened sea-anemone, and the big money had flown to the interior with the factories and the power: steelworks in Mongolia, quarries in Szechuan, chemicals in Xian, textiles in Hubei. The new regime has returned the initiative to the ports. They are to be the engines of economic progress, leading the country in harness; Special Economic Zones, where capitalism – free movement of goods, labour and capital – has been restored.

There was a sharp rattling at the doors onto the quay and the crowd surged forward with blind force, crushing an obdurate old man who fought back with staccato indignation and chops of his skinny arms. His neighbours pretended not to notice, and he remained trapped, a small explosion of blue and grey. The crowd leaned, holding all its heads high at once like a gaggle of geese, and the doors stayed shut.

A minute later we were through like pop from a bottle. At the quayside lay a boat with its gangway down. There was a wide passage amidships which we hurtled right through onto another boat, then through that, and the next, at breakneck speed. In each passage was a niche in which stood half a dozen grimy tea-cups below a brass hot water tap. The ships were identical, small and low, and at every moment I expected to reach something more substantial when all of a sudden, on the fifth boat through, everyone stopped running forward and began to scramble up the companionways instead, or to pour downstairs. I was whirled up with them (fighting, rather, not to be sucked below) to the enclosed upper deck, where I blenched.

I have only once before seen something resemble a mobile morgue. It was called a Rotel, and stood in the Sahara with thirty pink Germans poking their heads out of miniature windows along its side, smiling to camera – each guest sleeping in a coffin-sized compartment. On the boat the bunks were open-sided, but that was the only variation. By the time I had gathered my wits, calm had descended and I was presented with 600 feet, socked and slippered and bare and sandalled feet, in an unbroken line all the way to the furthest berth on the bottom row. I eased myself forward onto the woven mat, and calculated that, by twisting, I might just squeeze through the window if need arose. There was no other way out of the enormous crowded cabin.

To make things worse, even I could see that the ship was scarcely seaworthy. A big wash could have swamped her, and it was typhoon season on the South China Seas. Her decks lay a couple of feet above the water-line; her stanchion rails were buckled and there was no suggestion of watertight bulkheads, which the Chinese invented. I was reading *Lord Jim*, and the *Patna* with its quivering bulkhead sounded like the *Bismarck* by comparison. Our pilgrims were equally crowded, and looking down the length of the cabin I imagined a coolie ship, China's indentured poor on a voyage marked by the hourly splash of a fresh corpse in the water. I gloomily noticed that everybody carried bags of fruit, and cake, and tins of this and that; they had brought caddies of tea, and plenty of cigarettes. I had none of these things, and I felt hungry already.

At the ship's stern a gate ran across the deck. Behind it were coils of rope, and several nautical-looking bars and spars, and a bucket of sick, or congee, or soaking rags. In the galley a cook was hacking at a fish with a cleaver while his assistant brought a taper to the gas. There was one more boat like ours in the series which now cast off, and our rope was thrown aboard to decline stiffly on a basket of courgettes and onions. The outer ship made a lazy circle, waiting for us to move off. The tannoy burst out in panic; 'Kamera! Kamera!' and then once, calmly, 'Kamera – aa – a.'

I was slow this morning. Why did I suppose that navigation would have changed since Dr Downing took a bumboat from Whampoa to Canton? This was a river ferry to a larger ship. With that in mind I stretched out on my bunk, happy to tackle imminent pandemonium aboard the *Patna*. Meanwhile we chugged past a white pagoda on the western bank, the same halfway mark where sailors rowing up to the Factories had taken their tot. The banks were stacked with huge tree-trunks rafted down from the forests of the interior. Women swung long-handled spades from a barge: they appeared to be trying to fill the river with sand. Perhaps they were lunatics, waving as we puttered by. The river widened where a motley fleet of senile and misshapen ships rode on buoys: green-grey cargo vessels, graphite gunboats with domed turrets, container ships with their superstructure split fore and aft, and cranes in between. The banks were sandy and flat: far away the Pagoda Hills showed in faintest outline, a wavering smudge like chimney smoke. The water changed from brown to a rippling green, and we began to turn towards a creek choked with skiffs and dismasted fishing junks drawn up on the bank, with a puffing tug, and dinghies, and a cat's cradle of rope.

To let us in the tug had to move out first. Crowding the rails, we watched the tug's crew move at ease, hitching ropes and bringing crates aboard from the quay with bland unhurried motions. Our captain brought us in close, blared and shouted, and the tug-master threw a single glance over his shoulder and turned away. But when at last they moved out we had the satisfaction of watching them snag the painter of a dinghy and all but swamp it, and then manoeuvre disgracefully, like any Sunday sailor.

We disembarked here, 'a wretched, straggling place' as Whampoa seemed to Dr Downing, and it was not really much. Squeezed together on long benches in a great sunlit hangar we took hot water from a samovar for tea, and for the pleasure of wetting towels to wipe the stickiness from our faces and necks; and then we languished in bliss as the water evaporated coolly under the fans.

Amoy is a superb natural port with a harsh and unproductive hinterland. 'Amoy' is for locals and old China hands: a sea-dog, spice-laden, South China sound which makes me think of soy sauce and coolie hats, tramp steamers and palms. Mandarins and newcomers call it 'Xiamen', like a hiss from the political north. In fact Greater China lies beyond the highlands of Fujian, successive mountain ranges which have always been a struggle to pass. Even the Chinese language is corroded beyond recognition in its passage across the mountains: Xiamen, Amoy. Amoy looks to the sea. There was a port nearby called Zaitun, famous throughout the East, which gave us our word for satin, and then silted up, and was swallowed inland. Amoy grew upon its neighbour's misfortune. Europeans traded here for a century before the confinement of trade to Canton; the British, the Dutch and the Spanish of Manila had factories on the island. Green-eyed Amoy junks traded across the China seas. It was then that the herb the Chinese call *cha* was first sent directly to England, the tea the Directors expected to be 'extraordinary good, being for England'. In Amoy dialect, *cha* is pronounced 'te'. All the seafaring nations of Europe use the Amoy word today except the Portuguese, who settled in Macao, and first bought tea from Canton, which called it *cha*.

A day and a night after leaving Canton, we arrived in the Straits of Taiwan. Amoy Island lay to starboard and the wooded island of Gulangyu on the port side, from where a colossal statue planted on a bluff watched us enter. It looked like Queen Victoria.

I had been sharing jam sandwiches with a young Shanghainese whose father ran China's Sea Rescue Service. 'One of my father's ships,' he said proudly, pointing out a 70-foot motor launch so thoroughly consumed with yellow rust that sea rescue did, indeed, come to mind. A man in a vest promptly spat from its bridge, as if he'd read my thoughts.

There were no formalities, so we jostled down the gangway and through a gate on the quay. Outside, the cycle-rickshaw boys wobbled furiously into life, trying to manoeuvre their wooden sidecars closer to the gate; their efforts were frenzied by the appearance of a foreigner. Foreigners introduced the rickshaw into China from Japan a century ago, harnessing men between the shafts of a wheeled buggy. The Communists banned that particular contraption, but it didn't seem much better to sit in a converted orange box with the bare calves of the cyclist bunching and relaxing by my nose. The rickshaw boy leaned down. 'Change money?' He panted. 'One forty yuan?'

The need for *renminbi*, even at this encouraging rate of exchange, was still less than my need to find a place to stay. The bathroom on the ship *Chiang Liu* had been a reeking cavern of lemony mosaic and leprous chrome plumbing, and the canteen had served nothing but gritty rice and a choice of scrambled eggs in tinned tomatoes or tough beef strips in raw onion and liver sauce. My fellow passengers had forearmed – hence the jam sandwiches – and although a friendly steward had given me an envelope of Long Jing green tea I felt hungry and dirty nonetheless.

The Lujiang Hotel stood on the quay at the corner of the main road and the Bund. It was brighter and better appointed than the Love the Masses, and far more expensive. I arranged with the rickshaw boy to find somewhere cheaper after lunch, and meanwhile sat in the ninth-floor restaurant by a tinted-glass window to watch the view. The *Chiang Liu* was still mopping up the Shanghai-bound, but she had arrived late and now another passenger ship was advancing slowly up the harbour, hooting with impatience. The *Gulangyu* was a Scandinavian ferry bought by China to make the run from Hong Kong to Amoy. I knew her from another voyage: inside, everything was at ambassador standard. She was smart and clean; her loos smelled of bleach and roses and her stewards stood to attention to welcome passengers aboard. The *Gulangyu* dwarfed the *Chiang Liu*, and edged imperiously closer, hooting, conscious of her spanking white sides and superior bow thrusters and passengers who spent foreign dollars. The *Chiang Liu* was shamelessly bullied, and when at last she cast off and slid away up the channel she moved with the carefully mustered dignity of a poor relation going home, and sailed east, showing a rusty stern.

It was my signal to leave before new arrivals bagged all the rooms in town. The rickshaw boy was waiting on the steps, but not alone; for when the doorman swept his glass doors open, his outflung arm took in a dozen spivs in shades who murmured their litany *changemoneychangemoney* when I appeared. My guide had abandoned his rickshaw. Across the street was the ferry station, from where, every quarter of an hour, a ferry shuttled passengers across to Gulangyu Island.

The ferries worked in pairs, like all the best routines, and gave each trip a blithe, almost vaudeville air. On either shore a cage on the pontoon received passengers until the ferry docked and let the arrivals get off. Just before the gates to the ferry opened the gates to the gangway closed, with a warning bar or two of *Jingle Bells* tonked out incongruously in a tropical summer. At the first note someone would always be pounding down the gangway: it was free entertainment. The crossing to Gulangyu was free because you paid to get back; the outward journey was therefore classless, while the return could be made upstairs on a bench or downstairs amongst the crowd. First class was naturally breezier, and you could buy a soft drink from a stand. But whatever class you took – and it was generally easier to stay below – there was always the delightful shock of approaching the Gulangyu terminal, built to look like a white grand piano.

From the deck of the *Chiang Liu*, Gulangyu Island had looked forested and barely tenanted, but as the ferry approached it revealed a jumble of old buildings around the quay. The little island had been the foreign concession, run, like Shamian, by a Municipal Council which laid drains and enacted byelaws; it became a haven for middle-class Chinese as well. Sampans bobbed by the pontoon; a fishing-junk clunked away from us like a startled tortoise, while spray flecked its square-ended prow. (It had a painted number, but not the green eyes which once would have distinguished it from any red-eyed rival from Canton.) My guide led me along lanes that snaked between low buildings harbouring shops and restaurants until, skirting a small playing-field, we arrived at the guest house.

The receptionist had just cleaned her floor in the little gatehouse, and meant to take her siesta. After some debate she agreed to let me check in first; but the idea of siesta was firmly rooted in her mind and she seemed determined to take it, as far as was possible, while she worked. She yawned hugely, picked up a pad of flimsies as if it were a brick and slapped it on the counter. A small square of carbon paper dozed in a drawer; without waking it she brought it gently to its place in the pad. I could have a room for 60 yuan or half a room for 30 yuan. No, the rest of the room was empty. But if another foreigner came, she'd put him in with me.

The hotel had been built as a mansion for a tea merchant of Amoy who had chosen a site above the cliffs and the Botanical Gardens, fronting The Lawn by the Masonic Club. His own formal garden was elevated above the green, protected by a low balustrade and a screen of banyan trees. At its centre was a Taoist symbol laid out in box hedge and balustrade, with a defunct fountain in the middle. There were three buildings: one Chinese and one European villa flanking a central mansion compounded of good ideas from both. Out on his verandah, sipping tea in the breeze of evening, the old merchant could have looked through the banyans at foreigners working up a sweat at tennis or five-a-side, their handlebar moustaches slick and their faces red with exertion. The banyans were smaller then. Now they almost obscured the view of schoolchildren playing thirty-a-side.

Number Two Building, the European villa, was managed by a girl with slack eyes. She sent me down a dark corridor to a hallway stacked up with very small armchairs under dust-sheets; I had to lift a corner to make sure because the brilliant sunshine barely penetrated through the rose window of a disused door. A mop and bucket waited at the foot of the stairs as they had waited perhaps since the Liberation; even the spiders had moved on and the webs were heavy with dust. The verandah of my room on the ground floor had become a bathroom and the single window was monopolised by a gigantic air-con box and the roots of a tree. When I flicked the lights an orange worm glowed faintly somewhere overhead.

I took the number of the room directly above and asked the concierge

73

if I could move. She sent me back to the receptionist who was energised by irritation and jabbed the carbon rudely between the sheets of the receipt book.

'Sixty yuan,' she snapped.

'Not 30?'

She grumbled and changed the figure. Room 210 was a little brighter. Under a high ceiling two of the midget armchairs, ferociously antimacassared, were frog-marching a varnished locker towards the beds. The louvred doors were pitted with keyholes, but only one of them functioned. I peered at them with the enthusiasm of an archaeologist. The original lock from the beginning of the century had been plastered over, leaving only a small keyhole above which could have been the same vintage. Above that a new lock had been installed, perhaps during the Second World War, when the Japanese had controlled the island. The key had not been surrendered with the island, so a crudely joinered hole had been made higher up by the fleeting post-war tenants, who had vanished in turn with their key around Liberation. Perhaps it was now in Taiwan. The next occupant had run out of space higher up, so his lock had gone in below the first: it wasn't there any more, only a square gouged from the wood, with empty screw-holes half gorged with emulsion. Officiously removed by cultural revolutionaries, who treated privacy as property as theft? Someone had then added a pathetic wire hook to hold the door shut; its eye remained. Finally there was my key for a Yale-style lock. You had to yank the door open; it was warped and stiff.

I had a cold bath. Xanadu can be found in a cold bath in the tropics. 'Ice have finish': Crow's pidgin illustration struck me as an apt rendering of colonial despair.

The mansion at the centre of the three buildings which made up the guest house was masculine, heavily panelled in teak. A full-size billiard-table was draped in clean cotton, the baize immaculate beneath. I wondered how long ago the balls had vanished. Perhaps the table had never been played upon. Its survival into post-Cultural Revolution China was extraordinary. Red Guards should have been here, as they were everywhere, rooting out relics of the impure past. Perhaps the Party, which held meetings here, had extended its protection to this foreign frivolity. Perhaps it was too massive to destroy.

Beyond the billiard room lay a huge marbled verandah set with wicker armchairs and tables. In my mind's eye, as I remembered *Lord Jim*, Marlow's cigar glowed in the night and then spun out into the damp foliage beyond. Instead, a woman in a white jacket levered herself irritably from her white armchair.

'Not allowed, impermissible, forbidden, no entry,' she clamoured, using the comprehensive Chinese phrase *bu xing*.

'I'm staying here,' I explained.

'No no no,' she waved her arms.

'I want to look around,' I said firmly.

She yelled something at her companion on the verandah.

'Not on. Inadmissible,' she said, but she was grumbling now.

At the far end of the drawing room sliding doors were set with panes of coloured glass in the shape of a peacock. I peered through the crack and saw the room I really wanted to stay in.

The room was also dark, because the shutters onto the verandah were locked, but the heavy panelling, the windows pushed high above glass-fronted cabinets displaying treasures like old newspapers, a chamber-pot and several lidded mugs, the gigantic bedragonned fireplace, and the ceiling coffered nine inches deep, all exemplified the style of Oriental-baronial the Amoy merchant had set out to achieve. There were four beds, which halved the 30 yuan I paid. The sliding doors could be padlocked with a laminated bicycle-chain; but the further door, which gave onto a slender staircase of white marble, could not be locked at all.

The garrison the British installed on the barely inhabited island of Gulangyu during the Opium Wars was decimated by malaria, and the settlement was abandoned as part of the Nanking Treaty in 1842. But thirty years later it was properly reclaimed, with a Municipal Council to clean it up. The whole island – larger than Shamian and maybe four miles round – was above all a place of residence: the businesses and warehouses were grouped together along the Amoy waterfront opposite, beside the ferry terminal, in what had been the British Concession.

The foreign merchants and consuls built large villas on Gulangyu, with pantiled roofs and deep arched loggias screened by rattan blinds from the hot sun. 'Did the residents display as much wisdom in the furnishing of their tables as they have in the building of their houses,' said the Gulangyu medical officer in 1870, 'they might live as comfortably here – as far as health is concerned – for eight or ten years, as they could in Europe.' Europeans here avoided the terrible look of yellowed parchment that dogged them in the tropics; the doctor thought that 'a little languor by the end of summer, becoming more pronounced as a rule the longer one stays here, is perhaps the only climatic disease a sensible man need suffer from'. All this had distinguished Gulangyu from Amoy City behind the British Concession, where cholera and plague were brought on by 'the filthy state of the town, and the fact that the civilisation of the people has not advanced to the point at which the advantages of hygiene are realised.'

The doctor's criticism of the way Europeans furnished their tables was reasonable when a Victorian tea-merchant might sit down to a dinner of 'rich soup, and a glass of sherry; then one or two side dishes with champagne; then some beef, mutton, or fowls and bacon, with more champagne, or beer; then rice and curry and ham; afterwards game; then pudding, pastry, jelly, custard, or blancmange, and more champagne; then cheese and salad, and bread and butter, and a glass of port wine; then in many cases, oranges, figs, raisins, and walnuts . . . with two or three glasses of claret or some other wine.'

Fever or over-eating had been killing foreigners on the island since the first factories were established in Amoy. Robert Fortune 'stumbled upon the tombstones of some Englishmen, who had been interred upwards of one hundred and fifty years; their graves had been preserved by the Chinese'. Later an English captain had them all restored, earning himself the nickname 'Old Mortality'. Foreigners continued to leave their dead behind until they were driven from the island by the Communist takeover in 1949.

There are no cars on Gulangyu: no wheeled vehicles at all. Foreigners introduced the rickshaw into China but banned hubs and spokes from their island retreat, and the Communists have not changed that. Only barrows are dragged by gangs in harness, exclaiming their way up and down a hill with a load of stone for a new building. The cacophony of a normal Chinese street, the clanging and revving and cycling and shouting, is replaced on this tropical Sark by the two-stroke rasp of crickets, the cries of tradesmen and the hand bells of the ice-lolly sellers tinkling like halyards in a marina. One night it rained, and at first light the puddled ground was covered in tiny green frogs. There is a holiday atmosphere. The lanes run over the island between walled gardens and bleached villas, wrought-iron gates and slender lamp-posts. The wider lanes are full of restaurants which set out their tanks of razor-fish, crabs, and shrimps on the path: sometimes the shrimps go berserk, the water churns and dozens of them leap from the tank, skittering across the pavement.

The pavements were made with any local stone that came to hand, and one afternoon I saw beneath a scattering of shrimp a fragmented epitaph in Latin script.

EMORIAM

PH HUNTER

All over the island, each afternoon, piano music – scales, half-pieces and phrases – floats out of verandahs, slips through rattan screens, trips down alleyways, rustles in the trees, as in Prospero's island. Gulangyu is a musical island, home to two of China's greatest living violinists, but saunter down lanes at the siesta hour and it is pianos you hear: practising pianos, accomplished pianos, pianos which departing foreigners left behind. Big ships browse in the western roadstead, occasionally lowing a satisfied moo that carries across the island. Sometimes they are gently nosing out, or ambling in; and you think, majestically, of Landfall and Departures.

There were bathing beaches around the island too, scattered with chiselled rock which had supported gun emplacements. In a cove, dug into the stone, were the words HMS ACORN 1867.68.69.

Unbusinesslike then, Gulangyu is still an island of residence. The very sight of a plaque bearing the words 'Amoy Light Transformer Co Ltd' was a shock; it looked like bad form, and I imagined a Bateman cartoon railing apoplectically around it.

An English travel agent, unable to help devise anything so abstruse as a tea tour, had offered me a letter of introduction to Françoise instead. I had posted the letter in Hong Kong. Françoise was not on the phone, so the day after I arrived I made my way over to Amoy University.

On the Amoy side the minibuses congregated near the ferry terminal, and for twopence I got the ride to the university and a fistful of brilliantly-coloured paper tickets adding up to the correct value, which the conductress tore from a small board. We trundled down Amoy's Oxford Street, a street of colonnades and shops – barbers' shops and bookshops, tea-shops and department stores, apothecaries and bicycle-menders – to the crossroads, where for a moment we seemed to have been caught up in an armed insurrection. *Ratatatat!* The volley of automatic gunfire turned out to be firecrackers, set off to celebrate a wedding: the same sort of firecrackers which had sent off the *fanqui* from old Canton before winter.

Françoise wanted to go for lunch on Gulangyu, so we bussed back to the ferry again. She had been teaching French in Amoy for four years, but she wanted me to choose the restaurant. Rather nervously I directed her to a place where I had not yet seen the shrimps scooped straight off the pavement into a pot, and to my relief she seemed to approve; it was a family-run restaurant with fresh plastic covers on the tables, fans playing over the customers and chopsticks which you snapped apart for yourself. Françoise said that was important, because there had been 'red tides' washing along the coast – harbingers of hepatitis. We ordered tea and razor-fish.

We talked about the treaty ports. Françoise said that some of the foreign teachers were missionaries, the computer instructors in particular. In the old days missionaries had made converts with food: the rice-Christians. Now there should be computer-Christians, too – except that the Chinese government rigidly forbade proselytisation and the undercover missionaries had to keep very quiet about the Word if they wanted to stay on and spread It.

'A lot of them are good teachers. Really good, not Chinese-university good,' she said. Chinese-university good meant a teacher whose students consistently got high marks. 'It's absurd. If you mark out of 20 and give the worst student 15, your class will get high marks and you look good. If you give the best student 15, your students will get low marks and everyone thinks you must be a bad teacher.' Time and again Françoise had tried to find out how the department wanted her to award marks in exams. According to merit, they replied.

Françoise laughed. 'There is no key to the process. Right now it doesn't matter so much, because the students are simply assigned jobs when they leave. But when there's job competition? How will the employer make a decision when the same student might get 40 per cent from me, and 90 from a teacher in the next room?'

She made a face. 'My students aren't good at all, but I have to give them 70 per cent, 80 per cent, otherwise they get unhappy. It's not their fault. Most of them wanted to learn English, not French. English English English! French won't be any good for their careers, but there is a quota and they were chosen to fill it.'

Françoise enjoyed herself nonetheless. For a Parisian who had studied

Lacan and the rest there was something fascinating about people who did not accept that everything was text. The Chinese, she felt, were like Europeans of an earlier age, maintaining divisions between disciplines. 'A book is one thing, a TV programme is another. A programme has to be about one thing, very single-minded.' She thought TV itself might break down those borders with its magpie diversity. 'Content and utility are the ways to judge aesthetics here. It's poor education. Millais is a good painter because he paints peasants. Boucher is no good, because he paints courtesans. They see everything literally. After Huang Po in the fourteenth century there were no Chinese explorers. There is no attempt to reconcile or enquire. When Europeans go abroad they ask: Why aren't these people more like us? When the Chinese go, they say: that's what they're like.'

We finished the razor-fish, and I walked Françoise back to the grand piano. 'You know, I showed my students a postcard of the Rue de Rivoli. It's just like Amoy, they said.' She snorted. 'Like Amoy! You know the big new neon signs by the Lujiang Hotel? When they switched them on for the first time everybody went around very happy. They said: now Amoy's just like Hong Kong!'

Just before she embarked she told me to ring Tom, an English businessman who lived in two rooms built on the flat roof of a Gulangyu villa. The owner of the villa had been allowed to use two rooms himself after the Revolution, sharing the bathroom and kitchen with newcomers, but now, thanks to China's *volte-face*, he was repossessing the building piecemeal, cajoling and bribing the other tenants to leave, embroiled in a war of attrition with a family on the third floor who had installed an iron gate and refused to move; when they did, Tom could use his second room, currently used for storage. For the moment, the stubborn family dropped their litter into the owner's garden and stared at Tom's visitors through the bars of their gate as they climbed the stairs.

The last flight of the well-worn wooden staircase ended in a box opening onto a sunny terrace tiled in terracotta, where Tom had dragged out wicker chairs and made an impromptu cooler of his water tank. His presence here was accidental: he had studied Chinese at Durham University, and after a year at Shanghai he had come here to look for a job. He had worked at first for two New Zealanders who ran a consultancy for foreign firms setting up in the Special Economic Zone – Mark and Ann, who had come to Amoy after back-packing around Asia, fallen for it, gone home to sell up, and moved to China. They spoke Chinese pretty well, but not like Tom, who could pass for a local. Tom had pixie ears, quick humour, and a veiled shrewdness which now had him, in his mid-twenties, running a trading office for an import firm in Cardiff.

His girlfriend from Peking, Tsai, was staying, and Mark and Ann had come over for late tea. We sat out on the tiles, looking over the low parapet. Gulangyu spread away towards Amoy: the harbour between was obscured by trees. The evening sun spread over pantiled roofs, pale stucco, the bleached reds of painted rattans, and bushed tree-tops which turned the island, from certain angles, into unbroken forest.

Over tea our conversation descended to murmurs. I leant back against the wall: long cracks ran up its stucco sheath.

'It's not stucco, really. Isn't stucco always coloured?'

'This is a sort of, I don't know . . .'

'Cement.'

'Pebbledash?'

'More like gritdash, then.'

'Dustdash.'

A small piece, light as pumice, fell away and clattered onto the tiles.

Tom waved to a family on their loggia a hundred yards away. They waved back. He waved to an old man with binoculars who was leaning forward in a chair over the balustrade of his verandah. The man didn't move.

'That's Mr Ju,' said Tom. 'Always watching me up here, never speaks. The Gulangyu curtain-twitcher.'

We all waved at Mr Ju.

That evening Tom took me to visit Mr Lu, an English teacher, up a complex of stairs and passageways at the back of an old villa on the other side of Gulangyu. Tom left us to pore over a 1930s map which showed the island as my grandparents must have known it, calling it Kulangsu, just as my grandmother did. There were the consulates and the corporate headquarters. There was the Lawn, just outside my guest house. Next door was a classical villa which had seemed to be a playschool; on the map the spot was marked Masonic Lodge. Masons were yet another arbitrary set in the Venn diagram of colonial Gulangyu society, a way of producing a new slice out of the same old ingredients. And down on the southern tip of Gulangyu, near the best bathing beach, was a collection of shaded squares marked Asiatic Petroleum Company Ltd. That was where my grandfather had worked.

After the map had been folded away Mrs Lu brought in tea and we talked about English literature.

'Do you know the works of Somerset Maugham?' asked Mr Lu. He had made a study of Maugham at university in 1947; since the Cultural Revolution, when he had hidden the books, he had rediscovered the short stories.

Mr Lu insisted on walking me back to the guest house. 'You must learn the way to come tomorrow,' he said. At every junction he would make me guess the way, and then correct me: that was the best way to learn, he explained. There were few street-lights, and the dim lights of houses stood out in the darkness: glimmering archways of loggias, through which each domestic scene glowed in chiaroscuro, framed in sequence like the panels of a triptych. I was to meet him very early the next day. At the gate of the hotel he pressed a book into my hands.

It was a very battered copy of Somerset Maugham's *On A Chinese Screen*, with notes pencilled in English in the margin. I took it to bed and read a story about a *taipan* in a southern Chinese port. The *taipan* is congratulating himself on his own success, and dreaming of a retirement he plans to make somewhere near the racecourse in Shanghai. When he sees two coolies digging a grave in the English cemetery, he can't think who could have died. Mrs Broome's child has been poorly, but the grave is too large. All through the day it bothers him, and later at the Club he loses his temper, loses at cards, and finds people looking at him oddly. Nobody knows anything about a grave. That night he wakes panic-stricken, determined that when he dies it will be at home, in England, not in this sly and inscrutable country. He hates China. In the morning they find him at his desk, quite dead, clutching his letter of resignation in his hand.

In the margin by the title the young Mr Lu had written: 'Kulangsu?'

The word itself means Drum Wave Island; the sound of waves is made by the wind blowing around the rocky hill that stands at its centre. Mr Lu took me to the top as dawn appeared. He was cheerful because an article of his had been published in an international English teaching journal where non-native English speakers air their ideas in a glorious variety of styles from the elegiac, formal prose of a Tamil to the hotshot idiom of a Central American. Mr Lu had advised readers to approach English like a prudent general: attack, secure, hold. He did not approve of the modern notion of immersing children in a foreign language from the start.

The sea and sky met indistinguishably in mid-air, uniform blue-grey. A small island floated like a smut; a few lights burned unblinking across the channel on Amoy. While I sat and watched the colours waver on the horizon above the rail, Mr Lu commenced exercises. There were a few others up here, performing the same slow sketches in the air, the same motions of extricating themselves from a cat's cradle of invisible thread, which is tai-chi.

Tai-chi is not only physical exercise but also a way of harmonising the humours. Over days *chi*, the energy, wears thin, or lumps together like the stuffing of a cheap duvet, and tai-chi is the way to restore its balance. You aim to become as whole and even as a sphere. Since Liberation, I was told, tai-chi has been introduced to dialectics, and the result is cruder and more uncomfortable. Instead of a gentle harmony, like gathering armfuls of flowers, tai-chi is all about reaching limits, and straining to overcome them. One imbalance must be matched by another and contrary imbalance. So as the sky whitened and the rim of the sun bobbed suddenly from the skyline, I watched Mr Lu for enlightenment.

Mr Lu looked as if he held to traditional methods. He was as round as a ball himself, or rather three balls: a spherical head, and bandy legs knotted with muscle. He was quite as firm as india-rubber and there was nothing he liked better than to be punched in the belly or to bend his biceps for an admirer's prod.

He was sixty-four, and Gulangyu-born. His grandfather had come to the island to escape a landlord and at first sold firewood, but he was literate, and finally secured the post of cook to a foreign family which he retained, as he said, not because he was a good cook but because he dropped opium in their coffee to addict them to him. His son married the granddaughter of a Parsee from Bombay when Parsee firms had made up part of the British merchant contingent, and became for a while a passport agent in Manila. Mr Lu thought his father had looked down on him because he was short and ugly.

In his youth, Mr Lu said, Gulangyu had been safe and clean. Through the upheavals that followed the collapse of the Chinese empire a White Russian officer ran an island police force of fearless Shandong men; the British deployed Sikhs on Amoy. You had to be careful about the gangs: they wore black jackets, white vests, and clogs; they had their hair curled and they used knives. It was better not to stare at them. At best they would curse: 'Cry for your pa, he's dying.' Mr Lu shuddered at the memory.

Exercises completed, we stood to watch the sun bulge from the horizon and suddenly detach itself like a new amoeba. At 6.30 it was already warm. Lie-abeds toiled up the hill for exercises as we descended for a walk.

Near the ferry to Amoy stood the old British Consulate, gutted only the year before by an electrical fire. It stood roofless on high ground, its empty windows full of sky, a shell of sooty red brick and cement pilasters. The consul would have been well placed to catch a breeze and watch the arrival of ships. Captains would have called in by and by, to do paperwork, register births and deaths aboard, deliver newspapers or read them, get a briefing on the situation up the coast, air a grievance and demand to know what *he*, the consul, was going to do about it. Right up to the end of the nineteenth century the great Pacific liners would put in at Amoy to load tea for a clear profit, and the passengers benefited from a day ashore to break the monotony of quoits, gin and stale romance.

'I do not remember the British consul,' said Mr Lu. 'The Americans and the Japanese also had consulates on the island. The Japanese were very unpopular. The Americans were all right.'

'And the British?'

'They were much more popular than the Japanese,' replied Mr Lu diplomatically.

Along the shore road we came to the colossus of Gulangyu: not Queen Victoria but Koxinga, a Ming general who in the seventeenth century defied the Manchus from Fujian. He also defeated the Dutch, who wanted to make Taiwan their Philippines, and later he was driven by the Manchus across the Taiwan Straits to rule as King of Taiwan. His son succeeded, but eventually the island was repossessed.

The statue was very recent. The sculptor was a friend of Mark and Ann, and lived in Amoy. 'Not another fucking hero,' he said, when he received the commission. The resemblance to Queen Victoria which had struck me from the deck of the *Chiang Liu* was presumably unintentional, yet there was certainly a pride in Koxinga's chest that blurred the line between martial and matronly, with the swelling skirts and the thick cape holding him upright, while from a distance the warrior headgear could be taken for a starchy bonnet. Koxinga, overall, looked thoroughly unamused.

Koxinga deserved to be commemorated. That 'extraordinary good' tea had left Amoy for England in 1687 because Koxinga allowed it to. Koxinga fought the Dutch, and on the grounds of a shared enmity he permitted the English to begin trading in Amoy. The Amoy trade lasted nearly fifty years until Koxinga was dead and the Manchu emperor in Peking felt strong enough to bar foreigners from the port.

The modern Amoy authorities had not erected a new statue simply to celebrate China's first international tea salesman, though. Koxinga is a hero shared by Amoy and Taiwan, just across the Straits. Modern China is keen to find things to share with the Taiwanese, because it wants to persuade them to return to the fold. There are certain similarities between Koxinga and Chiang Kai-shek, the Nationalist leader whose armies and government were driven out of China into Taiwan by the Communists in 1949 (the nationalists still possess the small island of Quemoy a mile or two away from Amoy: on the top of Drum Wave Rock people queue at a telescope to read a quotation from Sun Yat-sen, carved in giant characters on a Quemoy hillside). Both Chiang and Koxinga fought civil wars, were driven south and finally over the Straits to Taiwan, and thanks to a change of mood in Peking, Chiang can nowadays be described as a patriot like Koxinga – if a misguided one.

In fact Koxinga has been put to work, here as a local Statue of Liberty, and all across the city in smaller copies. He has become a professional greeter, murmuring to every visiting Chinese from overseas, and above all to the Taiwanese: 'We are all patriots, aren't we? None of us are foreigners! Here in China we honour our people. Why, with Koxinga we've almost erected a statue to Chiang! In fact, we've gone further – Koxinga is Chiang without the divisions!!'

And the Chinese friends and relations pour in from overseas. There are millions living in the West and throughout the Far East, concentrated especially in Singapore and Taiwan, who can trace a connection to Fujian, if not Amoy. And being people who respect – even worship – their ancestors, they return to visit. Even native Taiwanese without family connections in Amoy come because they share a similar dialect and outlook.

For over fifty years until the turn of the twentieth century, Amoy exported tea and people for opium and remittances. The tea, mainly oolong, was grown in neighbouring counties and exported to Europe, America, Japan and to Chinese colonies overseas. It was a major export which provided work for thousands of people, but never enough, and because Amoy was a port and the land was poor, emigration was wide-spread.

But towards the end of the nineteenth century, when the empire entered its rapid decline, it became an exodus akin to the Irish famine emigration. In a turbulent region, the armies of rebels and imperialists marched across the tea gardens, scattered their cultivators and left the land waste. The trade's collapse was dramatic and catastrophic. In the Amoy district the quantity of leaf produced for sale fell while the tea itself earned a particular reputation for gross adulteration, crude picking and sloppy manufacture.

Amoy tea must have been very bad indeed, because the reputation of Chinese tea in general had been suffering ever since the abolition of the East India Company monopoly in 1832. By the 1850s expectorators had begun to approach the musters with positively shroffish caution. There were at least ten tell-tale symptoms which indicated adulterated or *ersatz* tea. One involved stirring the muster with a magnet to discover iron filings, which would give the brew weight and a good colour. In Canton, as long as the Company existed, the possibility of fraud was barely discussed: W. C. Hunter even claimed that 'the ingenious process of augmenting the brilliancy of tea by a clever facing of Prussian Blue or Chinese Yellow, of adding to the bulk by an admixture of chopped willow or elm leaves, of increasing its weight by iron filings, was not yet practised by those "heathen Chinee" '. Dr Downing believed that adulteration took place on a minute scale, if at all. He thought that 'the injurious effects which are universally allowed to arise from drinking Hyson or Twankay' were caused by the method of making green tea, which he assumed was dried more slowly than black, so that 'anything baneful in the living plants' themselves would be dried into the leaf, rather than driven out by intense heat.

Dr Downing might have asked how we should account for the complaints English retailers frequently brought against the Company, that tea at auction was spoiled or unfit for consumption. The appearance of green teas could certainly be improved by the addition of gypsum and Prussian Blue at the final firing stage, and in the 1840s Robert Fortune established the existence of this practice for a fact. When he questioned the Chinese as to why they 'faced' teas in this way, they 'acknowledged that tea was much better when prepared without having any such ingredients mixed with it, and that they never drank dyed teas themselves, but justly remarked that, as foreigners seemed to prefer having a mixture of

Prussian blue and gypsum with their tea, to make it look uniform and pretty, and as these ingredients were cheap enough, the Chinese had no objection to supply them, especially as such teas always fetched a higher price!'

When Amoy was first opened to foreign trade in the 1840s, seven or eight million tons of tea were sent out each year (chiefly to the US, which had a taste for peachy oolongs it retains). By 1899, when a mere 30,000 pounds of Amoy tea were shipped, the US Consul on Gulangyu was advising his government to discontinue shipments on health grounds. As tea exports dwindled, so the export of human cargoes rose: for the new emigrants had lived from tea, and when that failed they looked in the only possible direction, the sea.

I am toying with a menu in the orange and red restaurant of the Lujiang Hotel on Amoy. *Reddish been chease pigleg and peanut pot* could break me; I order Singapore fried noodles, full of diced leftovers. The waiter frowns. On a big round table a dozen people are holding a reunion. The host summons dish after dish after dish. The grandmother is dressed unmistakably like a mainlander while everyone else shares the same love of gaudy perms, sunglasses, Nike trainers and farming caps. Only the command of some of the diners suggests that for them eating out is a familiar experience.

The neighbouring table is invested by three fat brown boys, like young Buddhas, with Cokes and half a dozen plates between them. There is no mistaking them for locals. Their fat cheeks push their lips into pouts; their jowls are folded into their necks. Their friend waddles in, a twelve-year-old with a loose T-shirt and the belly of a fifty-year-old beer-drinker. He squats, his bottom flattens slightly on a chair, and with a lordly air he orders up Cokes, and the same again all round.

In Shanghai, welcoming an overseas relative is called stripping the pig. China welcomes them, and the huge investments which they pour into the ancestral country. They give scholarships, universities, sports stadia; they set up factories and agencies; they provide the bulk of the tourist revenue. There are perks, in return; and beyond the obvious advantages – the concessionary fares, the cheaper accommodation, bigger duty-free allowances and the like which officially go to anyone with a foreign passport and a Chinese face – there is the unspoken benefit. Conrad's Marlow says of Jim, 'he is one of us'. Wherever they choose to spend their lives, whatever language they speak or politics they hold, the overseas Chinese are Home.

I attack my noodles hungrily. Halfway through I revolt, finish my tea, and quietly depart. As I walk away I just hear the chubby boy click his fingers for a waitress.

Imagine a long, hot street, not quite straight. There are puddles in the gutter from a recent burst of monsoon rain. Pedestrians are lost in the black shadow of the arcades. The buildings are all of a height; two storeys over the arcades, cement-faced, hung with laundry, and there is not much traffic to raise dust, or leave behind a film of tar. Perhaps the street had a use, led somewhere; but things have evidently changed since then. Some of the arcade fronts hold shops, but not many, and alleyways lead off the street to tenements behind.

For the elderly who do not want to sit in tenements all day there is a tea-house under the arcades. Tables and stools spill onto the pavement: the stools are bamboo, and barely a foot high, chiefly to assist squatting; they are very comfortable. The proprietor lurks behind a clay oven, where a kettle hisses on a coal grate. Soot blackens the chimney breast, the wooden ceiling, the dingy walls. All around the tea man there are shelves and niches stacked with earthenware teapots, none larger than a plum, and thimble-sized tea-cups (without handles, of course) standing on ceramic trays. A great tin caddy, bald with wear, and dented in a thousand places, stands with them.

The tea-equipage is brought to the table. It is absurdly small – everything is so small that were it not for the soot and the old men and the grumpy proprietor, you could easily believe yourself attending a dolls' tea-party in a Wendy house. The owner stomps up with the kettle. He takes the lid from the miniature teapot, which is stuffed to the brim with tea, and fills it with a swing of the kettle. Four tiny cups surround the pot; he picks up the dainty pot between his thick fingers and pours out the tea in a circle over the cups. When the pot is drained he empties the cups onto the tray. This is called *washing the leaves*, a customary practice which is supposed to remove the bitter edge and encourage the leaf to expand, as well as warming the tiny cups. He refills the teapot, and leaves you to pour the liquor into the cups, with a circular motion, to maintain an even strength. Against the rim, the tea water looks clear, but if you look down into the cup it is dark. It is ubelievably strong and fresh.

The water sits briefly on the leaves, and the pot must be emptied completely on each round: four cups are provided, even if only two people are drinking. The first brew after the washing should last about half a minute; subsequent brews are given a few seconds. There is a limit to how much tea can be drunk like this before your heart races and your mouth begins to fur. It's tea's answer to espresso.

The style of tea is peculiar to southern Fujian and is known as kung-fu, which means hard work and mastery of a skill; for the tea used is supposed to be the finest. The earthenware utensils were black with deposits because the cups and teapot are never scrubbed; at best they are rinsed in boiling water. An aged pot is treasured: the tea deposit on the inside has been laid down by generations of drinkers, as ingrained as the soot on the tea-house walls. The pottery was not Yixing ware, which would be beyond the pockets of the old men, but although it was local and inferior, its age alone gave it value.

In Amoy nobody says 'zaijian', goodbye. 'Man zuo' they say, go slowly: take it easy.

The Amoy tea trade is still to be found on the waterfront, in the offices of the China National Foodstuffs and Animal By-products Import and Export Corporation (Tea Department). The branch is responsible for teas grown locally, not for all Fujian Province. A score of clerks work there, bobbing like sampans on a sea of papers, negotiating reefs of piled books and ledgers. They work on old tables under fans, where every paper has to be weighted, in shirtsleeves and shouting; some of them have the use of a telephone; some have their own offices, sparsely furnished.

The collapse of the Amoy tea-gardens in the 1870s was a blow to Chinese tea connoisseurs. Among the local growths was a tea known as Tieh Kuan-yin, or Iron Goddess of Mercy. According to legend, a tea-grower lived near a dilapidated temple dedicated to the Goddess of Mercy, who was represented by an iron statue. He had no money for proper repairs, but he swept the halls and cleaned the statues, and on the first and the fifteenth of the lunar month he burned incense. Kuan-yin appeared in a dream to tell him of a treasure hidden in the cave behind the temple. 'It is not for you alone. The treasure must be shared,' she warned. In the cave, instead of heaps of gold and jewels, he found a single tea-shoot in the soil. Disappointed, he planted it in his garden, and in time it grew, and the first brew he made filled the room with extraordinary fragrance. The travelling buyers paid well, and the grower grew rich. He had the temple restored, and gave his neighbours tea-seed so that they might share his good fortune.

The finest grade of Tieh Kuan-yin came from the tops of high tea-trees, growing in awkward recesses of the mountains; tradition held that it was plucked by monkeys. 'Monkey Plucked' became its name. Typically, the Westerners refused to let the story be: they would enquire, fret and speculate. They added their own footnote. The monkeys, they decided, were released up the trunks of the tree and, having reached the top, were pelted with stones. Infuriated, they tore away the topmost branches and hurled them down at the pestering tea men.

Without Taiwan the collapse of the Amoy tea industry would have been the end of Amoy port itself. Taiwan had plenty of tea similar to the mainland but no harbour suitable for large ships, so with the decline of the Amoy teas, Amoy merchants began to post representatives on Taiwan to buy and ship the teas to the mainland; during the tea season small steamers shuttled between island and mainland, bringing the chests to warehouse. As the port for the entire province of Taiwan, Amoy entered a period of unprecedented prosperity, when the great liners put in for tea, and foreigners and wealthy local businessmen built the majority of their residences and godowns. In 1873 the Hong Kong and Shanghai Bank opened an Amoy branch. By 1880 twenty-four foreign firms were operating in the city as general merchants (many owned by British Chinese from the Straits, doing business across the China Seas), with 183 Chinese wholesale houses, and six local banks.

In 1895 the Japanese seized Taiwan. Imperialism has been called a crude form of development: absolute power can make things happen faster. The Japanese built a new harbour on the island, suitable for big ships, and the boom on Amoy collapsed. By the turn of the century the city had almost stopped handling Formosa tea, and had altogether lost its way.

From then on, under scientific management, Formosa teas went from strength to strength. They had always been popular in the US, and the Japanese developed a liking for them, too. The whole system of buying tea was put on a rational footing. Between the wars foreign buyers could choose teas at a particular price and quality from the following preselected grades: Standard, Fully Standard, Standard to Good, On Good, Good Leaf, Good, Fully Good, Good Up, Good to Superior, Fully Superior, Superior Up, Superior to Fine, On Fine, Fine, Fine Up, Fine to Finest,

Finest to Choice, Choice, Strict Superior, Choicest and Fancy. A new tea was invented for the American market to go with the oolongs and pouchongs (flower-scented oolongs) which was marketed as Orange Pekoe Leaf Size. The new tea was in fact an oolong, fermented longer than usual to take on certain characteristics of black tea.

Since peace has returned to China the Amoy gardens are restored and lessons have been learned from the Japanese, Comintern and Mao. All Chinese teas for export are graded and priced by the State Inspectorate; buying is only a matter of a telex because the standard – though not the quantity or price of each grade – is constant. This I was told by the Amoy tea people; who observed, too, that the Japanese and the Americans were still their best customers. The fundamental lesson, though, had been learned from the Emperors: do business, if you must, from a distance.

Tom took me to meet an elderly friend of his who lived in Gulangyu. A wall sheltered a small garden full of blossom, and a yellow villa, where Professor Ge sat in a sunlit room furnished with broken-down sofas and a comic-strip armchair erupting with springs. Professor Ge was like a moorhen, with irrespressible tufts of grey hair and huge winged eyebrows. He had not shaved recently, and his white shirt was choppy with creases. If anything he looked Siberian, about six foot and broad. His father, in fact, had been German. He stood confusedly as we entered. Tom introduced us.

'Glad to meet you. GREAT to meet you!' He roared, pumping my hand. 'Sit down, sit down. I would have prepared some luncheon if you'd warned me.' Tom apologised for us. 'Eh?' He looked at me. 'Great to meet you! I'm afraid my wife is abroad at the moment.' He gestured airily. 'Canada, Buffalo, New York, Boston. She would have made some lunch. Would you care for lunch? Pot luck, of course.' His eyebrows shot up.

'This is really just a flying visit,' said Tom apologetically.

'A flying – I haven't seen you for days, or is it weeks? I expect you're working too hard. WORKING HARD? How's business?'

'I'm selling slate to the Welsh now.'

'They work you very hard, don't they? Working in the evenings now, I guess,' said Professor Ge, his eyebrows sprouting innocently off the sides of his face. 'That's the way for a young man to get on,' he told me. 'Have some more tea.'

Alice in Wonderland. Tom and I exchanged glances.

'But you have no tea!' There were a couple of odd cups on his desk, both cracked and ringed on the inside. He poured from a brown pot. Oolong.

'Excellent water,' remarked the Professor. 'I draw it from my neighbour's new well. Dug it himself. Excellent.' He took a fruity slurp from his own cup. 'Good, eh?'

We agreed it was good.

'Jason's grandfather lived on Gulangyu before the war,' said Tom.

'Chinese grandfather?' said the Professor in surprise.

'English.'

'Ah. What name?'

'Innes,' I said.

'Wasn't there an Inglis at the Consulate?' He asked Tom, as if they were both old men.

'Innes, Professor.'

'Innes? Innes? Innes, Innes, Innes.'

'That's right,' Tom was keyed up. Would his Professor perform? 'He worked here for —'

'Asiatic. Sold me a drum of gas. Strong man, well built. Bit stout. Yes, yes. Angry face. A red face?'

'That's him,' I said. Tom grinned.

'Where did he live? Asiatic Petroleum Company. Under the Rock, it's the Army San now. Innes . . . Had a huge staff. Is he well?'

'He's dead,' I said.

'Ah, well. We dined together at the Amoy magistrate's once. A Chinese banquet. You English don't like Chinese food.'

'I love it,' I objected.

'Too rich for you, of course. A Chinese meal. At the magistrate's. We had . . . duck's web. Innes did not, ah, appreciate it very much. Do you smoke?' He flicked half a dozen out of a soft pack. 'SMOKE?' He roared. One dived into my tea. The Professor didn't notice. Tom did. Avoiding his eye, I surreptitiously fished it out.

'These aren't bad,' said the Professor, not lighting one. 'My wife says I smoke too much. I love the smell.'

Tom, who had a meeting in Amoy, gave me a surreptitious nod. It was time to go. The Professor, meanwhile, sniffed the air.

'Lucky Strike!' he said suddenly.

'Professor —'

'Lucky Strike Means Fine Tobacco!'

'I think we ought to –'

'A MAN AND HIS LUCKY!'

'– be going –'

'TOBACCO AND FILTER – THE PERFECT MATCH!' bellowed the Professor.

'– to lunch.'

'Lunch? Have some of my jam.'

'Thank you very much, but I'm afraid –'

'It's home-made.'

'I'm sure it's delicious, but we do have to run.'

'Won't you have some?'

'Thank you.'

'It's very clean. Home-made.' He went out and reappeared with a pot of jam, yellow bread and a sticky knife. He cut two wedges.

'It's very clean jam,' he explained, dolloping it onto the slices. 'How long will you be in Amoy?' He stuck the knife into the wrong pot and it came up covered in cigarette ash and a spent matchstick on the blade.

'Oh dear,' he said, shaking the knife. The matchstick came unstuck, swung wide and clung to the blade's tip where he couldn't see it. He pulled more jam from the pot.

'Oh dear,' he said again when the matchstick appeared on my bread. He prodded it off with a knife. Tom and I sat rigid.

'Beautiful wife. Don't recall any children. And where are you going next?' He wrote out a letter of introduction in my notebook. 'Introducing Mr Jason Goodwin who is anxious to know the history of tea trade in China. Wonder if you could give him some help.' It was to a professorial colleague in Fuzhou, an old school-friend.

'Do give him my regards.'

We thanked him for his delicious jam. He insisted on showing us to the garden gate, pointing out the plum, lemon and cherry. 'I adore trees,' he said.

He wrung our hands. 'Come and see me soon,' he told Tom. 'Goodbye, young man. Glad to have met you. GREAT to have met you!'

I came off the ferry that evening, and went into the Lujiang, the hotel from where I had watched the *Chiang Liu* sail away.

Typhoons from Alice to Olivia had been and gone, and now Peggy rolled up in their wake, dodging inland to bring flash floods to southern Fujian: seventy people drowned. She was gathering herself up for a move east and her skirts swirled through Amoy and caught me on the rooftop bar of the Lujiang. Yielding ferns bent to her whim. Fag-ends jumped from the ashtray and an empty bottle skittered across a nearby table and crashed to the ground. Inside, couples were waltzing to forgotten hits played by the hotel band. The girls, on the whole, waltzed with each other, the boys wore dark glasses and fumbled on the tables for their beers. Peggy began to bang pots together on a neighbouring roof, enthusiastic but out of time. At the end of the verandah I pushed open a door I hadn't seen before, marked BAR.

Half a dozen stools around a horseshoe bar were occupied. There were no peanuts, no special lighting, and no conversation. Nobody looked up when I took an empty stool.

'Another beer here, Wilson,' said my neighbour.

Wilson?

'Are you on business?' I asked.

'Fella wants t'know if we're doing business, Joe.' He was Australian.

'Moot, Arnold. Very moot,' said Joe, a northerner. 'Are you English?'

'Not another bloody Pom.'

'Spoken like a convict, Arnold.'

It was an old routine, even before they'd got to it.

'I make – *bogs*,' said Joe, with defiant emphasis.

'Joe makes 'em for America,' Arnold explained. With Joe, Arnold had to be upbeat. Arnold was in his forties, with a thin moustache turned down the corners of his mouth, the moustache of a watchful gaucho. Arnold was plump and looked boiled.

Two stools away a man was wearing Richard Burton's face several sizes too large. A round belly smoothed his shirt. He said: 'You travellin', or workin'?'

He was a southerner – American south. I wondered if Joe and Arnold had a loos-to-America routine he wanted to head off.

'Working and travelling. I'm writing a book.'

The confession seemed to cause acute embarrassment. Joe stared at the vacant TV set; Arnold, who had been about to say something, shut his mouth; the American stared at his beer.

He scratched his chin.

'You a writer?' He said finally.

'Well, I'm writing a book about tea.'

'Now, that is a subject.' My neighbour chipped in. She was wearing a lot of make-up and had spooned herself into a tight black jeans suit. She spoke as if something else *wasn't* a subject. I asked her what that could be.

'Oh, few months back, had a writer up along here, raised Cain.'

Her bayou accent confused me for a moment. I had a vision of a man with a notebook running a sugar plantation. The real picture emerged in remarks and contradictions: someone in his cups had griped about his managers to a visitor; the visitor turned out to be a stringer for the *South China Morning Post* and the next day a story appeared naming names. The journalist left Amoy very quickly.

'The bosses were not best pleased, I can tell you,' said Joe. 'People in this bar,' he added, 'have learned the Art of Discretion.' He drained his glass. 'Pink gin, Wilson.'

The door flew open.

' 'Ullo, 'ullo, 'ullo, 'ullo, 'ullo, what, what, what?'

'Evening, Lydia!' everyone chorused.

'Have I had a time and a half!' chortled Lydia, who was Welsh. 'I was having supper tonight with Dan and Stan, you know, when I got the news about Ice Cream Frank. I mean, of all the unfortunate things! He only had another day or two before he was off, you know. Now he won't be able to go for weeks. And stuck in that hospital, too.'

'It'll hit him hard,' agreed Joe.

'Have you not been to see him yet, then?'

'No point. All dosed up.'

'In another day or two he might have been in Hong Kong for the treatment, rather than stuck up here, too. A gin and tonic if you please, Wilson. It had better be a quick one, they say the ferry may not be working later.'

'Is the typhoon so bad?' I asked, apprehensively.

'We had one once that stopped the ferry for forty-eight hours. Nobody could get across at all.'

'If you lived on this side you could have got off work,' observed Arnold.

'Now wouldn't that be a pretty thing, and all the children dying for my presence.' Lydia taught English at a school on Gulangyu. 'But I'd rather live on the island than in a shoebox here.'

Joe leaned foward and addressed me.

'I've been staying in this hotel for eighteen months. They don't even know my name downstairs.'

'Men!' exclaimed Lydia. 'Old socks and suitcases.'

Though she meant to stop only a moment it was much later, in a lateness measured in gin and boredom, that Joe suggested a video.

For twenty-five years Joe had worked in the East. He had gone Home once eighteen years ago; he had meant to go back again since, but somehow he never got around to it. He had delayed so long that now he was afraid. Like divided families meeting again in Amoy, he was afraid of the change. He had heard about that; out here, he said, he'd seen the bloody Empire futter out. He thought it was all right, it was meant to go; but he couldn't decide whether it had been given away generously or lost by mistake, by union trouble and smartarse bureaucrats. The England he read about in the papers, the England that was wrapped up in a video and sent out by some kind friend, had seemed a shambolic, indolent, confusing place — after working in the miracle world of Eastern economics, that was hardly surprising. Joe turned his back on it. He had stopped getting videos sent out, except of cricket matches, which could be played in any foreign field.

As Wilson inserted the video into the machine I wondered if Joe had seen screaming supporters flooding the pitch at Lord's, dark fudge stealing over a pristine green?

American Fred was torn between his wife and the boys. 'You okay, hon?' In fact she followed the game a shade quicker than he did. Arnold had seen live cricket at Perth that summer; Joe hadn't watched a match for about ten years. Fred didn't know much about cricket but it was a ball-game and he was determined to pronounce.

'Some ball,' he remarked as someone in a blue cap hit a four.

'Khan. Good batsman, demon bowler,' said Joe. He was admitting Fred by degrees. 'He'll be LBW now, you watch.' So Joe had already watched the video.

'Bowled by Foster,' added Arnold. Had he seen it before? Had Fred? There went the bowler, running fast nowhere up the foreshortened pitch. A moment later someone was on the ground. We switched cameras for the close-up: Foster, hand held high. We watched the whole event in slow motion. There . . . went . . . the . . . bowler . . .

'We'd better be running, if the ferry is,' announced Lydia. 'See you all at the TGIF, boys and girl.'

As the lift juddered to the ground floor she said: 'We've cut it a wee bit fine tonight.' Outside the door the black marketeers sneezed their questions – 'Chay – chay – change –' as we dashed down the steps. '– Money' floated forlornly on the air behind us. We hit the ramp just as *Jingle Bells* bleeped and triggered a Pavlovian burst of speed. We were better than the proverbial fat man: two foreigners, clean out of dignity, belting as hard as we could to the last ferry of the day. The gates began to slide; it looked as if we wouldn't make it. A young man hopped from the ferry, planted himself against the gate and hauled against it, vibrating with exertion; we just slipped through, and he relinquished his position with a clang. We thanked him profusely; everyone grinned. The motors thumped to work, and even Typhoon Peggy stood off to let us all across.

5
Treaty Ports 2
Fuzhou

I once stumbled off a Chinese train onto a Mongolian railway station in one of those new towns built around steel or coal, where everything is uniformly drab and hastily put up. I had spent the evening on the train drinking what looked like table water in the restaurant car with an American friend. I had spent the night mostly up. Now I had a staggering hangover. For a while I sat in the station waiting room, drinking jasmine tea through gritted teeth – the scent of jasmine, early in the morning, on a weak stomach, made me feel very ill. I had to walk about. The main street was lined with concrete blocks; it was a dust road, with a few camels parked outside a government office, but otherwise the place was deserted. I staggered along, a sorry figure still slightly drunk from the night before, until I heard the faint strains of music. It grew louder and louder, and a heavy bass line made my head thrum: *Funky Town*, played very loudly in a Mongolian city of militants. I went up into a building and followed the music to a pair of doors at the end of a corridor where the noise was deafening, and there, in an enormous hall, to the distinctive disco sound, hundreds of couples in blue Mao suits were doing the waltz.

The Amoy to Fuzhou bus was a modern Japanese affair equipped with air conditioning and a video machine. The passengers were mainly business-men, like the fruit-canning company buyer who sat beside me. The video blinked as soon as we started, and everyone insisted on drawing the curtains to see better, much to my disappointment. There was the sound of a ribald oboe over the loudspeakers, and the titles flickered up: *Early Bird*. With Norman Wisdom.

Wisdom is the local milkman with a horse, doing his rounds in a northern town. Consolidated Dairies want to take over his pitch with their electric floats. The horse gets sick: he puts her in his bed. He falls downstairs a lot, ruins the Chairman's game of golf, finds his boss is having an affair with a fat lady, creates mayhem in the Consolidated building, almost falls down a lift shaft, dresses up as a fireman, wrecks the offices, and finally delivers a proud and stirring Small Man's homily, which even the Chairman eventually cheers. The film was dubbed, and I couldn't follow the dialogue very exactly; but I was not at all sure if my neighbours could follow the premise. Within ten minutes those who had not dozed off were staring open-mouthed at the screen. Nobody drinks milk in China. Nothing is delivered, not in the morning or at any time during the day or night. Few could even dream of living in a back-to-back terraced house. There are no games of golf and the virtue of the small man and his old-fashioned ways are at odds with Party directives to embrace modern management, new methods and efficiency. Even the Fat Lady is an in-joke. The bus passengers looked pretty nonplussed.

The barrier was crossed once only, as Wisdom fumbled sleepily around the kitchen to make a morning cup of tea. But even that was spoilt: he had to add milk.

Fuzhou is the capital of the mountain province of Fujian; the city itself lies a few miles from the sea on the junction of the Min and the Oolong Rivers. In the days of the Chinese Empire the city's imperial governor would arrive by ship, ever mindful of the sea and the hills: for with Pagoda Anchorage Fuzhou was a port, a bib of tableland encircled by mountains. The governor would know he was hemmed in, from the tedium of the overland mails, the throng of wiry browned hillmen, and the mountain tea from Wuyi which took just three days to come down the Min River. But it was a cultivated, enviable imprisonment. The townsmen made beautiful lacquerware, called bodiless; the hillmen made fine tea; commands came slowly from far away; and the fishermen brought in superb freshwater mussels from the estuary to be simmered in wine and green pepper – mussels that are known only here and in Venice, Marco Polo's home town, thousands of miles away.

98

From beyond even Venice, though, the port had been marked out. Long before the Opium Wars, British merchants had realised that they could cut costs by shipping the tea from Fuzhou instead of Canton. It took only three days for Wuyi, or Bohea, tea to reach Fuzhou down the Min river, whereas Wuyi tea had to be brought overland to the Canton factories on a journey of nearly six weeks which added considerably to the cost. In 1814 they tried to have teas brought down to Fuzhou and then shipped along the coast to Canton, but the Emperor banned the experiment in favour of the long, slow, traditional route overland.

Nevertheless the foreign merchants insisted that Fuzhou be opened as a Treaty Port in the 1840s. The officials in the city had no wish to see their Eden breached by foreign trade, and for ten years they managed to block the foreigners' every effort to buy tea cheaply in the port. But the tide of trade was against them. Twenty years after the bursting of the breach, Fuzhou was the greatest tea market on the China coast.

It was dark by the time we arrived, three films later. The overseas Chinese hotel was getting a face-lift and all the cladding had been stripped from the reception area to make a cement cavern entwined with flex and naked bulbs, with a wooden desk for reception. A young Chinese loitering at the reception desk told me that I spoke good, clear English for an Englishman. He was another Tokyo Rose, a Voice of America graduate who thought BBC announcers spoke too fast. It is the general complaint in China.

'I'm John,' he continued, implausibly. 'One day I'll be running this outfit.'

'How do you know that?'

He laid his palm on the desk, with sincerity.

'I am very popular. I speak Japanese, English and some German. *Herzlich willkommen.* Welcome to our hotel.' He pronounced '*herzlich*' *hässlich*: hateful. 'I am very useful to foreign guests. I work very hard. The manager is a friend, and I'll take his job.'

'When does he leave?' I asked.

'Oh, maybe when he leaves. Maybe before.'

I digested this sinister information and signed for a room.

'I'm a popular guy,' said John.

'And I'm a tired one.' John had an owlish, bespectacled face and an oily grin. 'I'm going to my room.'

John wanted to come too. 'It's good practice for me.' I gave him a bag to carry, and pressed for the lift. There were four lifts, and they had no central brain. You took the first lift to answer your summons, but the other lifts never found this out. One by one they would stop on your floor and open. After a while they closed and beetled off to another empty floor. One lift was always full and three were always empty, and it made going up and down an unbelievably slow business. I watched the numbers light up, floor by floor, all the way to the sixteenth, and descend, floor by floor, all the way to the bottom. It took ten minutes.

'When I run this hotel, I'm gonna get new elevators,' said John.

My allotted room was under construction when we arrived. Flexes dripped from the ceiling and the beds lacked mattresses. The floor attendant looked at me appealingly, hoping I wouldn't mind, but ten minutes later we were downstairs again. I collected a new room chit and turned to find all four lifts invitingly open. Just as I bent down to pick up my bag all four lifts slid shut in front of me and went off to answer a summons.

Trudging up to the eighth floor had the unexpected bonus of losing John. He stood at the bottom of the stairwell, speechless.

It was all worth it to find a printed envelope by the thermos which read:

JASMINE TEA
WELCOME TO OUR HOTEL!
WISH YOU A HAPPY LIFE!

Twenty minutes later John appeared, to talk about himself.

He appeared again early next morning, with a list of new words he wanted me to check: INADEQUATE, DERELICT, POUCHONG, CONFUSION, STUNNING. I recognised them all, of course, from the previous evening. John had also fixed up a meeting with a tea expert, and a visit to the tea-scenting factory.

An hour later I was making tea in my room for Professor Zhuang, Chairman of the Fujian Tea Society, a sort of semi-official drinking club for veterans of the tea industry. In the old days, the Professor said, there had been tea-houses all over the city, because the coolies needed somewhere to go. Now there were none.

We sipped our jasmine tea, which tasted of chlorine. The Professor

admitted that Fuzhou water was pretty terrible: he always allowed it to
stand for an hour or two before using it. For special occasions he collected
spring water from Gu Shan, the nearby mountain. It wouldn't be worth
the trouble for this jasmine, which was only for the common people. I
asked if he drank fine teas with ceremony. He grinned. 'There is no
Japanese tea ceremony in China! We Chinese do not believe in God. It is
best to drink tea with two, three or four friends – sit and talk.'

On the whole the Chinese prefer green tea to black, which was more
popular on the coast and overseas – something to do with the pace of life,
the professor thought. Black teas were brisk (a formal taster's term), suited
to city life, but greens were subtle and quiet. At his time of life he
preferred green tea, the greener the better. Light in the cup, heavy on
aroma. Africans, the Professor said, preferred green tea to be deep-
colouring, with little aroma. That was because they added mint.

'Is there a system for classifying Chinese teas – a uniform way of grading
them all, and describing their place of origin?' I asked the Professor. It
was, as far as I was concerned, the key question. The thousand and ten
thousand kinds mentioned by Lu Yu might be arranged like a library,
with a code; or they could form a labyrinth.

The Professor thought for a while. 'There is a system. It makes about
eight thousand distinctions. Perhaps there are more exceptions to the
system than distinctions within it. I have seventy-three years in tea, but
I do not know the system.' He grinned again. 'In the West you use an
alphabet. In China, we learn characters. It is the same with tea,' he said.

When he had gone I plonked four books on the table and turned the
air-con to Arctic. Samuel Ball, Late Inspector of Teas to the Honourable
East India Company, had written an *Account* in 1848, riddled with good
sense and inaccuracies. It is still referred to as the 'standard account' of
China tea. Harler's *Culture and Marketing of Tea* had been the Planter's
Bible since it was issued in 1935 to rave reviews in the *Tea and Rubber
Mail*. *All About Tea*, by William Ukers, though, was the masterpiece:
two vols, bound in leaf-green, 1152 pages, 54 chapters, well over half a
million words, a fitting companion to Ukers' previous work, *All About
Coffee*. Ukers had beavered on through the death of Edward VII, the First
World War, the Russian Revolution, the rise of Chinese Communism,
Hitler's putsch, commercial aviation and the New Deal: twenty-five years
from research to final proofs. At the same time he had written *Tea in a
Nutshell*. To demonstrate how much tea was drunk in 1934, he had

commissioned a drawing of a tea-cup with the *Normandie* (the largest ship
of the age) floating on the surface like a broken matchstick. Harler and
Ball and Ukers had travelled with me and I had done my best to ignore
them, though it wasn't easy, Ukers weighing 20 pounds and growing
sticky in the heat, dyeing parts of my underwear green; Harler sulking at
the bottom of my bag for a week, to reappear dirty and unshaven where
fluff and old chocolate had gathered on his cover. Ball was nearly 150
years old, clubbable but inert. Nothing ever happened to him. Now I
drummed them up for a conference.

Everything they could say about China teas pointed to No System.
There was no literal key which would reduce the profligate chaos of names
to a few general principles, and I felt adrift.

The Chinese themselves group tea into reds, greens, whites, red brick
and green brick. Red is what we call black: we judge by the colour of the
dry leaf, rather than by the colour of the liquor in the cup. Some teas we
would call green give 'red' liquors. The five classes are divided by grade:
rough, tender, old or new; and can be well-made or ill-made. You now
have forty permutations, but as yet you haven't said where the tea is from,
or who made it, or whether it was picked early in the year or late. You
haven't said whether it's a blend. But add the Province and District of
origin alone and, as China grows tea in eighteen of her twenty-four
provinces, your classification has come up somewhere up in the eight
thousands.

The Sung-dynasty tea-tasting tournaments described by Professor Tea
in Hong Kong seemed more remarkable if the competitors were aiming
to know and remember all the tea in China.

Foreigners devised their own systems. The Western consumer was not
as nice as a Sung connoisseur. J. H. Wade distinguished twenty-two
classes of black tea and six of green. Torgasheff made out sixty-four classes
of black and forty-eight of green. Which system worked best? The foreign
merchants, on the whole, stuck with rule of thumb, common sense,
origins, method of manufacture, season of plucking, age of bush, size of
leaf, port of exit, 'all beat up and intimately blended together', as Turner
said of the Lama's tea. They made up a language to suit – a pidgin poetry,
vivid and transient like any good slang.

In the beginning, the seventeenth century, there were two teas: Singlo
and Bohea. Both were anglicised names of hills which grew green and
black tea respectively. Both words were stretched to include blacks or

greens from other regions, and eventually came to mean teas of the poorest quality.

As more tea left China, the merchants began to sophisticate their order-books. They called good black teas (as opposed to Bohea) Congou, from *kung-fu*, hard work. There were North China and South China Congous. The former were known as black-leaf congous, and as English Breakfast teas; poorer qualities were called Monings. They left through Shanghai. Good North Chinas included Keemuns, Ningchows and Ichangs, which were even called China's Burgundies: ragged in appearance but thick and full in the cup, with a rich aroma.

South Chinas generally came out of Fuzhou, so they were also known as Foochow Congous, or China's clarets: friskier than northerners. Paklums, Paklings and Panyongs were supposed to be the best sorts. Souchongs were black teas: the word meant 'small sort' in Chinese, and in Ball's day described excellent, small-leaf teas. By the turn of the century, though, souchong meant quite the opposite – what the Chinese call '*da cha*', big tea.

I followed my mentors as far as this, but I gave up on placing the Kintuck Monings, the Shantams and the Oonfas, the Hohows and Oopacks, silky black Chinwoos, tightly rolled, honest Soomoos, 'thick and full, albeit somewhat dull', high-fired Padres, whose leaf was black and crape-like, with the flavour of blackcurrants. Some of these words still exist, but most of them have vanished with the decline of Chinese tea.

All green teas were called Country Greens, except Hoochows and Pingsucys. Their generic names went partly by size and shape: Gunpowders, Imperials, young Hysons, Hysons, Hyson Skins and Twankays. Gunpowders looked like ball shot, and they ranged in size from pinhead to pea leaf. Imperials were like Gunpowders, but made of older leaf. The very best – the 'crack chops', as Ukers says – were the Moyunes; Nankin, Packeong and True Moyunes, which were once called Cowslip Hysons.

Cowslip Hysons were, another time, scented green teas. Oolong teas are somewhere between green and black teas; they come from Fujian and Taiwan. Formosa Oolongs are more black than green. Foochow Oolongs are, often, more green than black. When they are scented they are called Pouchongs. Scented teas are popular in northern China, but in the south on the whole they are considered poor.

I shut the books and opened a window. A gust of warm wet air met Arctic and fogged the glass. I invented characters and drew them with the end of my finger, slippery and fading. Real characters are meaningless, too, unless you know which sound they represent. You can't guess, you just have to learn. You see people everywhere reading newspapers with the help of a dictionary. It works both ways. You might need a dictionary to decipher the character for a sound you understand, but you can communicate with someone whose dialect is utterly different by means of writing – Xiamen and Amoy, for instance, look the same on paper. Stuck for the right word in a shop, I would often be handed paper and pen to write it down. So, perhaps, would a Shanghainese shopping in Fuzhou. Every syllable has four characters for each of the four tones; a clever person knows perhaps twenty thousand characters by heart, and looks up the rest. The older you are, the better you read and write – which may justify the Chinese respect for grey hairs. Professor Zhuang was right: Chinese tea and Chinese writing are the same. You added to your knowledge piece by piece, stone by stone like the Great Wall.

I was excited about meeting tea for the first time – tea the Commodity. The factory was no more than a concrete shed which stood in a muddy compound on the outskirts of Fuzhou, but the scent was heady enough for a Hollywood romance: an almost sickly sweetness of jasmine. Inside, on a swept concrete floor, warm tea-leaves are spread about two inches deep. On top they strew blossom – full-blown, without stalk or stem – until the base layer of tea is wholly covered. Another layer of tea goes on top, and then more jasmine – or magnolia or chrysanthemum or gardenia – and so on until the heap is a couple of feet high. The expiring blooms will impregnate the tea with their scent within the day; then, if the tea is good, the withered petals will have to be picked out laboriously by hand – if not particularly good, it isn't worth the trouble. The scented leaf is mixed with unscented, about one part to twenty; and for Western markets a few dried jasmine flowers are tossed in, just to show that the whole thing is natural.

John had given me quasi-official status and the visit passed in a sort of bland official bonhomie, like 'Jennifer's Diary': 'Mr Hu Wo Bang is the general manager. He very kindly allowed me to see the export godown, where the Oolongs, lovely scented teas which he told me interestingly were called Pouchongs, and green teas were all stacked very neatly in chests. Everything was very neat and clean. Next we visited the bagging shed, where Miss Lu Fo Da showed me how she puts the tea into half-kilo bags with a special machine. The machine came all the way from Italy, which astonished me. Miss Lu seems very nimble, and like all the girls in the factory she wears a white mob cap, which is more hygienic and nice to look at.'

It was at elevenses that I began to come unstuck. They hoped, they said as we sipped our tea, that my visit to China was interesting. Most interesting, I said. There was a pause. They thought they had shown me everything in the factory, they said. Yes, thank you very much. Even though your factory is so large, I said. That's right, they said. A pause. The teas, er, looked wonderful, I said. They smelled wonderful, too. Ha Ha Ha, they laughed, genially. Genial laughter simmered for as long as decently possible, and then died. A pause. Would I be visiting anywhere else? Not in Fuzhou, I said.

A pause.

Would my order be very large?

I looked at John, who continued to smile blandly.

'I'm afraid I can't say yet,' I countered. Big mistake, for then I was parrying questions about the size of my company, its name, what arrangements I would be making for shipment and payment, qualities sought, probable date of purchase, my position.

My position.

'Er, junior executive,' I said.

I think it went over wrong in translation. They looked dumbfounded.

'How old are you?' they said.

I asked them to guess.

'Twenty-nine?' said one.

'Sixteen?' said another in English, proudly, and then looked confused.

Sixteen felt about right.

John considered he had earned an English-language session. For an hour or so we looked for new superlatives to describe John's attitude to work, friendship and modern China. John worked so hard he had no time for girlfriends. He swotted up on his irregular verbs at home after a twelve hour day. Most Sundays he had free, but no holiday. It was his duty to his country to become important as quickly as possible.

'A big cheese,' I suggested.

John looked doubtful. 'Big cheese?'

'It's American,' I explained.

'But I have American friends.' He paused, avoiding my eye. 'Big cheese is good? My American friends call me — small potatoes.' He looked anxious.

'Slang,' I explained.

'Yes,' he said quietly.

'It means . . . it means — you will be a big cheese soon,' I said, lamely.

Fuzhou's roads are six-lane highways, but only bicycles, buses and a few taxis use them. Like Salt Lake City, laid out through Brigham Young's divine inspiration on a colossal, improbable scale, with perfectly straight roads, as though they knew the automobile was on its way. Fuzhou's pavements are wider than most London streets, but they are potholed and muddy and largely go to waste. For the thin traffic there are police-boxes at every junction, looking like big stripy hand-grenades, and a motionless policeman inside every one, wearing white gloves. Saplings planted along the thoroughfares are prematurely wizened and covered in soot, like Victorian child sweeps. While some of the new buildings are up, and some haven't yet begun, most seem to have topped off mid-way, as if further building were promised but in the meantime the bamboo scaffolding had simply mouldered off. The successful new buildings were all hotels, because new hotels are *de rigueur* for Development; but they appeared to be full of Chinese boys playing Space Invaders, and Chinese girls in cheongsams straightening menus in empty restaurants, and generally keeping the investment warm. And in our hotel, the biggest and newest, I read a notice at the door which seemed to have the Fuzhou flavour of expectant make-believe to a T:

HONOURABLE GUEST! THE HOTEL IS NOW AT THE ACTIVITY OF 'SMILING ENVOY' SERVICE. PLEASE KINDLY GIVE YOUR COMMENTS ON THE SERVICE THE SMILING ENVOY PROVIDED. WHETHER THEY HAVE OFFERED YOU INITIATIVE. WARM. PATIENT. THOUGHTFUL AND ASSIDUOUS SERVICE WITH MODERATE SMILING ON THEIR FACE.

One afternoon I took the road 12 miles off to Mawei, the Pagoda Anchorage. I was glad to see hills and the sea instead of the dreary half-formed buildings, and the moderate smiling. The road tunnelled through the encircling mountains to the east, and emerged onto scrub on the hills, red clay and rocks tumbling towards a chunk of glittering sunlight which wasn't the sea but the estuary and mud-flats on the far side. We passed a goods yard, and a container quay; a single-track railway ran to a marshalling-yard stacked with steel boxes; and there was the pagoda on a small hill overlooking the port.

I paid a few pence and climbed up. From one balcony to the next the stone staircases grew narrower, and near the top they smelled damp and close. The pagoda had been built, it was said, by the wife of a sea-captain, so that every day she might climb to the top and watch for her husband's sails. The years passed without a sign. And then one day, just as the sun was beginning to set, she saw the familiar sails turning up the estuary towards her. But the husband saw the pagoda and thought he must be in the wrong place, so he sailed away again.

With the abolition of the Company's monopoly in 1833 the slow East Indiamen had gone and quicker ships were brought onto the China run by private companies, to whom time was money. In 1849 Britain repealed her Navigation Acts, which had required British-owned imports to enter Britain in British bottoms. By the 1850s, when Fuzhou's intransigence began to show signs of breaking down, tea had become a highly competitive business and ships of every registry could tender for the run to London. The demand for tea itself had never been bigger.

In December 1850, 1600 tons of tea arrived at the West India Docks, aboard the *Oriental* out of Hong Kong. The *Oriental* was an American clipper. Setting out against the monsoon she had made the Hong Kong – London run in ninety-seven days, beating British merchantmen by a couple of months – and carrying tea at £6 a ton against their £3 10s. It was a blow to every idea of British naval supremacy – a challenge, *The Times* said, which could not go unanswered. The Admiralty had to request permission to take off the *Oriental*'s lines in dry dock.

The clipper itself was not entirely new: in India they had been building smaller ones to run opium up the China coast for years. But no one had attempted to build a great cargo ship for extreme speed. The old tea waggons had been slow but very stable; the clippers were slim and their bows entered the water like a knife, prone to cutting too deep and sending their bows under water; in a following sea they were tricky to handle. Fast but dangerous, they needed crack crews and skippers of the first chop.

The port at Pagoda Anchorage is triangular: the Min flowing down from Fuzhou at one point, and in one direction lies the sea, through an estuary that clippers found hard to navigate. Fuzhou became the favourite clipper port nonetheless. It was closer to the teas than Canton or Shanghai; and closer to London than Shanghai, advantages in the race home with the new season's teas. And it was a race. A year's supply of tea no longer had to be kept in London at all times, so the arrival of the tea ships was a great annual event which staved off the prospect of shortage. 'New tea' could be sold at a premium on an assumption that the freshest teas were the best. The Chinese thought differently, and liked their teas aged a little; but it was true that the clippers leaving China in May and June carried the first and finest pluckings of Spring. The tea sold on razzamatazz and hype, as Beaujolais Nouveau sells nowadays: tea from *Ariel* or *Fiery Cross* was a talking point which had cachet for snobs.

Not all the tea carried by the clippers was top-quality either – over the shingle ballast they would usually lay a protective 'ground chop' of low-quality tea held over from the previous season. Before the crack chops came down from the gardens the shingle was laid smooth and slightly cambered towards the centre, so that the chests would lie in a very shallow arch: they were put in from the outside towards the middle, and the last chest was hammered into place with a wooden mallet, as a sort of keystone. The fit was so tight that the outer chests became moulded to the curve of the hull, and it was done partly to stow as much tea as possible and partly to keep the trim of the ship precisely even, for a list would slow her down, at best, and make her handling uncertain. Everyone agreed that Chinese stevedores were the best in the world.

All this was done as the teas were coming down. Weeks were then spent haggling for chops, especially in Fuzhou. The Chinese knew that the Fuzhou buyers were eager to consolidate their natural lead over ships from other ports, so they tended to be slow about fixing acceptable prices. Every season brought the same agony of delay. The buyers in one port were naturally anxious to pay no more for teas than their rivals and colleagues in the next. Meanwhile they negotiated for cargo space on the clippers, whose fees were set according to their track record as racing ships, or the experience of their skipper, or some novel ingredient of their design. The man who bought space on the favourite, at an inflated price, would be anxious to close his tea deal first. So everybody watched him closely. It was a stretched out, high-stake game of poker.

At the top of the Pagoda I sat with my back to the wall and squinted out over the water. There was not a single ship at anchor there that day, though below the hill was an International Seaman's Hostel whose corridors I had seen placarded with snaps of maritime festivities: last year's Christmas party, a sailor's birthday, landfall. After a few weeks in China the rollicking figures already looked alarmingly alien. 'Barbarian' was an apt word for the Nordic revellers, with huge blond moustaches, beery red cheeks and hairy, hairy, hairy; or the dozy Indians, heavy-lidded with drink; or the wiry Irishmen with T-shirts gaping at the waist, white bellies peppered with hair. They had red flashbulb eyes, too, which didn't help much.

Out on the anchorage sampans like pointed slippers glided slowly, engines knocking. An ugly dredger, all scoops and cranes, worked silently in the channel, and a locomotive hummed in the yard below. There might have been fifteen clippers or so anchored here during the season, their hulls as black and glossy as lacquerware, copper sheathing burnished and oiled, deckboards holystoned to white, each yard exactly squared with braces and the rigging freshly blackened, the agent's house-flag flying from the mainmast to guide the chop boats, and the Stars and Stripes or the Blue Ensign waving from their sterns.

Sooner or later, in the night as often as not, one of the buyers broke and closed a deal. Everyone raced to a price. In Fuzhou the chests were weighed and labelled in forty-eight hours, and chops ran them down-river to the Pagoda Anchorage, bursting upon the clipper fleet with shouts and trumpeting and the wail of chop-men calling for ships. No observer was ever quite sure how they found their destinations, but at first light the 'going ships' would be already surrounded by chops, and the stevedores would be working for the next forty-eight hours or so to load the chests aboard.

It had begun as a race between the British and the Americans – 'between father and son' as *The Times* had it. The Yankee clippers put out of Boston or New York to carry prairie-shy gold-diggers round the Horn to California. From the West Coast they made the run to China, picked up a cargo of tea and raced it on to London, or back to New York. The British ships spent more time in China, using the wait for teas to carry cargoes locally, earning their keep in a way that the old merchantmen, which were unable to tackle contrary winds, never could. American ships dropped out of the running during the Civil War; in 1866 the sixteen ships waiting in Pagoda Anchorage were all British, racing to London. *Ariel* was the favourite that year and her agents closed on a deal first; she finished loading and left under tow at 5 p.m. on 28 May. Ninety nine days and eleven thousand miles later, the *Taeping* beat her to the London finish by just ten minutes.

The first teas of the season off the winning ship could be sold for sixpence a pound more than later arrivals. Sampling clerks would be on the quay as soon as a ship was reported off Gravesend, ready to snatch the sample chests for delivery to brokers and wholesalers. Bids were taken as soon as the tasting was done at Mincing Lane; duty was paid, and by the following morning the tea would be on sale in the great cities.

In fact the owners of *Taeping* and *Ariel* had become so nervous about the outcome of the race up the Thames that they had agreed to split the bounty paid to the first ship to 'break bulk' by hurling her tasting chests onto the quay, so both crews took a bonus. It was a mingy decision, really; but the race had a mingy finish, and a prophetic one. Both ships took on steam tugs in the estuary, and the faster tug settled the race.

Steam wasn't new: steamers had landed British troops in China during the Opium Wars. But Suez was. When the canal opened in 1870 it solved the problem of coaling for steamers to the East. There were steamers in Fuzhou the next season, loading the crack chops, while clippers went begging for cheap cargoes to Australia. The steamships were not necessarily faster – for the first few years most made slower times through Suez than clippers around the Cape – but they were new and exciting and comparatively safe. Nor were they governed by winds. They worked to a timetable, and made regular trips back and forth, and could carry much more than tea alone.

The 'new season' conceit died with the romance of the clippers, but it was not the only casualty. Steam tolled for Chinese tea in general. For over two centuries tea had arrived once a year in England, and the wholesalers would release it gradually, maintaining steady prices which enabled the buying agent in China to predict costs and the quantities required. Steam meant all-year deliveries from India and Ceylon as well as China. The broker tried to sell his teas as quickly as possible to the wholesaler, in case a new delivery glutted the market; the wholesaler sold on fast to the small dealers, who sold on fast to the grocers. The fear of collapsing prices in a market where prices were sinking overall, in the words of a contemporary, 'has continuously forced the pace and driven the tea into the consumer's teapot'.

Good news for the consumer, with his Aladdin's teapot endlessly replenished with cheap tea, but disaster for the exporter in China. In 1879 China exported more tea than ever before but in the following year, for the first time, exports of tea from the British Empire overtook those of China. Within twenty years the tea industry in Fuzhou was suffocating.

Camphor and tea had always been inimical – camphor forbidden on tea ships because it tainted the leaf: now there was no leaf left, and camphor was taken up wholesale as a desperate resort. Sail and China tea were mothballed.

A young couple came up onto the top parapet of the pagoda to share a can of Shanghai Cola. I remembered that Professor Zhuang had said that their pace of life was too fast even for black tea. 'Young people don't drink tea any more,' he worried. It was probably true. A decade of Coca-Cola culture had made more of a revolution than a decade of mass mobilisation against 'feudal thinking' and old habits. Even the Red Guards had needed their tea. But their children didn't want tea or Peking Opera or Chinese legends any more than they wanted mass mobilisation and Mao suits. They wanted crocodiles on their T-shirts and TV and fizzy drinks and for China to beat Hong Kong at football.

Their leaders are working on it. A week or so later I visited the Tea Research Institute in Hangzhou, whose director very solemnly unveiled his secret weapon in the battle for youth. It was a small glass bottle with goosepimples and a pressurised top. The director opened the bottle, pushed it across the conference table and gave me a straw. The liquid was brown, and tasted minty. I was just about to say how nice, when my mouth involuntarily puckered. I was so surprised I could only put my hand up to cough. It was as if I had rubbed my gums with fermenting banana skins. I couldn't think what to say.

'Tea Cola,' muttered the Director, looking down. 'I don't think we're quite ready to launch it yet.'

By the turn of the twentieth century, the clippers gone and the tea merchants packing up, the Bohea and Twankay of Dr Johnson or Sydney Smith were going to be forgotten words. China was entering a century of revolutions which would end with Shanghai Cola. I leaned back against the pagoda wall and half-closed my eyes to imagine the harbour ridden by glossy black ships, and the chops coming down with a drawn-out cry: 'Eeeeee-wo! Eeeeeeee-wo!' for Jardine's, and 'Wha-kee! Wha-kee!' for

Turner's. But there was only the ugly dredger clumping home, and the
screech of a loco shunting waggons up the line, and when I opened my
eyes the harbour looked empty.

A friend in Hong Kong had given me an introduction to Mr Wang, a
retired schoolmaster who spoke beautiful English and insisted on showing
me around. Mr Wang was very enthusiastic about the past. 'I remember!
I remember!' He cried as we passed through the gates of the old Anglo-
Chinese college on Nantai island, into a quad of balding gravel. 'Smith
House,' said Mr Wang, pointing to a colonnaded white pile. 'My dorm.'
There was the teaching block, and the brick chapel with a tall spire and
padlocks on the doors. Old Mr Wang led very nearly at a scamper, though
he was old enough to remember wearing a queue. 'Here, somewhere, we
used to come . . .'
   Later we stood in a little square at the top of a hill. It was a Mediterranean
retreat: a walled lane wound up at one side, and descended at the other
to a church whose spire could be seen, uncrossed, over the shoulder of a
gnarled yew tree; a folding-in of walls, and a rotting mansion which
overlooked the river and the swooping pantiled eaves of the Chinese town
below. Over the river lay Fuzhou proper, connected to this island by the
Bridge of a Thousand Years, and in the distance the Black Pagoda, which
Consul Lay had fitted up to be his residence after the British discovered
him in 'low' accommodation, Unbefitting to the Dignity etc, near the
bridge; a place which had been closer to the trading ships, and the
up-country tea boats. Eventually, of course, the consuls and missionaries
and businessmen moved across to Nantai Island. Foreigners always moved
to an island: Shamian, Gulangyu, Nantai.
   'This building was airy and light' said Mr Wang, holding me by the
arm and pointing to the decayed mansion. He wanted me to guess what
it had been. The shutters had seized up, and rattan screens were tacked
across the windows. 'The Club, of course!' Inside it was dark and mean,
a warren of partitioning and flatboard, the hallway clogged with furniture;
a semi-naked youth raised himself from a day-bed and regarded us slackly,
leaning on his elbow. 'It's all changed, all changed,' murmured Mr Wang,
as our eyes adjusted to the gloom. Dozens of families fought for space
behind crude partitions which failed to meet the ceiling or the floor. A
woman with a bundle of laundry came down the staircase – a wooden
staircase dusty and scuffed which had once, I supposed, been slippery with

polish – and greeted us cheerily. She said something to Mr Wang, who chuckled.

'She says you can have it all back, you know, whenever you want.'

When Mr Wang said he had visited the club only once, I imagined a conventionally imperial scene – an Aziz-like figure under the porch, driven there by reluctant necessity, faced with the sanctity of baize and brandy, where cigar smoke balled in slatted sunshine. But it wasn't like that. In the early part of the century when Mr Wang was a student at the Anglo-Chinese college, an Anti-Foreign Movement was sweeping Fuzhou. He had argued with more radical students that they should put education before politics, but they insisted on a boycott. Later, at the height of the convulsions, Mr Wang had crept to the Club on a dark evening; for safety's sake he entered through a side door to meet the College Principal, Mr Ward, while his elder brother lurked protectively under the great tree in the square. The occasion was a graduation, without mortar-boards or speeches or proud families; Mr Wang took his diploma, and the diplomas of classmates like himself who had not joined the boycott, shook hands, and was gone.

He had his diploma framed, once it had landed him a good job as a comprador for Customs on Gulangyu Island. He got on well with his British and American superiors. 'China was a very backward country, you must remember. When I was young, my father was sent to work in Kunming, in Yunnan Province. We had to go first by boat to Hong Kong, and then to Hanoi by ship, and take the French railway up to Kunming. Do you see? To travel in China we had to go to a foreign country!'

Mr Wang saw a bright future for Fujian tourism, which would help the nation and, perhaps, underline the point that he had been right about foreigners, and everyone else had been wrong. To develop that future, Mr Wang wrote about the province, and the stories he wrote were set in the past. They were legends and traditional histories. He handed me sheaves of lined paper, done up in brown paper wrappers, covered with his own spidery handwriting. 'I don't want any recognition for myself,' he would say. 'I just want people to hear about this. I would like you to try to have them published in England.'

6

The Nature of Bohea

Early one morning I arrived at Fuzhou railway station. I had a third-class ticket to Nanning a few hours up the line, where I could pick up the bus to the Wuyi Mountains. I sat on a hard green seat opposite a little girl with grey teeth who stared rudely and spat melon-seed like a machine-gun. Third-class air-conditioning was the open window, which I like best, even though I was covered in grit and clinker smuts by the end of the journey. I could see the smoke streaming from the engine whenever the line curved, which was often, because we followed the course of the Min river, which carried craft mottled and colourless as moths: fishermen's sampans, poled Oxford-style from the stem, or houseboats, larger versions of the same pen-nib design, with the bamboo awning tight and round over the stern. I'd expected the river to be moribund – perhaps I was growing too used to abandonment and decay as I found it among the European remnants of the coast. This wasn't an old house but a Chinese river which would be needed as long as it continued to flow.

For millennia, in lieu of decent roads, most goods in China were transported by water, either along the coast or through the web of canals and rivers inland. China shelves from the Tibetan ranges in the east and the Pamirs in the north towards the sea: the country is riddled with rivers and her civilisation grew up on them, fed by them, but fearing them, too. The great rivers do not tame easily. Flood and famine have so terrorised China that her heroes have been river tamers and irrigators. It has been

114

said that the colossal, unprecedented unity of China reflects the need to match the scale of floods with an equivalent grandeur of effort and resource. Tea is mainly cultivated in rice-growing country to the south of the Yangtse River, where the paddy fields have to be deep in water, making seasons when the whole countryside is in flood, not only on the plain but uphill on terraces banked to retain water carried there by hand. The Chinese peasant must understand water to survive: the building of tiny dams, the control of miniature sluices, and the times of flood and shortage.

The Chinese had tried to regulate the timing of foreign trade, to confine trade to a single channel; they saw trade as a seasonal repeat to be understood by reference to 'oula' custom, old custom.

Like water beyond a dyke, the barbarian at a port or trading post could be watched and contained (so could his natural ally, the Chinese merchant, who sat near the bottom of the social pile because he neither governed people nor fed them). There were other reasons for confining the trade. When almost every official in government service was expected to have sticky fingers there was at least a limit to what a few pairs of hands could carry away; while constant dealings at a single port would create a pool of experience of dealing with the foreigner.

The option chosen by the Japanese, of banning foreigners altogether, had been closed to the Emperor of China, who had a duty towards them as the one universal sovereign. He could do no less than acknowledge those who came from afar, because they came to bring him tribute and to purchase some of the blessings of the Han: tea, silk, porcelain. It was this view of the world which allowed Dr Johnson to drink hyson, and the London beauty with 'Her two red lips affected Zephyrs blow/To cool the Bohea, and inflame the Beau'. As a secondary benefit to China there was some money to be made, though not a lot; there was employment in manufacturing and transporting silk and tea, better than idleness among the common people.

There had been anxiety, too, behind the Canton system: although China's political system was stable and continuous, individual ruling dynasties could be challenged by a border people who had grown independent and insubordinate. It was how the Manchu Ching dynasty from Mongolia had come to power, and like their predecessors they used the promise and threat of trade to encourage dependency amongst outer barbarians who might try to mimic their own success. In port, as far as imperial intelligence could fathom (and that not very far), they had had no reason to expect trouble from the western ocean barbarians. Coming so far, so plainly eager for trade, so necessarily restricted in numbers and power, and hemmed in by the wisest regulatory safeguards that could have been devised, the barbarians had seemed in no position to challenge the Dragon Throne.

China's concern through millennia has been to keep floods and barbarians controlled. The Great Wall of China was like a dam to hold back people. Dynasties fall when they fail in these aims: disaster portends the withdrawal of Heaven's mandate. Mao first enchanted his people by conquering the foreign flood that spilled from the bursting of Canton (bringing down with it the last imperial dynasty). He expelled the Russians in 1962 when they threatened to breach the boundaries. Mao was the Yangtse tamer, as well; yet stories of flood and earthquake devastating a region near Peking circulated months before his death, like traditional omens of a failing dynasty. He had outlived his competence.

From the train it was hard to gauge the river's breadth. The river dissipated scale so that the hills opposite could have been massive and dotted with pines, or merely heaps of scree with clumps of gorse and grass here and there. What first appeared to be a fisherman's sampan would suddenly balloon into a ferry, grey, wooden and flat-bottomed, carrying a hundred people or more. It was summer and the water level was low, exposing grey shingle, and the sandbanks wove orange strands into the flow, and the ferries took the rapids like the sampans, askew.

Banks of jasmine grew between the line and the river, and sometimes a village announced itself with a sudden smell of pigs, and a glimpse of flying eaves or a running child; laundry on a line, and women walking along the verge with baskets of jasmine blossom in their arms; bamboo piles sunk into the river-bed near the bank to retain the sampans, and buffalo subsiding in the shallows like melting chocolate. On the opposite bank, where the hills were higher, pines were lopped from the hillside and shaved and rolled into the water to make log rafts, and these were floating down with a shack on top and steered by two men with poles.

The line crossed the river on stilts of broken stone and curved through a town. At the station I disembarked and outside, where dozens of coaches had attracted an impromptu market for melon-seeds and cake and ice lollies, embussed and sat high behind the driver, hoping for a good view over his head.

The bus had a horn and a honk. We struck the horn to push through vendors and punters, but on the open road we preferred to honk. The horn was minibus equipment. The honk was shattering, pitched to rise clear above the rush-hour cacophony of a Tokyo street and to crumble the walls of Jericho. It lifted me off my seat every time, and I scanned the road ahead for warning, although the driver seemed to have abandoned the conventional rules of honking. We drove very fast and honked at anyone shambling along the verge who might not have seen us. We honked at people already running for cover. We honked at an oncoming bus, and the bus honked back: we locked honks and charged, blaring, until the other driver blenched and swung in and swept by sucking the air from our windows and sending our purple curtains rattling and flying in the wind. We honked a bicycle into a ditch and a baby into tears. When the traffic thinned we found other things to honk about: our breakneck speed, blind corners taken at a roll, the river bed below us, the narrow road and clumps of trees. We startled a gravel truck up to its gunwales in the river like a buffalo. The driver craned left and right to find new things to honk at, and he turned in his seat to gauge the effect. From time to time we merely horned, to establish the grandeur of our honking.

When we stopped for lunch the bus took revenge and disappeared around the corner to have a puncture mended. My companions on the bus, young holidaymakers from the southern coast wearing baseball visors and designer sportswear, insisted I join them in the village restaurant, where they pressed frog and octopus upon me, filled my bowl with soup made of Wuyi mushrooms, proposed tea toasts; I gave them my store of new chopsticks, recommended by Françoise in Amoy as protection against disease. When the bus did not reappear we sat outside in the dusty road on little stools, an object of dull interest to villagers, who stood slack-jawed and stared. They were fascinated by a Taiwanese woman with a perm and Hawaiian shirt, but not by me. I took strolls up and down the street. After a while I grew so hot that I took off most of my clothes and sat discreetly in a basin in the restaurant, spooning cool water over my head, humming songs.

I hummed a coffee song and a tea song alternately, to test my theory that coffee gets all the best lines. There's an awful lot of coffee in Brazil, I crooned, and switched to 'Tea In Chicago'. I poured more water over my head. Now I was Sarah Vaughan singing 'Black Coffee', swaying slightly in my basin; now I was a digger on 'Waltzing Matilda', roaring cheerfully at the ceiling. It is a tea song: in the outback tea was boiled up in a billy-can. You let it bubble for about five minutes; you threw in Carnation and sugar, and you were ready to pan, or go walkabout. Coffee got honourable mention in Piaf, but there was 'Polly Put The Kettle On'. 'Brown Sugar' may be a coffee auxiliary.

The bus finally returned, meekly tooting – a chastened vehicle. It crept along, even across a plateau where the road was frequently straight and lined with trees. Brilliant green paddy stretched for miles; here and there clumps of bamboo marked a well and a hamlet. Sometimes we skirted the hills, and then the road would cross depressions like dried up rivers, terraced and sunken. A farmer drove a flock of ducks and ducklings in front of him, using a long bamboo with a bunch of streamers at the end to dab them into formation. The afternoon light was soporific, and soon I began to nod, and when I woke up we were in hills again, heading towards mountains.

One of the mountains had adopted a less serious pose. It was wider at the top than at the bottom. It had a quiff and a hump or, as the Chinese prefer to say, it looked like a crouching lion. Parallax gave it a weird vitality, and it rushed out from behind hills, or peeped coyly around trees, or bounded over the crest of a rise until we flushed it out and, approaching up the valley, found our hotel at its feet.

Robert Fortune, in Chinese dress, carrying Ward's Cases for transporting tea bushes, approached Wuyi from the north – from a height. He was a hardened Edinburgh rationalist with high mileage, but even he gave way to the sight: 'Never in my life had I seen such a view as this, so grand, so sublime. High ranges of mountains were towering on my right and my left, while before me, as far as the eye could reach, the whole country seemed broken up into mountains and hills of all heights, with peaks of every form.' His gaze is interrupted by the sight of a huge pine tree which he finds to be a variety already introduced into England by himself.

The hotel was a collection of wide-eaved buildings around little open courts which contained rock-pools and goldfish. A young Chinese interpreter offered to act as a go-between with the manager, whose advice I thought I would need.

For weeks, humping baggage around the old ports, I had dwelt in a sort of chronological haze. The hotel manager brought me briskly up to date. He found the idea of a tea book suspicious, regretfully so. He spread his hands and eyed me anxiously. I had come a long way to explore the mountains, I said. His muskrat sadness grew more pronounced. '*Mimi*,' secrets, he said sorrowfully.

'Every year we get a visit from a Japanese tourist,' he explained. 'He seemed to be a tourist, anyway, when he first came. But we discover that in Japan he grows tea. He knows many things about our tea, but not everything. He asks questions. He tries to give money to our workers. Now we know he is stealing our secrets, and we do not let him find out anything. He has to buy our teas, not make them! So I am sorry.'

Early the next morning, anxious to avoid the manager's suspicious eye, I walked down to the hamlet by the river – no more than a widening of the road and an assembly of eating shacks on a concrete plinth. Most of them were closed, and the choice fell between a shack run by a crabbed woman with a wicked face who importuned me disgracefully and a large man in a vest who simply indicated a table with an outstretched arm, like a waiter in a French café. His establishment had *ton*: three whitewashed walls and a hardboard ceiling, a glass counter for selling tourist knick-knacks like fans, teas, kung-fu swords, film, and bamboo walking sticks; two fridges (one brand new); a number of tables and stools whose legs were made from gnarled tea bushes, as I later found to my satisfaction; a kitchen at the back in which two huge black woks were set into an oven, a *kang* such as the northern Chinese sleep on at night, when the embers are still warm (the two woks could accommodate the washing-up, too, in boiling water); and various hangings on the walls: a blackboard menu, framed certificates of hygiene and a licence to trade, a silvery pennant wrapped in yellowing cellophane which proclaimed its owner a disciple of a certain Hong Kong chef, and two framed prints of the Wuyi Mountains at sunset and sunrise. There was an uncompromising photograph of the proprietor, too, against pine trees, standing stiffly with a stick and a frown in a brown suit rather pinched at the knee and a white shirt buttoned to the collar. After seating me he handed me his card: The Wuyi North–South Eating House. His name was Chen Ping.

Every nation has its own unyielding idea of a breakfast. I lost track of the times people apologised to me for not providing the Western supper or lunch I didn't want, but it never seemed to occur to anyone that it was their breakfasts of oily peanuts and rice gruel I couldn't stomach. To Chen Ping's growing astonishment I explained the principle of a boiled egg. He went off shaking his head and came back a few minutes later with a bowl of billowy albumen in hot water. He was looking at the egg with a sort of horrified pride, half eager to see it eaten, half braced to be repelled. We were all apologetic. I should have said . . . and I boiled the egg myself in water at the bottom of a wok. Chen Ping sat with me over a pot of strong Oolong and we struggled into conversation, swapping cigarettes and discussing, after a fashion, the chance that had brought Chen Ping, a Northerner, to Wuyi. As the restaurant grew more busy Mrs Chen suggested that her husband start pulling his weight, so we arranged that I would come again in the evening. He had a very special dish for me, if I liked it. He showed me a white haunch lurking in the back of a fridge. It did not look familiar, but I said I'd like to try.

Looming over the hamlet, the mountains were how I imagined Disneyland would do China; too fantastic. Just above the hamlet I dived into a former temple hung with scroll paintings inspired by the mountains. They showed ledges jutting out over cloud, pagodas at the top of zigzagging flights of steps, thorny gnarled trees. Poems cascaded down the paper. I'd always mistrusted scroll paintings, thinking them merely conventional, like the Alpine pictures produced by the million on Swiss chocolate boxes. But here I had to admit I was wrong. Of the Wuyi mountains they were almost photographically accurate – the more because the same art had worked over the mountains they depicted. Zigzagging stairways took you to pagodas from where you could admire the view and meditate on nature; and should you need prompting, appropriately meditative poetry was on hand, boldly carved into the very rockfaces it described, the characters limned in red. Nature and art circled each other. The calligraphy would take its rhythm or style from the subject of the poem. There is a bamboo style, for example, and a rock style. The impression was of walking through a fabulous picture into a more fabulous reality, a landscape of metaphors.

Between the mountain pagodas and steps and cliffs ran a tributary of the Min called the Nine Twisting Stream. It is the name Dante gives the Styx, that 'bourne from which no traveller returns' which divides the world of the living from the world of the dead. I sat on a ledge and looked down on it, kicking my heels in space.

Professor Zhuang had told me that Wuyi tea was unique – utterly loyal to what a vintner might call its *terroir*. Because the yield of Wuyi tea planted among rocks in the mountains is very low, attempts had been made to produce Wuyi tea elsewhere, on the plain or on shallower slopes. It had been started by aping the exact methods of manufacture in the hills, but when that failed to reproduce the flavour, plants were cloned. Cloning is the same as taking a cutting, and theoretically allows you to grow a plant identical to the original – a much better method than planting from seed, which produces offspring who, as in life, may or may not much resemble the parent plant. To some extent, anyway, the Chinese think that Wuyi tea is so good because it is so old; for while most tea bushes have a useful productive life of a century at most, many Wuyi plants are a thousand years old. The cloning experiment was not a success, although chemists came and matched the soils to within a minute of pH; the botanists looked through their microscopes and declared one bush the spitting image of another; meteorologists counted rainfall by the milli-metre and sunlight by the hour. Nobody, said Mr Zhuang, really knew why tea from the new garden tasted different. But, yes, the difference was there.

By the end of the nineteenth century Western botanists had robbed China of thousands of tea bushes and suffered a Mummy's Curse in their attempts to grow China tea outside China. Fortune sent thousands of young plants to the experimental tea-gardens in the Himalayas and other parts of India, but most of them died. Only stubborn and persistent transplanting, at great expense, brought a few plants to maturity: then the Curse struck from another angle. The native Indian 'jat' or strain of tea, the Assam variety, was discovered to be eminently superior for Indian production, rather as certain grape varieties better suit certain wine regions: it produced more abundantly, and it made a tea which the British consumer preferred. The mature China jat, grown with such difficulty, was declared a waste of effort – too late, for it had crossed with the native type already, and became a sort of shrubby Frankenstein's monster, popping up all over the place and spoiling the planters' rest.

Chen Ping's special dish had been lurking in the back of my mind. Back at the shack I drew an armadillo as best I could and showed him. He grinned and jabbed it with a big finger. 'That's right!' It came chopped in a soup; it was very, very chewy and tasted like strong beef. Chen Ping suggested that I just drank the soup: he would use the meat to make a stew tomorrow, which would be easier to eat. We sat again over tea and he explained that as a young man he had joined the army – a good job, which paid well and gave you a chance of seeing China. But he had been a sick man. He gripped his stomach to emphasise the pain: an ulcer, perhaps. He'd been in and out of hospital all the time; eventually he quit the army and looked about for a new job. Private enterprise was flourishing after the overthrow of the Gang of Four. He had no cooking experience but his wife cooked well, and a restaurant doesn't need much to set up. They settled in Wuyi because it had no hospital, and he began to learn to cook from his wife and from books. One day a chef from Hong Kong had visited the mountains, which are famous for their tea and their mushrooms – ear mushrooms grown on bamboo stakes – and fell in with Chen Ping. The Hong Kong chef enjoyed himself because he was able to use ingredients which were either unavailable in Hong Kong or prohibitively expensive, and in return he gave Chen Ping cookery lessons. Now he came up once a year, and gave them both refresher courses. Chen Ping had gone on to win a cookery scholarship to Peking, where he studied for six months. Then he returned to Wuyi and his little restaurant.

Wuyi was famously healthy. It was the air, he thought, and the good climate. The water was excellent and pure. Above all, said Chen Ping, the tea was a life-preserver. Wuyi tea bushes, after all, contained something that allowed them to live a thousand years: why shouldn't humans derive some benefit from that? Wuyi Oolong tea is drunk particularly by the elderly and the infirm. That was why there was no hospital here, because everyone drank the tea and never needed one. He punched his stomach. There was the proof.

We drank the tea from a fair-sized pot in tiny cups: it looked very orange, and tasted thick; but it had a lasting aftertaste, a sort of fruity sweetness. Professor Tea would have approved.

The first person I saw back at the hotel was Miss Wei – 'but you may call me Wendy' – who had appeared at my elbow in Fuzhou announcing that it was her job to help foreigners like me to get about. As she had arrived in Fuzhou from Peking only a day before me it was rather a case of my helping her, with my guide-book and money: it was like showing the city to a debutante, not least because Miss Wei had a very particular way of speaking.

She appeared to have learned her English from an expiring Edwardian aristocrat. In physical form Miss Wei was rather tight and tubby, yet her remarks were made in the languid drawl of a Sargent hostess reclining on a chaise-longue. The brisk patter of a professional guide was transformed into upper-class *politesse* with a Chinese accent, and I could never quite get over it.

Miss Wei was here to shepherd a party of Singaporean tourists around the mountains for a few days, but she was soon co-operating with the manager to find ways of keeping me off the tea terraces. Short of actually tying me up they sought out any distraction to occupy me during the hours of daylight. The manager announced one morning that there were certain excursions which were automatically charged for, and that I had better go on them or lose my money. I called his bluff and offered to pay regardless, so he let it drop.

Miss Wei was the first to discover that I had a friend in the village. I met her one evening on the drive where she was mooning about in a big sun-hat she had forgotten to remove.

'Where are you going?' Miss Wei had never shied from the direct question: with her peculiar accent it always sounded grand, not rude.

'I'm going to have supper,' I replied.

'You did not eat in the hotel,' she said reproachfully.

'The food is terrible.'

'Where will you go? It will be very dirty.'

'There's a Northerner in the village who runs a place. It's cheap and very, very good.' I sounded ridiculous. We found such a wonderful little place, you know . . .

'You must be back here early,' she trilled, bossy to the end.

But the next day, while the manager was insinuating that it would be better to eat in the hotel, Miss Wei waded in with fruity irony: 'Do you feel well today?'

'I have my own chopsticks,' I said with dignity. She nodded approval at that.

'Wuyi food?'

'Some Wuyi mushrooms, yes.'

'They say the mushrooms are very good,' she replied guardedly.

I met her again an hour or so later.

'Just mushrooms?' she asked.

'Mushrooms, and fish. Cooked in a northern style.'

'Big fish?'

'Small fish. In a soup.'

'Small fish? Grey?'

'In a clear soup.'

'Oh!' She almost seemed to blush. 'Those are famous in Beijing!'
Miss Wei, I realised, had a weak spot after all.

Chen Ping led with his alpine stock. We cut down a defile and switched
back and forth across a stream on stepping stones. Tea grew higgledy-
piggledy among runner beans and boulders and cabbages; but it had been
partly tamed by pruning and plucking over the years which kept each
bush little more than waist-high, and gnarled about the stem. Every ten
or twenty years, Chen Ping said, you had to hack the bush to a stump or
it grew too large and the flavour dropped off. The special flavour was the
work of the mists which hung about the bushes for seven months of the
year, and the peculiar nature of the soil. The government forbade fertilisers.
The tea is hand-made as it always has been in the villages. There are three
villages, about seventy families who have been in tea for generations. From
April they begin work at five every morning – April is the busiest month,
when the tea puts out its first spring flush of young leaves, and everyone
has to work hard to get them in. The experience of the villagers is very
important. In slack months the government employs them as guides or
loggers.

The Wuyi equivalent of a château was a pinewood chalet with huge
overhanging eaves and a sloping shingle roof. It was only two storeys
high, with a long verandah on the ground floor and a balcony above; its
shutters were decorated with cut-out shapes, and had been thrown back
to admit the light. It was brand-new, made without a single nail, with
strong pine pillars, wooden pegs and dovetailing, and end-beams carved
into scrolls. The teas stood in bins in a shuttered room, and although each
bin was closed with a heavy lid the smell of tea was strong under the
sweeter smell of pinewood. Our host sauntered from bin to bin, lifting a
lid, sticking his head in and inhaling deeply; he invited us to scoop up
handfuls of dry, springy tea. In the main room a bird had nested in the
beams over our table, and it flew in and out of the great barn door while
we sat and tasted teas, brewed at great strength in cracked and stained
teapots, which Chen Ping named and explained, although I understood
not a word. Gradually a rime of tannin settled thirstily over my teeth and
gums and tongue. The tea man obviously expected me to buy something;
so I took half a kilo of good *yen cha*, rock tea, and paid about a fiver for
it. It was as little as I could decently buy, but the plastic bag looked
disconcertingly bulky and I wondered how I was to get it home. Chen

Ping insisted on carrying it for now: he had a further hike in mind.

Fortune had sweated across the hills and saw tea everywhere – and Japanese cedar, and hydrangea, and abelia, and weeping cypress, azaleas, camellias other than *sinensis*, roses and jasmines. He saw the lettering on rock-faces and the grotesqueries of rock; he did not find the chariots which an earlier traveller, du Halde, claimed had been drawn up into inaccessible places by the priests to amaze the ignorant; he dismissed, too, the old stories about tea and monkeys and Ball's suggestion that inaccessible bushes were dragged with chains to dislodge the leaves. I stumbled along after Chen Ping in Fortune's wake, gradually stripping to the waist, my mouth puckered to a rusk by the strong tea, trying to concentrate on what I knew about the mountains.

Ball, I remembered, had got a soil sample from 'Bohea' which he had Michael Faraday, the electricity man, analyse in London. Faraday published his analysis and a Dr Guilleman became very enthusiastic about growing tea in Brittany. Fortune wouldn't have approved: stuck in the factories at Canton, Ball had no way of knowing whether the soil had really come from the Bohea Mountains or whether the collectors had simply pocketed the expenses and taken a sample from the next town.

Wuyi was supposed to be the origin of black tea, and produced the first tea known in Europe. It was partly Wuyi's fault that Britain had gone to war with China in 1840 – to haul the merchant closer to the source of his teas. It meant not just a drop in transport costs, but a readier market for British goods. Canton may have been awash with foreign silver but the city was only a distant door on greater China: the man who sent his teas from Wuyi to Canton was unlikely to ask for unheard-of barbarian goods by return. It was a forty-day journey to Canton by river boat and coolie: two chests to a man, who carried them slung over his shoulders on a split bamboo. The finest tea never touched the earth: a chest was fastened between the ends of two bamboo laths which were tied together at the other end, like a wishbone. The coolie carried the chest on his shoulders with the poles running forward, so that to rest the weight he had only to dig the point into the ground and hold the bamboos upright, with the chest suspended. They could be leaned up against a wall or a tree for the night. Of course a single man didn't make the whole journey: he merely relayed the load across his patch. Only Cantonese buyers – those wily city folk – sometimes made the whole journey.

The great Tea Highway ran southwest to Canton and, later, northeast to Shanghai as well, from the watershed home of tea in northern Fujian. It was, in places, fearfully narrow: Fortune's chair-bearers were delighted when he proposed to walk.

Whether I looked up towards the pass, or down on the winding pathway by which I had come, a strange and busy scene presented itself. However numerous the coolies, or however good the road, I never observed any two of them walking abreast, as people do in other countries; each one followed his neighbour, and in the distance they resembled a colony of ants on the move. At every quarter of a mile, or sometimes less, there is a tea shop, for the refreshment of those who are toiling up or down the mountain.

Fortune had an odd experience on this pass, when he was offered a cup of tea with a curiously-shaped spoon in the cup, and the tea sweetened with sugar. He had never seen such a thing in China. Had he been recognised as a European? He felt his disguise was pretty impenetrable; and he was left to wonder whether we were not indebted to the Chinese 'for our mode of *making* tea, as well as for the tea itself'. Later on his disguise was very nearly blown by the arrival of some Cantonese tea merchants he knew from Shanghai. The Cantonese, it seems, got around.

The move to Fuzhou and Amoy cut time and the merchants' costs but didn't much increase their penetration of the markets. The British government decided that there was too little cash about in the ports, and actively encouraged early Victorian Britons to drink more tea so that the Chinese could buy Birmingham goods in return. The British needed no encouragement to drink more tea, but I think the extra cash never saw Birmingham again. It just leaked away into the vastness of the Chinese interior, scaling pockets on the way.

There was another reason for coming to Wuyi. From this area of about eight square miles comes Great Red Robe and Hairy Crab; Buddha Hand; Clear Fragrance; Kung-fu tea; Great White; Black Heap; Red Border. Chen Ping said that a thousand years ago the best tea in China – and thus the world – came from here. On a mountain top, hundreds of feet high, tea was plucked before dawn for the emperor's sole use. At the foot of the mountain there had been an express dock on the river, from where, before sun-up, the tea was punted away to the imperial manufactory.

I had read somewhere that in Chinese the tribute tea (Canton's Padre Souchong, perhaps) was called Great Red Robe, Da Hong Bao. The story was that an imperial supervisor had become so excited by the tea that he

removed his red court robe and hung it on a tree while he climbed higher
into the mountains; another version reintroduced the monkeys, who were
supposed to pluck the tea wearing red robes in honour of the emperor.
But when I asked Chen Ping if he meant Da Hong Bao he looked surprised
and said no, that was a low-grown tea, not a *yen cha*, a rock tea. I was
confused again, because the Chinese honour high-grown teas especially.

The same stories cropped up again and again. I thought of Balzac. Did it
matter if his tea was Da Hong Bao or Padre Souchong? Did it matter if
he had stepped out onto the Rue Dragon and bought half a kilo from a
tea-shop there? Drawing on rumour and his own imagination, he gave his
tea its own *terroir*. Goslan had described his tea as *'parfumé'* by the
tale. Balzac concertina-ed the whole business of embroidering truth and
invention into a legend, which is properly the work of generations of
storytellers. In the tangled Wuyi stories, in the monkeys, rocks, ancient
bushes, the robes, the emperor, in all the business of boats and virgins
and mist, lay a pattern over time and place which might not be discernible
to any human eye. To recount the tales, to drink the tea: these were
glimpses of a pattern. And I could see why the Chinese, who do not
believe in God, found pleasure in their tea.

Then Chen Ping stopped to mop his brow. Through sweat-prickled eyes
I admired the view, two or three hundred feet above the stream. Bluffs of
smooth rock bulged like a parade of operetta sergeants; the vegetation rose
between them, plastering wide crevices at their feet and squeezing finally
to thin, watery cracks. On our side the slope was shallow enough to
support a pathway, but we had reached sheer rock and the path skirted it
to the south, in the direction of the stream. The hats of holidaymakers
popped up from dips or emerged from brush below, and the woven hats
of tea-pickers bobbed through the brilliant green tea.

When Chen Ping stopped again, I sat down to wring the water from
my hair.

We were on a ledge a hundred feet above a pool, in the scoop of a
hollow cliff. The ledge was occupied by a wooden tea house; and a thin
stream which flung itself from the overhang above and scattered, beyond
reach, to pepper the pool below, had been harnessed at its head to a stone
basin: the water trickled down the rope and filled the basin to the very
brim, so that for a moment it seemed empty. I splashed myself, and then

drank. Chen Ping said it was the best tea water here, and so, having rinsed my mouth, we ordered a pot.

As Professor Tea had said, tea marries with water rather than merely floating in it, like coffee, so it must be a good match. Jonathan Swift called tea 'water bewitched' (as a criticism, in fact, of a particularly weak brew). In England, until recently, most grocers would blend their own tea to suit the local water; nowadays our water is so treated and recycled it hardly seems worth bothering.

Lu Yu, author of the *Cha Ching*, recorded the traditional mantra of the tea-drinker: spring water is better than river water is better than well water. There were springs and springs: mountain springs burbling up through pebbles were the best. One treatise enumerated twenty classes of water from the best to the worst. Some amateurs had famous water brought from its source in crockery jars over great distances, all very expensive but further justified by the belief that a tea is best made with water from its local spring.

Chen Ping made no effort to praise the tea. He ran a rival establishment. We did not try much talking; sitting in a curve of rock, midway between water and the sky, there was no call to break the spell with our hard-won banalities; we felt like ancient hermits, drinking tea, and sitting for our own portraits, on a scroll.

Chen Ping walked me back to the banks of the Nine Twisting Stream, where we found a collection of sheds surrounded by tea bushes.

I saw the bright green leaves, freshly plucked, spread out on platter baskets to catch the sunlight. Suddenly, from a blue sky, the clouds clamped down like a cauldron lid, with a shudder of light beyond the mountains and the boom of thunder down the gorge. All hands ran forward to pull the tea-trays under cover as the wind began to gust and rip; when of a sudden the wind collapsed the first fat drops of rain began to spatter on the rock before the clouds broke and the water streamed in shallow arcs from sloping roofs, and a light wind drove the rebounding spray hither and thither over the rock like a watery sand devil. In ten minutes it was over, leaving an odd silence, dripping eaves and a clear sky. The water shrank from the rock, and the new tea sparkled on the bush. The platters were put out again.

Chen Ping opened the door of the shed onto '*poey*', drying. Inside, a dozen waisted baskets like wicker hour glasses were set over charcoal fires;

the tea in bamboo sieves rested in the narrowing waist of the baskets. There was very little smoke, just a hot breakfast smell of tea and toast. The workers swarmed up like angry bees when we opened the door because there was a danger of fanning the charcoal and drying the tea too fast, and even Chen Ping, who commanded respect locally on account of his size, I suppose, was unable to placate them once they had seen my face. I was a foreigner against whom the spirit of *mimi* worked inexorably, and we had to beat a retreat.

Later that week I was in Hangzhou, capital of the green tea province of Zhejiang, where Gunpowder is produced. With meetings and investigations too tedious to describe I reached a shed where tea was being made by a man rolling a handful of green leaf in a hot wok set into a charcoal stove. The backs of his hands were white but his palms were tanned; his work was swift, monotonous and skilful, and he puffed incessantly at a cigarette, eyes half closed against the smoke. Suddenly the room flooded with electric light and a busload of Japanese, masked by popping cameras and video-recorder proboscises, burst upon us. As soon as they had gone the roller stood up, took the cigarette from his lips, spat, and walked out without a second glance.

Back at the hotel I consulted my books as to what I had seen.

Ball, in his book of 1848, was reaching the conclusion that green and black teas were made from the same plant, and that they were distinguished only by their manufacture. Given that by Ball's day Europeans had been drinking tea for over two centuries it might seem remarkable that they took so long to reach the truth. But China was closed and the error began early, couched in a form that was almost irresistible to men of the time: the Scientific Pamphlet.

The pamphlet in question was written in 1753 by an Englishman called John Hill. At various stages in his career, Hill passed himself off as a philosopher, an actor, a gardener, a pamphleteer, a botanist and a baronet. Sir John Hill, the botanical baronet, published his *Treatise On Tea* between the publication of Editions I and II of Linnaeus's *Species Plantarum*, which laid the foundations of all plant study and classification. Edition I contained the sum of current knowledge about tea: the species *Thea sinensis*, the common tea plant. Another, supposedly unrelated genus was named *Camellia*, after a Moravian Jesuit called Kamel who wrote on Asian plants. In Edition II, on the authority of the Enlightenment con-man whose treatise he had just read, Linnaeus divided the genus *Thea* between *Thea viridis* and *Thea bohea*: between green and black. Nobody could enter China to test the specification for many years; when they finally did they could never make up their minds whether the secret of green and black tea lay in the bush itself, as Hill maintained, or in the manipulation of the leaf, or in the air or the climate or the soil or in a combination of two of these or more. As the East India Company began to investigate the possibility of growing tea in India, an end to the confusion was being sought by men like Fortune and Ball.

The solution (to consider the green and black tea plants as being identical and calling them *'Thea bohea'*) coincided with a new dilemma for botanists when tea was found growing wild in Assam: was it the same bush as the Chinese or something altogether different, *'Thea assamica'*? The confusions multiplied. The genus *Camellia* stole back to rout *Thea*. By the turn of the century the botanical name for the tea plant was beset with variants, and it took an International Code of Botanical Nomenclature to solve the problems in 1905. All *'Theas'* were actually *'Camellias'*. *'Assamicae'* and *'boheas'* were one and the same, and combined as *'sinensis'*. Tea's real name is *Camellia sinensis (L.) O. Kuntze.*

Once all tea plants are recognised as broadly alike the mystery of *terroir* deepens. Keemun, that rich black China, was a green tea until a bureaucrat got the sack and set off to learn a skill in Wuyi a century ago. Returning to his native Keemun he began producing black teas as he had been taught. A green tea *ordinaire* became a black tea *grand cru*, and his neighbours naturally copied his success. The *terroir* found expression.

The great difference between black, green and Oolong teas lies in fermentation, while the secret of tea itself – why it tastes fragrant rather than vegetably like any other leaf – lies in manipulation. Freshly-plucked leaves are juicy and brittle; they snap if they are bent; if rolled, they would become a fibrous mush. The fibrous mush market remains untapped so tea is withered, often in sunlight, until the leaf becomes flaccid like a cut flower. The correct 'wither' cannot be predicted – it depends on the *terroir* and the season – but roughly the tea is withered when the leaf can be folded without breaking.

Black and Oolong teas must ferment. This process has nothing whatever to do with fermentation – there is no alcohol involved; it is rather the oxidisation of the leaf's juices. To give the juices a chance to mix with oxygen and each other, the leaf has to be knocked about a bit, bruised and battered. This process is called rolling, which also gives the tea in your packet its shape. The rolling process can be done by machine or by hand; either way it seems astonishing that it succeeds at all. Cuban women rolling cigars on their thighs have a certain erotic charm, but the business of rolling every single tea-leaf along its length like a furled umbrella beggars belief. Look at a tea-leaf (a good big one, not a tea-bag's innards) and you will see that it is tightly rolled. Drop it in hot water and it gradually unfurls like a Japanese paper flower: tea men call this the 'agony of the leaves', and the tightness of the roll the 'twist'. A tighter or closer twist generally indicates how much trouble the planter thought worth taking over this tea.

Green teas are rolled and dried at the same time. Only black and Oolong teas go from a cold rolling to fermentation, when the tea is spread out, green and sticky, to oxidise. It starts to brown like a sliced apple. Its natural fragrance ripens. Oolong is not fully fermented. The Chinese like a 14 per cent fermentation on their Oolongs; foreigners often prefer a fuller fermentation, say 60 per cent, bringing it closer to a black tea. Some people maintain that the 14-per-centers should nowadays be called Bohea, not Oolong, since the mountains are still the main source of the tea.

Fermentation has to stop at the right moment, after a couple of hours at most. The Chinese stop it by tossing the whole lot into a red-hot wok where it steams and crackles. It is moved about very fast to prevent it burning or sticking. Every now and then it is taken out to cool and be rolled again, and each time it is put back into a progressively cooler wok. The tea is finished off in the baskets that Chen Ping and I had seen in the shed, over a charcoal fire which gets smaller and smaller until the leaf is crisp and dry.

The Chinese call fire the teacher of tea, as they call water its friend. A green tea's upringing depends more than black tea's on heat: the right amount at the right time will either bring out the nature of the tea or suppress it. Black teas encounter heat much later than green: fire is black tea's finishing school.

Green tea is not fermented. Instead of being rolled or bruised after withering it is simply put in the wok and rolled back and forth over a diminishing heat. Now and then it is removed for rolling. This rolling and roasting process is called tatching, and when the leaves rustle like paper it is done. The twist of green teas varies. Gunpowder, for instance, is rolled so close that it becomes ball-shaped. The youngest leaves make the smallest balls, known as pinhead; old leaves make pearl. But a famous tea from Hangzhou, called Long Jing or Dragon's Well, is without any twist at all in the best grade, Lark's Tongue, and lies perfectly flat and even-sized. Green tea tends not to keep as well as black; the Chinese often pack it with a small hydrophilous stone to keep it free of moisture.

This is the manufacture of Chinese tea in broadest outline. Even now very little about traditional Chinese practice is known outside the country; there are methods which are known only to certain Chinese regions. Yunnan Province, bordering Burma and Assam, produces 246 teas alone – including Professor Tea's aged variety. Much China tea is produced like *vin de pays*: a peasant grows a few bushes among his vegetables, takes what he needs for his family, prepares it at home, and perhaps sells the surplus to the state. It has always been the way in China: the lack of scale and efficiency has been the bane of the trade.

Chinese legend abounds in stories of poor men who discovered a wonderful tea bush and became rich and happy. China's language, water, tea and myth change from one valley to the next. The prized teas are rare. Lark's Tongue, for example, is made only by the Dragon Well. The quantity produced is minute, and a half-kilo costs as much as two weeks' wages for a well-paid Chinese. Yet none is exported. It can only be made with water from the Dragon's Well, even if the Ch'ing emperor Chi'en-lung, breaking convention as only a master of the conventions can do, believed that the water from his Jade Spring near Peking, a thousand miles to the north, was a better match for Lark's Tongue.

I surprised Miss Wei by asking to join a trip down the Nine Twisting Stream. The Singaporeans had turned the minibus into a florist's window, their shirts and blouses bursting with tropical blooms. We drove to the head of the river, where it entered the mountains, and Miss Wei decanted us professionally into a tourist shop by the bridge. It seemed an odd place to buy electronic gadgets, but there they were, twinkling rows of them, and the Singaporeans were buying them, too. A swaying toddler gripped a chair leg and surveyed me. I smiled in a friendly way. The baby's lips quivered. I grinned winningly. The baby's mouth popped open in an enormous circle and bellowed. Naturally I tried to move away unseen. The Singaporeans were too busy to notice, but Miss Wei sniggered. 'Your face frighten him.'

In our funny hats, toting cameras, we clambered aboard rafts made of lashed bamboos with curving prows, and sat in rows on tiny armchairs. Everything was made of bamboo, like so many things in China. You can sit on a bamboo seat at a bamboo table in a bamboo house. Bamboo guttering drains the water from the roof while a man in a hat and cape of woven bamboo carries two sacks of rice slung from a yoke of split bamboo to the bamboo house. You pick up your bamboo chopsticks and dig into a dish of bamboo shoots. The walls are hung with paintings of bamboo. If you are a Chinese diplomat, even your foreign policy is predicated on bamboo: those pandas eat nothing else.

The river was low but diligent boatmen had been out damming it in sections and channelling the flow through the rapids, so that tourists would continue to disburse. Only tourists; it was a long time since any tea was carried from Wuyi by boat. These days it is trucked to the railway at Nanning, and only poor-quality stuff in no hurry goes down the Min. The raftsmen wore gondoliers' boaters, and punted from the stern; their calves were like knuckly fists. The Singaporeans sat with their feet as far up above the splash as fat allowed, cameras clamped to their faces, swivelling to and fro in deep focus to pick out distant pagodas. They would have missed a mermaid swimming around the boat. We were punted on two rafts, and the boatmen named each rock and Miss Wei pointed her finger at it and all the Cyclopean eyes followed her arm and clicked, before returning, like a sprung mechanism, to rest.

On the reaches the rock soared from the water, and on the inside curve smaller rocks lay wrecked on the pebbly beaches. They were Jade Girl Peak, and Looking Glass Rock, Goddess of Mercy Rock, Water Tortoise Stones, The Rock of Three Monks, and so on. There was no system here, either: the naming could have been done by Professor Tea in a surreal mood. We passed a smallish grey rock with big ears and a trunk. 'Elephant Rock?' I guessed. Miss Wei asked the boatman. 'That rock has no name,' she drawled, Lady Glencora withering a bore at a soirée. We swept past a cylindrical rock that rose sheer 300 feet. 'International Hotel,' said the boatman, grinning. A man in the neighbouring raft waddled to the prow to have his picture taken in tight shorts and a baseball cap, and the gondolier remarked unkindly that he looked like a fat woman. Miss Wei had a giggling fit.

Miss Wei was enjoying herself very much. She was wearing one of those wide-brimmed cotton hats which figure-of-eight into a small circle, and she looked rather like an Edwardian Girton girl being punted up to Grantchester. She went so far as to lean slightly to one side and allow her fingers to trail in the water until the boatman told her about the poisonous floating snakes and she hastily snatched them out again. I was still smarting from the bawling baby episode, so I did a bit of sniggering myself.

The stream did twist nine times and would have twisted more if we'd gone any further, but when twelve people had taken four hundred and thirty-two pictures of the same things and each other we disembarked on the bank. Miss Wei clapped her hands imperiously to announce that we would be going to look at the sky through a crack in the rock. The minibus door swung open.

'I think I'll just walk back to the hotel,' I said firmly.

'I am the guider here,' said Miss Wei in a muffled voice. We glared at one another until, with infinite graciousness, she added: 'You can.'

Chen Ping's neighbour was negotiating with a boy holding a bucket. He reached in and pulled out a glorious golden fish which gleamed like molten metal and twitched suddenly. Outside Chen Ping's restaurant an owl sat in a birdcage, blinking studiously at the sunlight: for a moment I was tempted to desert Chen Ping that night. (Later I hadn't the crust; but I flapped my arms and hooted and said, I don't want, I don't want.) My companions from the bus passed on their way to have a swim, so I joined them on the river bank where we floated downstream until we touched the slimy wall of a waterfall. The water was clear and fast-moving – second-grade tea-water.

Back in my room I looked at an etching in Ball's book entitled 'A Chinese Bird's Eye View of the Stream of Nine Windings and Strange Rocks'. The kinks in the course of the river had been shaken out to fit on the page, and it ran from top to bottom without perspective and the trees lying flat beside it, like a medieval map. The bridge was there at the top of the page, lined with houses like old London Bridge, and boatmen were punting the same rafts. At the bottom, nearly hidden by a thorny tree, a man might have been setting out a basket of tea to wither.

Ball got his information on Bohea from members of the Amherst embassy, Cantonese friends and Jesuit missionaries. On the whole it was sound, and he quoted often from Chinese manuscripts. One described 'a range of mountains which encompass and shelter those of Vu-Ye. These mountains are also of the same nature as those of Vu-Ye, and the tea is prepared in the best manner. It is fragrant in smell, and sweet in flavour.' In the concentric ring of outer mountains was a Ptolemaic vision of geographical neatness. I read: 'This tea is called Puon Shan, or Mid Hill tea, and is gathered to be made into Souchong.' This was all ancient hearsay and I would have skimmed on had Ball not commented: 'Here, I imagine, most of the East India Company's best Souchong teas, such as the chop, Lap Sing, &c., are made.'

In London I had spoken to the head of an august tea firm who had hinted, without being prepared to say outright, that his Lapsang Souchong was the Queen's favourite tea (I thought it was hardly headline material but his discretion was touching). We chatted about the tea, and he admitted that he didn't know anyone who had actually seen the stuff being made. He was vague as to its origin. A south China, obviously, he told me; probably from northern Fujian.

All the same I had doubts. For a start, I had no idea whether the outer mountains really existed. Although the change from Lap Sing to Lapsang was easy, in Ball's day Souchong was a small-leaf tea (it meant 'small sort' in Chinese) and it was only later that, in English, it came to mean the opposite, what the Chinese call *da cha*, big tea. Yet Lapsang Souchong looked like a big tea to me. Moreover, if Ball's Lap Sing Souchong had come from nearby, modern Lapsang Souchong might come from somewhere entirely different, keeping only the name. There were more twists and turns in Chinese tea than on the Wuyi rivers.

The hotel under-manager was a young man with a grasp of English whose father had been a tea-lover, working all his life as a taster in the nearby town of Chong An. Puon Shan, he said, wasn't far away, and it did produce some famous teas. Lapsang Souchong meant nothing to him. 'Smoke-flavoured *da cha*?' He would, he promised, ask around.

He came to my room early next morning. 'What name for your tea? Lapsang Souchong? English name! Made in Puon Shan!'

'That's wonderful!' I cried excitedly. 'Not far from here?' I jumped out of bed and started to dress.

'I am sorry. I try to organise visit at Public Security Bureau. It is impossible for foreign friends to see Puon Shan. I say you are good man, write a book. A new *Cha Ching*, no-yes?' He laughed. 'But no permission.'

I sat back on the bed, thwarted. The under-manager looked at his shoes. I bit my thumbnail. Then we both said 'perhaps —'

'Perhaps if you did not know it is forbidden,' he said slowly. 'You can find taxi . . .'

I did not find the taxi. At ten o'clock it appeared and tooted outside the main door: an electric red Honda called, by its badge, Cedric. Miss Wei had gone off with her troupe and the manager was managing somewhere out of sight. Cedric's driver wanted cash in advance: the trip was off the register. Only when my new friend had slammed the door and waved me off down the drive did I start to wonder why Puon Shan was forbidden to foreigners. Because of some mega-*mimi* over the tea? Then Wuyi should be off limits, too. For a moment I wondered whether the Chinese were treating their bushes with a secret ingredient to turn the Queen into a Maoist revolutionary. But on the whole I knew of only one reason why governments of all complexions like to put fences around mountains. If I was about to blunder upon China's top secret satellite-proof nuclear silo system I was thankful, at least, that I had left my camera behind.

A ludicrous prudence kept me squashed down into my seat through the hamlet, where Chen Ping was taking down the empty bird-cage. Robert Fortune had travelled in forbidden areas, but not, for choice, in a loud red car.

We took the up-river road, but instead of turning towards the bridge and the tourist shop we continued northwards, leaving Wuyi with surprising abruptness for a plain of level paddy watered by the river in a slack, meandering fashion, the whole view enclosed, as the manuscript foretold, by hills beyond.

As soon as the road began climbing we were wedged between a high gorge and the river which was growing younger by the minute. The mountains were not like Wuyi but alpine, making a funnel of woods and granite; blue smoke rose from chalets, mist rolled up towards the col where the gorge widened. The road clung to the escarpment, and sometimes there was room for a tiny, strung-out hamlet of chalets, barns and logpiles, where the ground was strewn with woodchips like a carpet of Assam tea. The people were brown, kept dogs, and grew roots and beans on the lower slopes. Fifteen miles up-river there were tea clumps on the terracing.

We passed beneath a red arch bearing a legend in gold characters. The driver slowed down and looked at me questioningly. I shrugged and nodded for us to go on. Did it say Foreign Trespassers Will Be Shot? We overtook a dozen men walking single-file up the road. Their heads were shaved and they planted their feet heavily as if they were treading on ice; then I saw the leg-irons and a soldier in PLA green who looked me right in the eye – the telltale round eye. The driver tut-tutted, but I couldn't decide whether it was meant for me or the felons. And all of a sudden the road passed to the opposite bank and we pressed on, bumping Cedric along a dirt-track scattered with broken wood.

The track ended at the foot of a barn. A few planks were laid across the brook and on the other bank stood a long cabin – the village residence, I supposed – and a handsome chalet with a balcony, from where a man was waving in our direction, as though we were expected. At the sound of an engine children raced from the long house and bounded over the brook to admire Cedric and look at me with startled eyes. The man on the balcony went in and appeared again at the door below to invite us in.

The floor of the chalet was not yet laid, and the new wood smelled resinous; it was big and new enough to suggest that good times were coming to Puon Shan. Where the individual responsibility system has replaced the commune each family does its own plucking, pays for its own fuel, and sells a portion of its production to the government at a fixed price. Chen Ping had told me that there were plenty of fiddles to evade quotas. Surplus is sold at market rates. The Puon Shan hamlet looked at first sight like a brigade headquarters. Living was evidently communal. Upstairs, in sunlight streaming through the balcony door, half a dozen elderly men and women were sifting dry tea, picking out stalk and grading the leaf. A heap of tea lay on the floor between them, and each sifter held a round bamboo sieve; as the tea fell through the mesh of one sieve it was swept up and passed on to be sifted through a finer mesh. Grading tea is done partly to improve the appearance – a uniformly-sized tea looks better than a tangle of sizes, and fetches a better price – and partly to offer a range of liquoring speeds: the smaller the leaf, the quicker it brews.

Grading the villagers was more difficult. I discovered they were members of a single family. Chinese has more words to express degrees of kinship than any European language: words for third brother, or second aunt, or fourth cousin twice removed, who bear the clan name. The elderly sifters were brothers and sisters, and husbands and wives, and everyone else in the place descended from them or had married in. In recent years they had improved the quality of their tea enormously, especially compared to the days of the Cultural Revolution, when intellectuals had been sent from

137

the cities to learn peasant wisdom, and tea was made on weight alone. The new building was the fruit of their success.

There was no mistaking the smoke and pitch aroma. Lapsang Souchong is probably the classic China. Bonzes and stupas, pagodas and mandarins decorate its packaging, promising a flavour of Old Cathay, the mysterious Orient; in the packet is a big black twisted tea. But I think of it now as alpine, like Swiss chocolate.

I wanted to know whether the smoky flavour was natural to the leaf, or impregnation. Stepping outside with my guide I looked up the col, beyond a forest of conversational bamboo to dark pines, and had my answer. The mountains produced a coarse tea but the pinewood compensated. My guide swung a latch on the old barn and showed me tea-leaves drying on slatted shelves in flat baskets. A flue from ovens under the barn snaked across the floor, open in places, and thick smoke filled the room. The tea was fermented, half-dried in woks, and finally placed in here to cure, like a ham. Lapsang Souchong, in fact, has a distinctly kippery relative called Tarry Souchong.

I took a cup before I left – hastily, because I was terrified of being discovered, and the chain-gang might be moving this way. The tea was disappointingly weak, almost flavourless, although the aroma was unmistakable. Perhaps it was too fresh and needed to settle and develop for a year or so, as the Chinese claim. Or perhaps the June plucking lacks flavour: the smoke only binds with qualities inherent in the leaf, and does not simply coat the tea.

Twilight was falling as we rolled away, with only the expensive sound of tyres drumming on the tar: Cedric was saving fuel. Shadow had long since crept coldly up the gorge, and I stared at the road ahead, trying to decipher the twilight greys.

I found Wendy Wei wandering in the garden with a handbag, eluding the hour between dinner and the bar-disco where she was expected to accompany her group.

'Too noisy,' she complained with a *moue* of distaste. 'I do not want to go.'

I offered to give her supper instead. She said no, clutching her bag a little too tightly.

'Was the fish – very good?'

'The *jaozes* will be even better, I expect.'

'*Jaozes*,' echoed Miss Wei.

'Come and have some. Come for a walk, anyway, and you can watch me eat them.'

She considered. Her knuckles whitened, then relaxed.

'All right!' she said brightly. 'For a short while.'

As we approached the shack the smell of cooking reached us and Miss Wei's voice folded like soft beancurd.

Chen Ping made us comfortable. We took beer from the fridge, and *yen cha* from thimble cups. When the *jaozes* were put in front of us Miss Wei clapped her hands and cried: 'Oh! These are famous in Beijing!'

'You must have some,' I insisted, and I had barely spoken when there was a clack of chopsticks and a digestive whump, as Miss Wei sank gratefully into the trough.

After supper Chen Ping sat to talk, very straight-backed against the wall, his big hands resting on his thighs. Now that we could speak properly through the medium of Miss Wei our conversation sped up and grew precise. We traded information about ourselves, clearing up misapprehensions, confirming suspicions. But the sudden ease flattened the shared effort of past conversations; for every new piece of information there was a loss of intimacy as we exposed ourselves in a borrowed voice. The conversation eagerly begun grew desultory; less and less was translated for my benefit, and when Mrs Chen joined in the triangle was complete.

Sometimes Miss Wei would sketch the direction of their conversation for me: they were giving her advice. Chen Ping prodded his remarks with the butt of a Holmesian pipe, and his wife grew animated, eyes shining, as they steered Miss Wei to an awareness of her opportunities. There were things she had not learned at tourist school. Miss Wei sat stiff and serious. They gave her the secrets of common corruption: the backhander, the squeeze, the commissions. She should not, they seemed to say, *be too muchee foolo*, like those stubborn magistrates on the opium coast: like them, she was invited to consider how much depended on people like herself.

I poured her some more beer.

'I do not want to drink,' said Miss Wei. 'I want to cry.'

But the exposition ground remorselessly on. I dare say she was an investment: she could repay the advice by recommending the restaurant to her tour groups. It was disturbing to watch the seduction, before which Miss Wei fell with a sort of swooning complaisance: Lady Glencora between the covers of a penny dreadful. She began to nod, and press for details. Chen Ping spoke less now, though ever calmly, without a glance in my direction; but his wife spoke with an eager excitement, like a procuress.

On the way back to the hotel, Miss Wei asked what I paid for the meal. When I told her, she asked if it was true that I had bought some tea. How much? 'That is expensive,' she said.

The road was pitch-black. Bullfrogs growled in the sunken paddy. The river on the plain glowed silvery in the starlight. Now and then a three-wheeler squeaked by, picking out the curves in the road ahead with its Cyclopean beam, until a twist in the road took it behind a spur, and the light and noise snapped off. Once we nearly collided with a couple of cyclists who came up behind us with a swift swish of tyres that was inaudible above the natural din; but luckily I heard their murmuring just in time, and we banked for the roadside until we felt gravel beneath our feet.

I looked in later at the bar disco. My young bus friends wanted me to join them in a drinking match: they waved fistfuls of cash beneath the barman's nose, asked for the music to be turned up, displayed their designer labels, danced expertly. The Singaporeans sat on low armchairs; the women with fizzy drinks, the men with their beers. In the corner I saw Miss Wei staring miserably at the floor. I started towards her and then stopped. Coloured lights glinted in two ribbons down her cheeks.

Chen Ping gave me a sudden shove from behind. It took me about a yard into the scrum on the bus – away from the folding doors, at least, which clattered shut behind me. I managed to struggle round, and he passed my bags through the open window. When we lumbered off around the corner I glimpsed him in the middle of the road, in his vest, waving slowly.

Boston

'Who knows,' asked John Rowe, 'how tea will mix with salt water?'

Lu Yu, one assumes, would have politely ignored the barbarian. The question was not so much rhetoric as a coded signal, for no sooner had the words been spoken than a large body of men were seen approaching from the direction of the Green Dragon, a harbour tavern. From their buskins and moccasins they appeared to be Indians. It was Boston, Massachusetts, on the night of 11 December 1773.

'Behold!' says Carlyle, 'Boston Harbour is black with unexpected tea, and now DEMOCRACY unfurls her black wings and announces, with death volleys and to the tune of Yankee Doodle, that she is come and, whirlwind-like, will envelop the whole world!'

The rant forsakes accuracy. Boston's Tea Party – and New York's, and Greenwich's, and Charleston's, and Philadelphia's, and Annapolis's, and Edenton's (this one led by patriotic ladies) – was made with green tea, as Oliver Wendell Holmes scrupulously records in the otherwise fantastical conceit of 'The Ballad of the Boston Tea Party':

> The waters in the rebel bay
> Have kept the tea-leaf savor;
> Our old North-Enders in their spray
> Still taste a Hyson flavor;
> (And freedom's teacup still o'erflows

With ever fresh libations,
To cheat of slumber all her foes
And cheer the wakening nations!)

Green or black, it belonged to the East India Company, and it carried duty of threepence a pound.

With the British victory over French Canada in 1763, George III and his ministers took the view that the thirteen colonies had been protected and that the colonists themselves could be expected to bear a portion of the cost of their defence. The Stamp Act of 1765, taxing tea and other goods, was seen on both sides of the Atlantic as unconstitutional. In Parliament Pitt and Burke challenged the house's right to levy a colonial tax without the consent of the local assemblies.

While the Act was repealed in 1766 the Declaratory Act upheld the disputed right of parliament, and duties on paints, glass, lead, oils and tea were re-imposed the following year. The new levies were short-lived: colonists boycotted British goods and anxious merchants lobbied Parliament until all the duties were repealed, bar threepence on tea. The colonists remained unsatisfied and, turning to Dutch smugglers for supplies, left the East India Company facing a glut on the London market and no business with America.

The powerful monopoly received support from Lord North in the shape of the Tea Act of 1773, which permitted the Company to export tea from England for the first time, without paying the normal British duty. The colonists would thus get tea cheaper than anything the Dutch could supply, the Company's profits would be saved, and the revenues would gain. The losers were the middlemen.

The point of principle remained. The boycott, too, held fast and spread. In parts of Massachusetts it was impossible to buy tea without a permit:

Sir:
Mrs Baxter has applied to me for Liberty to buy a Quarter of a pound of Bohea Tea. I think by her Account of her Age and bodily Infirmities it will not be acting contrary to the Design of our Association to let her have it & you have my full Consent thereto.

I am Yrs & c.
ELISHA WILLIAMS

Historians will point out that it could have been any sort of tax – a tax on lead, or duty on salt fish, or a levy on wig powder – rather than tea.

But carried into sitting rooms the length and breadth of the thirteen colonies the tea boycott must have been most conspicuous. When patriotic daughters of liberty offered Liberty Tea made from the four-leaf loosestrife, boiled, stalked and dried, they thrust the issues under the noses of their guests. Nor would a wig-powder tax, say, have involved the East India Company, the sort of bloated monopoly that liberty-lovers everywhere loved to hate.

The outcome of the tea-parties is well-known: a great nation turned to coffee. And imperial Britain turned to India.

7

Calcutta

India sprang aboard with the scent of combustion and vegetation, incense and the prickly smell of the insides of old cars — no respecter of Dacron headrests or airline plastics, like an old dog snuffing about a new house.

Across the tarmac the name CALCUTTA glowed in thin red neon.

I sat on my trolley by the carousel, sleepily eyeing the crowd around me. There were a few sari-ed women, comfortably folded at the midriff and standing as if their spines were a sort of post to lean on, but the majority were men. Some in suiting and shirting, with brilliantined hair, chunky rings and tinny watches, others in Nehru jackets buttoned to the neck like Mao suits, only tailored more closely with tight arms and ample belly-room, and worn with white cotton leggings which sagged at the thigh and gripped below the knee, the original jodhpurs. And there were men in *kurtha* pyjamas, long-sleeved shirts reaching to the knee, the democratic uniform: these were men who could wait with cold patience, accustomed to command.

And between their legs a splay-toed sweeper came sidling crabwise on his hams, with a stripy tea-towel around his waist and his head bandaged in a red cloth. There was half an acre of empty lino in the airport but he was making his life hard by sweeping around the carousel, using a broom of dry and bleached palm leaves. He sidled and swept, with his arm across his knees, trailing the dust, and as he came past me his friend arrived and handed him a glass of tea.

I smiled and tried my new word: *chai* – the overland caravan word, brought through the plains of Central Asia and over the passes of the Himalayas. Tea was always welcome to the people who lived on the northern borders of India and the western edges of China: the first Darjeeling tea-gardens were planted with the modest intentions of satisfying their wants, spreading British Indian influence northwards in cups of tea, checking the Chinese competition. In Tibet, the coarse brick tea made of compressed leaves, stalks and rubbish which the Chinese sent overland on the backs of coolies was often used as money (as was the top-quality tablet tea, made of compressed tea-dust, sent north to Russia within living memory). Tibetans still calculate Himalayan distance in teas: a four-cup or twenty-cup journey. Nothing else can express the gradient so well.

Nobody seems quite sure when India began to drink tea: the accounts of early travellers are silent on the subject. It's true that Marco Polo says nothing about tea in China, either; but it seems likely that tea was unknown in India before the seventeenth century. Adam Olearius in Persia finds his hosts drinking 'tzai', which he says they boil and drink bitter with fennel, aniseed, cloves and sugar. 'But the Indians only put it into seething water, and have for that purpose either Brass, or Earthen pots very handsomely made, which are put to no other use.' These were 'Indians' in Persia; a member of Olearius' party pushed on to Surat and found tea 'commonly used . . . not only among those of the country, but also among the Dutch and English, who take it as a drug that cleanses the stomach.' In those days tea wasn't grown in India so it had to come from Canton and Tibet, too far to be cheap. It was a rich man's drink.

Without warning the sweeper's friend brought me a glass of tea as well. It was milk-chocolate brown and thick as syrup, altogether different from the Chinese leaf in water. It was black tea boiled up in Carnation milk and sugar, laced with cardamom and maybe aniseed. And thus tea is drunk from Cape Cormorin to Chandigarh, the length and breadth of India, half a cup each day for every man, woman and child.

It wasn't what I would call a nice cup of tea. Lu Yu would have called it the slop-water of a ditch. A Chinese would find barbaric any attempt to mask the flavour of tea: in fact, a barbarian could as well be defined by his propensity to do so. In Russia and Poland tea is sweetened with sugar and honey, but drunk black; Americans have been drinking it mainly iced with sugar and lemon ever since the Chicago exhibition of 1888, when an Englishman took advantage of the heatwave and refrigeration to shift his uninteresting stock of Indian tea; North Africans and Arabs drink Gunpowder with sugar and mint; the British and their descendants add milk, often sugar, sometimes lemon; and continental Europeans, it is well known, cannot make a proper cup of tea at all, but float a bag in tepid water, and serve it up in a tall glass.

What the Chinese would probably like least in India is the habit of treating tea as a single product, like onions or curry powder. Indian *chai* makes a mockery of the thousand and ten thousand kinds. Tea is not familiar to every landscape as it seems to be in China; it is not cultivated by every farmer, in small amounts, differing from valley to valley. It is grown in far-off regions, on large plantations, using machinery to ensure it conforms to standard. Tea is one of the largest employers in India, itself the largest tea-producing country in the world. For many years it was the country's largest export, and even now it ranks in the top two or three foreign currency earners, whereas Chinese tea accounts for about 1 per cent of the total value of her exports. Tea in India has fallen from first place because production has had to meet a growing internal demand. Indians are learning to like the stuff.

It was a vile cup of tea but I grinned my thanks and found, in fact, that the sweeper's *chai* revived me: as Captain Turner had once observed, a cup of tea is always welcome at the end of a long journey. Indian lorry drivers get theirs with a splash of arrack measured by how far they mean to go before they stop again. Five-mile *chai*, ten-mile *chai*, hundred-mile *chai*. There is even one-metre *chai* – which does not refer to a tea-shack crawl but to the distance between the cup and the spout of the pot: cooler tea for a man in a hurry.

I picked up my bag from the carousel and as I approached the barrier fence a throng of youths pressed forward and shouted, waving their fists in the air. I was just passing through the gap when they decided to stampede through it, roaring and shouting and stabbing the air with clenched fists, whirling me about in a knock and shove of flying elbows and bony hips which carried me breathlessly almost to the feet of the politician they had come to welcome home. They hoisted him upon their shoulders, a complacent fellow in *kurtha* pyjamas, and threw garlands around his neck. He raised his hands and beamed and I, expelled from the press, crept out of the airport and into the first taxi I saw.

'Metre?'

'Metre, sah!'

He stabbed the milometer with his finger.

'One kilometre, eight rupees sah!'

'OK,' I said rashly, 'let's go.'

There was no question of going immediately. The Ambassador is a rugged car, based on the 1957 Morris Oxford: ours was an early model. It sagged dismally on its springs. It had to be push-started and it felt its way out of the airport on a single working headlamp. On the straight we briefly hit 30 mph, while other Ambassadors swung wide and overtook, and every pothole was a steely clunk. The road ran along a strip of water, and the verge was lined with single-decker buses brought here for the night. Under the blue flare of street-lights, with their windows barred, stripped of paint, they looked skeletal, a busman's *danse macabre*. Black figures crouched between their wheels, washing stones and grit from their tyres. We bucketed through a series of potholes. My jaw ached, and I realised that my teeth were set as I hunched on the rear seat.

Calcutta. Trees and houses and the glitter of water as we pass. A man in a *lunghi*, walking his dog. Lurching across cobbled tramways into a closer street, doorways dark and padlocked. A broad concrete step covered with a mat, and a prone figure upon it, sleeping out on a hot night. Two men in dirty headcloths, squatting over embers. From time to time, waist high in a wall, a cube of light shows a cubby-hole with space for cigarettes, cola, muck and truck and *pan*-leaves, and the stallholder recumbent on cushions; and generally a few people are standing on the pavement there, chatting quietly, taking advantage of the light and the stall to meet, keen to give us directions and unable to make them correct.

The driver promised to search for my friend's address for one, two hours if need be. I started to relax. In half an hour he was suggesting a very good hotel, very clean, yessir. The street was almost empty. We asked again, but the driver's enthusiasm for the hunt was draining fast. Very good hotel, sah!

It was two in the morning, when even my driver might prefer sleep to more kilometres on the clock. We drove once more down a long walled-in street, but our hearts weren't in it, and the relief when we scuttled down a back-alley to a small hotel was palpable. The manager showed me to a room. There were no windows, and two pubic hairs snaked across the sheets, but there was a shower through a gap in the corner of the wall and in the morning the manager himself brought me 'bed tea' and the paper.

147

I drank them both greedily: the tea was brewed English style in a pot. *The Statesman*, successor to *The Englishman*, carried a report on the return of a political delegation to China. Calcutta is run by the Communists. They sounded a little shaken by the change they had seen, smiling and garlanded though they had appeared at the airport. A leader writer blimpishly opined that 'the Chinese respect strength and firmness above all'. Page two promised ACTION ON BUS EVETEASERS: an article about bottom-pinching. On the inside pages a report on yesterday's tea auction began: 'The Orthodox section obtained elegant and fancy prices . . .'

'And do you know who discovered tea in this country?' said a nun, leaning forward until a shaft of sunlight from the broken roof suddenly illuminated her white habit. I had been wandering through the New Market with my Calcutta friend, down brilliant covered avenues of books and jewels and spices and cottons contained in something like a Victorian railway station. The nun had crept up as soon as we stopped for a glass of tea.

'Major Bruce, yes.'

'A Catholic,' she said with a nod. My Calcutta friend, lapsed herself, began to edge away.

'Major Bruce was a Catholic?' I wondered.

'A Catholic,' said the nun firmly. 'Of course.'

Robert Bruce was up-country in Assam in the 1820s, close to the Burmese border, when he found what he thought was a tea tree. At the time it was not known that tea of any sort existed in India: the report of the eminent botanist Joseph Banks in 1778 had recommended importing Chinese bushes. Bruce's bush grew in jungle controlled by a tribal chief, the Beesa Gaum, who promised to collect seeds and whole plants for the Major's return. But the Major died, and it was his brother, Charles, who collected the plants when he skippered a small steamship up the Brahmaputra at the outbreak of war with Burma. Some he sent to the Commissioner of Assam, David Scott, who planted them in his garden in Gauhati, and the rest he planted in his own garden in Sadiya.

In 1825 Scott sent seeds and leaves down to the Botanical Gardens in Calcutta, where Dr Wallich pronounced them to be merely a variety of camellia. Learned botanists were still urging the importation of China plants; Dr Christie, a Company surgeon in Madras, procured several Chinese bushes and planted them in the Nilgiris, a range of hills in south

148

India, but his death led to their dispersal. Wallich received more plants from Assam which he identified as camellia.

In 1832 the East India Company monopoly on the China trade came to an end. There was a possibility that the Chinese would react by closing Canton, jeopardising the supply of an article which had already become indispensable at home. From England a Mr Walker wrote to the Governor General:

For many years the consumption of tea has been increasing in this country; it has become a luxury to all, and almost a portion of food to the common people, who in some districts drink it three or four times a day. Its use is so intermingled with our habits and customs, that it would not easily be dispensed with.

It is therefore of considerable national importance that some better guarantee should be provided for the continued supply of this article, than that at present furnished by the mere toleration of the Chinese government, which, although the Chinese have at present a monopoly, it will be easy for us to destroy.

It was, too, of considerable commercial importance to the Company, about to lose the bulk of its domestic revenue. Lord Bentinck, the Governor-General, appointed a Tea Committee in 1834 to look into the possibility of making tea in India. It consisted of eleven Englishmen, two Indians, and a Dr Lumqua, a long-term Calcutta resident presumably included as an expert on Chinese manufacture.

In 1835 the Tea Committee's secretary George Gordon, arrived from China with three loads of tea seed, supposedly from Bohea, which the Chinese had forbidden him to visit himself. His ship, the *Sea Witch* of Calcutta, almost certainly an opium clipper, had been attacked by pirates on the return journey. They showed no interest in the seed.

In the meantime the Committee had received not only leaves and seeds from upper Assam but a living bush sent by the new Commissioner, Captain Jenkins. This time Dr Wallich identified the shrub as tea and the jubilant committee had 'no hesitation in declaring this discovery to be by far the most important and valuable that has ever been made in matters connected with the agricultural or commercial resources of this empire'.

Opinion now divided. Dr Wallich, the zealous convert, wanted to see the indigenous bush cultivated in the foothills of the Himalayas. Dr William Griffith and a geologist, Dr John McClelland, preferred to have China seed planted in Assam. The experts spent a frustrating and acrimonious three months in the Assamese jungle, led by Charles Bruce, and returned with their opinions confirmed. Griffith and McClelland won the argument, with momentous consequences. Chinese tea bushes, they pointed out, were surefire producers; people had drunk Chinese tea for centuries; the Assam bush might, or might not, produce good tea. For nobody in India or England had a very clear idea of how tea was made. Ball had not yet written his 'definitive work' – and even his information was to prove sketchy, his soil analyses, his second-hand descriptions of good tea soil and good tea climates, of proper planting and tending, proving the confusion and ignorance that surrounded the whole business.

Gordon was sent back to China, and over the next decade China tea seed poured into Calcutta. The first plantings were made on a sandbank near the Brahmaputra where the plants shrivelled and died as soon as their tap-roots hit sand. Later the boffins were accused of choosing the only patch of land in all upper Assam where tea would not have thrived. The few survivors were replanted at Chabwa:

It is a matter for profound regret that this garden did not share the fate of its predecessor, for it proved the Chief means of disseminating the pest of Assam – the miserable China variety – all over the province . . . the hybrid variety which now forms the great bulk of the plant found not only in India but also in Ceylon.

Once the bushes were growing, the problem of how to turn them into a drink was solved by inducing Chinese shoemakers and carpenters from the bazaars of Calcutta to go up into Assam. Most of them came from the south China coast and had never seen a tea plant in their lives. They were supposed to instruct the local tribesmen but fought them instead on the way up from Calcutta and eventually had to be deported to the Isle of France. Those who did arrive on the garden behaved 'saucily'. But tea of sorts was manufactured, and methods improved gradually. On 10 January 1839, at Mincing Lane in London, eight chests of Assam tea were sold at decidedly elegant and fancy prices to a Captain Pedder. A London broker described the lot 'as good tea as may usually be imported into this country from Canton, the only difference appearing to us being in the method of curing or drying the leaves, and the sample submitted to our inspection has been over-dried and evidently has not been treated in the way the Chinese prepare their teas. We character the tea in question as preferable to but middling tea or brisk slightly burnt flavour (not objectionable) and possess strength; the leaf is of a large dull black pekoe kind value 1s 10½d to 2s and at this valuation we should have no objection to enter into a contract for five hundred or a thousand chests.'

It was the first contract for Indian teas.

Calcutta was the capital of British India when the tea experiment was conducted, growing to become the second city of the Empire; and it remains the headquarters of the Indian tea trade. The largest auctions are here. The companies which own gardens, the brokers, the shipping agencies, the packagers and distributors are all based in Calcutta. It is also the shipping and distribution centre for the tea-gardens of northeast India, the largest and by far the most important tea-producing area in the country. It's as though you were wearing tea-tinted spectacles, for Calcutta is the colours of tea: browns and yellows, mostly. The whole city might have been steeped in the stuff, like a forged palimpsest. Calcutta, which looks as immobile and permanent as a geological feature, isn't all that old – a surprise to many people, who think Calcutta, like Indian tea, must reach back into prehistory. Her stucco villas, Italianate and sprawling, sit behind walls daubed with the latest slogans, the clenched fist of Congress, the Hammer and Sickle of the Communist Party of India (Marxist).

There are *chai* shops everywhere. Around the University they seethe with students in pursuit of the Bengali tradition of *adda*, tea and talk. Four or five people form the ideal group, and while participants come and go the talk must continue for as long as the money holds out. The wealthy conversationalist orders tea, toast and a three-egg omelette – a mumlette, as it's called; poor students combine to have a double-half – one portion of tea but two glasses. The conversation veers between argument and discussion, between politics and mechanics, Gibbon and Tagore, religion and luncheon, the larger the leap, the defter the turn, the quicker the idea, the better.

The house where I had been asked to stay was designed towards the end of the eighteenth century by one of the Italian architects who came out here to make their fortunes. In daylight the taxi driver (same man, better deal) found the address with ease. The car came to a stop beneath a colonnaded porch surrounded by long grass, the stucco so patched and faded it was hard to see that once it had been vermilion, like a Chinese temple wall. Stairs rose from the marbled hall to a great window, and divided and turned to reach the vestibule above. On my left, three pairs of double doors led onto a terrace above the porch; on my right, five slender pillars enclosed the drawing room, which was huge. Here I had to pause.

It was really the sight of a dog turd on the boards. Carpets were rolled back in sausages against the wainscot: a wise precaution, I thought, until I saw that they had become frayed and moth-eaten where they lay. A dark picture suggested a girl's face: but when I peered closer she blistered beneath bubbling paint which had begun to slide from the canvas. A silvered mirror had cracked in its huge gilt frame: it showed me a surprised face spotted with rust. There was a marble bust of a fleshy maharaja. Two autumnal chandeliers had pulled cracks through the ceiling, and were shedding their tiny lobes and leaves of coloured glass on the floor. A Louis XV sofa in shredded chintz was trapped in a slapstick pose, waving one leg in the air while tumbling backwards onto the stump of another. A tasselled bell-pull waited for the summons that would end it all by snapping its last thread.

There was, on the face of it, nobody here to summon. I thought I heard a few notes of song: and then footsteps seemed to track the skirting board behind the fireplace. But my shouted hellos went unanswered. I pushed through to the verandah beyond, where marble paving dipped and knocked beneath my feet, startling a rook on the balustrade which flapped away over the lawn and the great tank beyond to settle finally on a classical urn sprouting grass. The tank was completely covered with algae and looked more like an extension of lawn – of any lawn but this one, which was jungly. I thought again I could make out high-pitched singing. There was a sort of scratching sound and a fat brown sausage-dog tip-tapped by, its claws patently neglected. I followed it through a dining room furnished with carved blackwood chairs and table, into a study lined with books, with a kidney-shaped desk and a leather swivelling armchair. On top of the desk was a bottle of dried-up ink, a silver pen-stand shaped like a racehorse, and a pane of glass which held down a selection of family photos. The study was the end of this particular avenue, so while the dog deposited a fresh turd under a coffee table I pulled down a book, disturbing a lot of dust, and turned a page. For a moment I thought it was written in foreign script, or braille; but it was only a labyrinth of tunnels and alleyways made by generations of worms. Back on the verandah I discovered a tiny young woman carrying a tray of tea cups. She took no notice of me following her like a Bisto kid into a room off the verandah. My host and hostess were sprawled on a bed, and on the floor around them sat some twenty servants, all absorbed in a Bengali movie. Before nightfall I had discovered that every book in that study had been eaten, except a volume of 1934 GWR railway timetables. And that it was unfortunate that the dog crapped under the table. It was my bedroom.

That night it began to rain. The mugginess had grown unbearable through the afternoon and with the first pattering of rain a thin breeze seemed to come through the open windows. The overhead fan clattered monotonously, whirling on its axis like a gyroscope. When it flew off I hoped to be protected by the mosquito netting which I had scrupulously tucked around the bed: it was the only excuse for the netting, which was pierced by dozens of holes the size of cigarette tips. Mosquitoes have a blind method of finding them out, doggedly butting the outside of the netting with a plaintive whine until they sail through a hole and into their dinner.

I stayed awake to fend them off, reading an old Victorian city guide. Calcutta was established on a night like this, I read as I twitched, maddened, under a sheet alive with mosquitoes. Established on 24 August 1690, 'with the rain falling day and night, on the site of the abandoned village of Suttanultee', by Job Charnock, the Right Worshipfull Agent (of the East India Company), Mr Francis Ellis and Mr Jeremiah Peachie, gentlemen: 'in consideration that all the former buildings here are destroyed, it is resolved that such places be built as necessity requires and as cheap as possible . . . these to be done with mudd walls and thatched till we get ground whereon to build a factory.' Charnock remains an elusive figure, though he founded a city which was to be synonymous with horror, as well as intertwined with the story of empire. Charnock had his servants flogged 'when he was at dinner, so near his dining room that the groans and the cries of the poor delinquents served him for music'. Charnock rescued a young widow from performing suttee, and married her, and was said to have sacrificed a cock upon her grave when she died. Charnock sat dispensing justice beneath a great banyan, which was felled to make way for city improvements in 1827.

I pulled the wires of the lamp out of the socket by my bed, and yanked my hand back under the net. Strange that a man given such a sternly biblical name should make pagan sacrifice to the dead. It was dark in the room, rain splashing outside, the decrepit fan clattering overhead. A mosquito buzzed in my ear and the bedsprings popped like corks as I slapped my head. Was he a just man? What drove him to rescue his widow from her husband's pyre? In the scant tales Charnock appeared diabolic, angelic, a man of appetite: perhaps the perfect colonist.

The success of the London auction of 1839 prompted the incorporation of the Assam Tea Company, which took over the tea gardens and more land on easy terms from the government and began planting China seed in 1839. The government of India, the East India Company, was eager to pass the business over to private enterprise. Most of upper Assam was jungle – unproductive, sparsely populated, barely worth policing; with tea they would beat the bounds of the empire. The British had come as traders into a cultivated country; they stimulated the activity of the regions under their control and founded Calcutta, but before tea they had made no unique contribution to the economy of the country. They were no more than rulers taking over from other rulers and injecting a little life into the business as a result of their connections.

By the 1830s the mood was already shifting towards one of empire proper, of settlement and development and the imposition of particular – avowedly superior – standards upon an alien people. That Charnock married a Hindu was, in the late seventeenth century, eccentric; two hundred years later it would have been unthinkable. The blunt edge to the new mood was suggested by Macaulay, who arrived in India as a lawmaker declaring that a single shelf of Greek and Latin classics was worth a library of Oriental literature. Tea was a beneficent aspect of the imperial mood. It was an export and an earning which simply did not exist before the British brought it in, and it was a secure employer – a voracious employer. The early days of tea planting were dogged by the paucity of labour, for the Assamese jungle had never sustained a large population.

But tea also brought out men without long experience of the country; men who were not required to trade and ingratiate but only to manage: men who were made reasonably well-off in controlling men and women who were poor.

Ball cites this as an argument for growing tea in India, rather than buying tea in China. 'We find the Hindoo satisfied with a small mud hut or shed,' he says, 'which he hardly inhabits by day, preferring the shade of a palm or other tree.' He winds himself in a piece of calico, which serves him as a bed at night. He eats his vegetarian diet with his fingers, and 'furniture he has none'. 'The Chinese, on the contrary, has a good substantial mud or brick house, generally thatched, but not unfrequently tiled.' He has chairs, stools, tables and a bedstead; plenty of utensils; even books. 'And, like a highly polished people, to whom the Chinese have been compared by experienced judges, he closes each meal with his petit verre, or small cup of samshew or spirit, but taken before his tea instead of after coffee.' The Chinese therefore, Ball thinks, is an expensive workman; whereas the Hindoo, 'slender as are his means, they are adequate to his wants'.

There could be no doubt that tea was imperial. The Viceroy, Lord Lytton, spelled it out to a gathering of European planters in 1876, in what is now Pakistan: 'In the excellent results of the tea plantations . . . I recognise imperial benefits. Your undertaking has afforded lucrative employment to thousands of the population of this district. So far as its social and political influence extends, besides being eminently creditable to the British character, it is also conducive to the stability of the British Raj.'

By 1841 the Assam Company had produced 29,000 pounds of tea in all, rather less than a single shipment from Canton; worse, those 29,000 pounds had cost £160,000 to produce. The gardens were being run by Bruce and a 'tea expert' called Masters, who wrote that 'a passionate European, entirely ignorant of the language and of every part of his duty, can be worse than useless'. In 1843 Bruce and Masters were dismissed. In 1846 the Company directors, whose own confidence was fading almost as fast as their investors', paid a ten-shilling dividend; nonetheless a year later £20 shares were trading at half a crown.

Further cutbacks were made. The hope of driving the Chinese tea trade out of the running overnight was abandoned. Concentrating on high yields and smaller quantity, the Company struggled into profit in 1848, and paid a genuine dividend in 1852. After the disasters of the first decade it seemed that tea could pay, after all.

In the morning rain pattered gently on the flooded streets. The tank overflowed onto the lawn and a paddy heron on stiff legs caught whitebait on the sodden grass. A small cormorant torpedoed over the roof and disappeared beneath the cracked green surface of the tank. It had rained in the house, as well, leaving shiny slicks of water which slithered across the boards and dripped down the wooden staircase; an internal courtyard had filled like a beaker. Pots and pans had been put under some of the most obvious leaks, but not necessarily under the most serious. The marble maharaja wept. The porch was flooded to the second step, leaving the cars to squat ruminatively up to their chassis in the grey pool, a long way from Coventry, *circa* 1957. Outside in the street they were taking off the manhole covers in an effort to drain the city: and tomorrow we would read of people who had waded to work and suddenly vanished, with a short cry and upflung arms, into the municipal sewers. The French trade attaché struggled over for lunch with a handful of videos, and remarked that to be flooded up in one of Calcutta's big houses was the very best way to relax he knew. He was hoping for another cloudburst and a waterlogged engine to trap him here, out of reach of the Quai d'Orsay. They call May and June, before the rains, the dog days. The monsoon relieves the awful oppression, but very nearly puts a stop to going out. It is like settling in for a long train journey, and the falling of water makes a companionable sound like the rumble of train wheels.

A lot of the furniture in the house had once belonged to Warren Hastings, an impeccably energetic Governor-General. Now it was arranged to face a TV set which was supplied with fresh videos each day by a sharp young man with a suitcase full of bootleg American movies. The films were improbably bad – the Calcuttan video is a sort of life-support machine for films which would have died under normal circumstances. The family sat rapt and immobile upon bursting sofas, watching the grainy images until they fell asleep or staggered away to sprawl drowsily on bedsheets under a clattering fan, or simply moved to another room to carry on with their Sidney Sheldons. Sometimes the servants came and watched, too; the rest of the time they lay low, fetching the odd cup of tea. There were forty of them. Many were too old to move about much, or had pared down their activities so successfully over the years that now they were almost forgotten, and only emerged to collect wages that were paid automatically. I looked around at the festering dog-shit, the books crumbling for want of dusting, brocade rotting, hinges breaking, cupboards unopened ever since a key was lost.

That day we ate 'rains food' – whatever was available at market: kebabs, *kutharee* and potato fritters – out on the verandah, and vied to identify the birds which hung around the garden, and when the rain stopped altogether I got a lift with the trade attaché into town. The house phone wasn't working but there was probably a good connection from the Grand Hotel. The Calcutta phone system works erratically, at best. Lines fail because the exchange is old, because someone has borrowed your line (you pay his bills, he pays the operator), and because the number of people in the city has exploded since the phone system was installed. Small ads in the papers announce that J. P. Gupta has been reconnected; that M. J. Das can after all be called at his office.

The car pushed like a snow plough through the flooded streets, raising two fans of water which spread over the mudguards and fell like wings. There was some traffic. Rickshaws such as the Chinese banned were in demand. Running taxis were soliciting a rains supplement. The trams were working, even the buses, those battered double-deckers whose survival Geoffrey Moorhouse called a testament to Leyland: that was seventeen years ago. They are always so crowded that passengers bunched on the footplate tilt them to one side, and the Maidan, Calcutta's park, parade, racecourse and cricket pitch, was a lake over which the buses seemed to be sailing close-hauled to an invisible wind, while nearer the trees naked children played porpoises across the lawns.

Without the Maidan, Calcutta would appear no more imperial than London, which grew, after all, in much the same way, piecemeal. London had to be all but rebuilt after the fire of 1666; Calcutta began twenty-four years later. Both cities revolve around a business quarter, close to the docks. Calcutta, though, is no longer the capital city; no longer a great port; no longer growing failing, in fact, to repair the ravages of time and overcrowding. In the early 1970s people wondered at the city's survival. There was no investment. Businesses were folding. Refugees from the Indo-Pakistan war in neighbouring Bangladesh were pouring in. Emerging out of fanatical *adda* the Naxalities, Maoist terrorists, had paralysed the city and accelerated the departure of foreigners and wealth, and revolution was in the air. The city was rotting. It stank of death, like its terrible namesake, Kali, the death goddess. Its past became a litany of death: the Black Hole; the murder of Gandhi; Partition pogroms; foreigners now hurled alive into the furnaces of Kidderpore.

And yet, like the improbable buses, the city lasts. You are even told, very cautiously and with every hedged qualification, that things are not getting worse – that in some areas, in certain ways, they could be said to be improving. The revolution faded away. The Naxalite threat was abruptly curtailed by vicious and fairly indiscriminate police retaliation. The electrification of rural Bengal, and the concentration of resources on the countryside, and the awfulness, even, of Calcutta, perceptibly shifted the balance between the country and the city and slowed the stampede into town. Calcuttans explain that there are fewer beggars because they, the Calcuttans, are so mean: and I do notice that no one gives less than Calcutta's upper classes. But in the countryside electricity brought brighter evenings and TV sets and gave couples something to do apart from making children who would be forced into the city, the so-called Bengal safety net. And in Calcutta the whirlwind of humanity must have settled slightly as the influx died down: silted up like the port itself. It is a terrible state of affairs still; but it is a state, at least. The city is filthy: an estimated 880 tons of pollutants are pumped into the air here *every day*. But power has become almost reliable, and the city is plunged into sweaty darkness less often. When it rains it is dirtier still, as the middens of compacted earth and rubbish dissolve, and the almost-septic tanks overflow. If the city is saved from plague (and it is not, quite), it must be because of the scavengers, winged, canine and human, which survive on recycling scraps. Everyone seems to be deferred to by someone lesser than himself. It was not until I had been in Calcutta for a week that I realised that the House servants themselves have servants, so incredibly mute and humble they seem physically negligible.

At James Murray, in Murray House, I rootled through cabinets of precision instruments, microscopes and Admiralty charts, and had my glasses fixed. The gentleman who mended them waived a fee. Behind me a quiet pendulum clock told the seconds on one face and the hours on another. It was exactly right. The faces were inscribed James Murray and Co, London and Calcutta 1814. At the Oxford Bookshop on Park Street I bought my copy of *Hobson Jobson*, the great dictionary of Anglo-Indianisms compiled by Colonel Yule and Dr Burnell in 1886, and made a necessary pilgrimage to the Park Street Cemetery, where 300 years of European death are commemorated in funerary urns, broken columns, sarcophagi, temples, cupolas and pyramids. Some of the monuments had been restored to creamy elegance, but most were greeny-black with moss and damp, and the red bricks revealed the pretensions of stucco.

The Victoria Memorial, though, remains pristine. Raised at Curzon's command to be Taj Mahal of British India, it dominates the Maidan in isolated splendour, dazzling white. There are tanks and lawns and flower-beds around it, and benches for the weary visitor to rest and contemplate Queen Victoria herself, bombazined and overdressed, plumped on a high-backed throne, grasping her orb and sceptre and gazing east towards the racecourse. There is Edward VII, *Rex Imperator*, riding atop the arch at the Kidderpore entrance, and Curzon gazing viceregally towards him from the Memorial steps. Inside this preposterous domed edifice is a collection of imperial memorabilia. 'Look, Viku, this is Lord Curzon's cloak.' 'Chaya, have you seen this letter? It is from the Queen, her very last letter to India before she died.' 'See this, it is the Delhi Durbar.'

It seems incredible that the memorial remains, when every street-name has been changed to eradicate the vestiges of the Raj. Harrington Street is renamed Ho Chi Minh Sarani, which presents some of its occupants with a nice difficulty. The British and the US Consulates have solved it in separate ways. The Americans have opened up their side door on Shakespeare Sarani. The British pretend nothing has happened, and carry on writing to and from Harrington Street without incident or criticism because after all it's what everyone in Calcutta does, with nobody about to call Dalhousie anything but Dalhousie: certainly not Binay, Badal, Dinesh Bag.

'Your Bengali is a lazy fellow,' said Seroj Mehra, telling me something I would hear again and again from well-born Bengalis. Mehra is handsome and well-built with close grey curls and amused eyes.

We drank whisky sodas on a balcony overlooking the city. Calcutta's grand families used to build great stucco mansions for themselves, bungalows and villas with huge cool rooms, and gardens, and high walls and a *chokidar* standing at the gate. They appear to have given up the struggle. Mehra has followed the retreat of the rich from the street to a condominium created by razing a single mansion: speculation here is devouring what yet remains of one of the most beautiful cities in Asia. Mehra once returned to Calcutta to find great swathes of the city cleaned up in readiness for an official visit by a Soviet leader. The walls were weeded and the roads repaired. Louvred shutters were painted up. Drains were covered. Guttering was fixed and the bleeding pigment and gaping wounds on stucco walls were smoothed as if plastic surgeons had tended the whole fabric of the city. It was, he recalled, a terrible shock; but he had comforted himself with the thought that in a few years Calcutta would reclaim itself. And so, of course, it has.

Seroj Mehra had been a director of James Finlay & Co., later Tata-Finlay and now just Tata Tea. His front door bears the Finnish coat of arms because the consulship traditionally goes with a seat on the Finlay board. He is Norwegian consul, too, but for some reason the plaque isn't there.

159

He freely admits that he doesn't have an awful lot to do: it's a long time since bearded Scandinavian captains sailed up the Hooghly.

'The position has its advantages, though. It gets me to Delhi now and again for some interesting parties.'

'Are there no good parties in Calcutta?'

'Of course there are parties. But this is a pretty staid city.' He smiles and gestures beyond the balcony wall, to the rooftops and trees. Further off there are smoking chimneys, cranes, and a single office block, put up by the Metro builders long before they managed to lay an inch of track.

'Its image is more latter-day Babylon,' I objected.

'You find what you are looking for, don't you think? Foreigners tend to see only the extremes, black and white. They see, what is it, the rich man in his castle and the poor man at his gate. It's one truth, but if that were everything some sort of revolution would have occurred. The rich might have employed the poor, and developed the city. Or we could all be working in production brigades, like the Chinese. Although I hear they've given all that up now.

'Instead the place is inert. It's dominated, you see, by the Company *babu*.'

I looked up *babu* later in *Hobson Jobson*: formally it is a term of respect attached to a name, like Mr, but 'in Bengal and elsewhere, among Anglo-Indians, it is often used with a slight savour of disparagement, as characterising a superficially cultivated, but too often effeminate, Bengali. And from the extensive employment of the class, to which the term was applied as a title, in the capacity of clerks in English offices, the word has come often to signify "a native clerk who writes English".'

'Nothing can be done without them,' said Mehra. 'It is they who decide who holds power, not the poor in cardboard boxes, or the rich, in boxes like these.' He paused, and grinned. 'Nothing can be done with them, either.'

'They vote for the Communists?'

'Oh yes,' he raised a forefinger. 'The Communist Party protects them. They love to demonstrate, wave their flags, shout slogans and all that. They love to talk. But they are the biggest conservatives in India. After all, writers' jobs are often hereditary. Some families go back to the days of the East India Company. The father intends to hand the job over to his son, and the son looks forward to the day he takes over. He learns just enough to do the job. Ambition and mobility do not exist for these people.

As long as they needn't fear poverty, they have no desire to take risks.

'In the long term, of course, Calcutta stagnates. Twenty, twenty-five years ago, Calcutta had jute, coal, engineering and tea. It was the second city in the Commonwealth.' Mehra counted on his fingers. 'Unions destroyed engineering. Coal was nationalised – in other words, Delhi took it over and never re-invested here. Why should they help the CPI? Jute? The mills were British-owned. Every mail-bag in the world, every potato-sack, came from Cal. Partition left the jute fields in Bangladesh and the mills in Cal. The British sold out to Marwaris, who have always been middlemen and small traders. They'd made fortunes in the Korean War. The Marwaris worked their bargain as hard as they could and invested the profits in other enterprises elsewhere. So when the world demand for jute collapsed, they didn't fight it. Everything was finished. That leaves tea. Tea production is labour-intensive, yes, but only out on the gardens. It was never a major employer in Calcutta.'

Calcutta lies moribund like the Emperor Hirohito, whose life was prolonged by massive and repeated blood transfusions.

Thirty years ago tea rather looked down on jute and engineering. It is said to have been the last of the great trades to open to Indians after Independence: the list of chairmen of the Calcutta Tea Traders Association suggests it. The years 1888 to 1956 pass in an unbroken line of British names: Campbells, Lloyds, Taylors, Surreys, Jarvies; there are Nicholl and Blair, Peppercorn, Duncan and Brent. In 1956 there is a K. Ghosh. And then, by golly, another six years of Postlethwaite and Duckworth (Sir Richard) and Whitaker and Hales and N. S. Coldwell. Then Ghosh again. Then Brock and Smith and Scott and the last European name there: M. S. Christie, which takes us to 1968, one of the better times to be anywhere in the world but Calcutta, particularly if you were white and looking forward to a quiet retirement. The Company names barely register a blip: Duncans, Finlays, Lipton, The Assam Co (India) Ltd, Harrisons and Crossfield (India) Ltd, Macneill and Magor Ltd . . . They're all there still, trading and broking and planting out of Dalhousie.

Dawn is the best time to approach Dalhousie, Calcutta's Number One district: Cal 7000-01, precisely. Here you find the grand old GPO building, where scribes will later assume positions outside to take dictation and seal your letter with many ounces of fiery red wax. The Telephone Bhawan, Writer's Building and the High Court are here. The banks are quartered here, banks which can certainly *babu* the simplest transaction into a complex of forms and queues and 'waiting, pliz', during which you anxiously follow the progress of your traveller's cheque and passport from desk to grille to desk to counter, gaining weight all the time with clips and forms and receipts and triplicated chits until it arrives at its destination as fat as a healthy brief. In and around Mangoe Lane most of the tea companies have their offices, in newish buildings of painted concrete.

Although nobody lives in Dalhousie buildings, any more than they do in the City of London, people have come at this early hour to wash clothes in the tank in the centre of Dalhousie Square, or simply to squat by it with a tin mug to sluice themselves, as they will do all day. It is possible to wander across the roads of Dalhousie before the cars are out, the breakfast vendors set up their stalls, and the *babus* flood into work at Writer's Building or the banks or tea companies. Then it becomes Babel, and a roasting frenzied hell: peons rushing between offices, plump idlers in pyjamas mooning about food-stalls, trucks from Howra Station belching over the bridge across the Hooghly into a thick jam of Ambassadors behaving like queeny third secretaries and hooting, pushing, negotiating the press of bodies and vehicles and wobbling bicycles. Then there are calm figures ferrying their paunches astride Bajajes or mopeds who take to the pavements; and beggars planting themselves under everybody's feet, or hanging on each passer-by without ever touching him, a sort of human treacle melting in the heat and oozing through the streets.

The tea companies manage to operate in the chaos. They actually seem efficient. There are not, of course, the smart girls paddling at the keyboards of electric typewriters in fitted offices; I never saw a computer; and the lifts don't ride you up in an Airwick hush, but they seem busy for all that. There is generally a great open office cluttered with desks, piled with papers; there is the whirr of rotating standing fans and the odd *ping!* of a typewriter, but only one telephone in the whole room, because the writers aren't required to speak to anyone. That goes on in small side offices, where the directors have the day's prices relayed to them now and again by their man at auction over the phone.

At McLeod Russell a dozen pickets were standing in the entrance hall carrying placards, and posters had been plastered over the doors. Four Worker's Resolutions . . . Urge upon reactionary management . . . Demands . . . Betrayal . . . Conditions.

As I pushed through the glass doors my way was blocked by a man with a placard. 'Workers Rights Abused! Management Must Respond To Resolutions!' it screamed.

'You are looking for McLeod Russell?' he asked.

'Yes, I've come to see Mr Dayan,' I confessed.

'Follow me, pliz.' He propped his placard against the wall and led me upstairs. The stairwell bellowed its angry protest. 'Unity Is Strength! Support Comrades in Struggle against Opportunistic Management!'

'What is happening?' I asked.

He looked at me blankly for a moment. I pointed to a poster. He stared at it as if it surprised him.

'Industrial dispute, sah. This way, pliz.'

Plenty of people seemed to be at work in the writers' office. My guide knocked on a door, and waited for a reply before he ushered me in. I thanked him and he returned to his demonstration.

'What is that all about?' I asked Mr Dayan.

'Annual pay review,' he replied briskly. 'Sorry you had to come at this time, I hope it didn't inconvenience you.'

Mr Dayan took off his glasses and rubbed the bridge of his nose.

'Jolly good. It runs like clockwork. We make our offer, they mount a demo for a few weeks, demand more. We give in a bit, they give in a bit. Honour restored all round. The unions are happy, the company's happy. It'll be over by next week. Would you like tea?'

It didn't take long to realise that Calcutta life revolved around the Clubs. Membership of these clubs is restricted to the anglicised upper classes, an upper ten thousand (if, indeed, so many). There is a Calcuttan passion for organising and subdividing. My local guide book listed associations and societies in their thousands, from the All Bengal Dislodged Minorities Association to the Calcutta Tea Chest Fitting Manufacturers' Association, but the Clubs are the backbone of Calcutta society. When the exclusive 400 Club was founded in London a 300 Club opened in Calcutta. It cannot be accident that the first completed section of the new Calcutta Metro should run from Dalhousie to Tollygunge, where members of 'Tolly' can play golf, tennis, billiards, go riding and swim, and wind down afterwards with a drink at the open air bar. Tolly is a family club run by an Englishman known as the Viceroy. The Saturday Club is fairly sporty, for the younger crowd. The Calcutta Club – founded as a place where Indians and Europeans could meet – is distinguished, but not as eminent as the Bengal, which has reciprocal rights with the Athenaeum and the Shanghai Club, and has most of the government in its membership. Tea men are everywhere, but *en masse* they like to hang out at the Sports Club, a fairly scruffy establishment with a bar and a football pitch.

I had a few contacts to pursue from London; within a day or two of my arrival I had several more. My friends weren't in tea themselves, but gradually it became clear that you couldn't throw a chickpea at dinner without hitting somebody who was. (Throwing things at dinner was a Calcutta fad for several years towards the end of the eighteenth century, until an injudicious pelleting ended in a duel and a ban). I made arrangements to visit tea-gardens in Darjeeling; Assam, convulsed by border disputes with Bangladesh, was out of bounds, but the Dooars, I was told, were all but the same thing and there could be no objection to visiting there, within a stone's throw of Assam proper. And there were gardens in the South: the High Ranges, and the Nilgiris, where I could meet the last white planter.

An Englishman in India is perpetually brushing against the familiar amid the exotic and strange. The familiarity, though, is almost all nostalgia. The Ambassador is a fifties Morris. Pillar-boxes are red. The upper middle classes remind you of Shire English, and public-school men. They remind you of the clubland heroes of Buchan and Sapper. They call each other Bunty and Junior and Bobby. They do indeed meet at the club. They work hard, play hard, drink stiff ones and use a vocabulary that got shot down over the English Channel in 1942. Even when I spoke to someone my age I had the impression of speaking to my grandfather as a young man.

In the army, the Civil Service (rechristened the Administrative Service), the law, and tea, the British left a strong mark. They founded public schools, like the Doone, to provide the right sort of manpower to the institutions. They made, in effect, an Establishment in their own image: perhaps the only genuine unity that exists across India is the bonding of the elite, pegged down by the weight of pan-Indian institutions created by the British. Even the Pakistani surrender in 1971 turned into a sort of club reunion of generals who knew each other as Bunty or Banjo, and hadn't met for years.

While the British were here training for the professions was the quickest way to get on. Now the accent is shifting. I went to a party of young people in Calcutta. 'We are a class created by the British to take power,' I was told. 'Look around this room. Everyone here comes from a wealthy family. Every single person here is studying at an American university. I'm at Stamford, doing a course in Design and Communications. Saatchi have offered me a salary of 47,000 dollars when I finish, working in the US or Britain. Whatever I do in India, I'm not going to earn much above two or three thousand rupees a month. That's about 1500 pounds a year. In the States I've bought a Golf on holiday earnings.

'OK, it's not just the money. It's the work. I'm using a Compaq which is so advanced it can only be exported to NATO countries. Let's say I do get permission to take a Compaq out of the States. I've got a friend who got funded to study in America by the Indian Government. 20,000 dollars a year. But he couldn't get an import licence to bring a lousy 4000 dollars worth of equipment back into the country. So he gave it up. He's working in New York.'

At MacNeill Magor I met Michael Rome, as far as I know the last Englishman to hold a position in a Calcutta tea firm, apart from a handful of apprentice tasters on secondment from London. He is a great bear of a man, six foot two, with a firm handshake and a big bass voice. He was due to retire the following year: back to England, of course.

'They used to say that when you got out to the gardens you were made if you lasted two monsoons. Diphtheria, malaria, cholera – you had to work up the antibodies, or be your own doctor. If you were really sick they'd get you down to Cal, but the journey wasn't much fun.'

He jumped up and pulled down a book to show me a passage I remembered from Ukers, an early planter's description of jungle planting:

Sheep could not stand the climate. The Hindu population debarred beef. Religious prejudice forbade the milking of cows. So planters had to live on the skinny fowl of the country . . . The planter's daily routine was to go out only after the day was well-aired. After the morning quinine, he drank his coffee and ate what he could. Then with a pipe under his nose to counteract the miasma, he sallied forth to oversee his clearing, and all the countless jobs, which brought around the morning meal. Followed the afternoon siesta, or bout of ague as the case might be, and then the evening inspection. And so *da capo* from week to week, till it was time for the trip home to recruit, or else for rest in the grave.

Rome laughed. 'It wasn't that bad by the time I got here. I came out in '49. My company had sent me along to the Army and Navy Stores in London. I told them I was going to be a planter, so they asked if that would be Africa or India. They showed me to the India Room – extraordinary. They knew exactly what was needed, you know, three shirts (flannel), two trousers (twill) and so on, and you just gave them your size. It was all wrapped up in less than an hour. The only thing they got wrong was the topee. You see, by 1949 the topee had been killed off by sunglasses. The lads all laughed when I arrived with my topee. Anyway the colour was wrong. It should have been khaki, but I'd got a white one. Very dangerous, because elephants don't like white hats, for some reason. Pulled your head off.

'A lot of the young chaps nowadays have taken to hats again. Even topees. That's because of *gerao* – when your workers simply surround you when you're out in the open. That's all they have to do. It's usually about wages, but they don't realise it isn't really up to the planter to sort it out. Anyway they just stand there, and he can't move. No violence usually, but if he's out in the sun without a hat he's a raving loony pretty soon. They change the guard as it were. It happens in Cal, too. Used to happen all the time at the university. Nastier there, more violent.'

I asked him if 1949, two years after Independence, wasn't an odd time to be recruiting Englishmen on the gardens.

'These were basically British companies at the time, the Agency Houses. I suppose it was a question of satisfying the shareholders. The devil you know, and that sort of thing. There was also the problem that the tea companies hadn't prepared for Independence, and there weren't all that many trained Indians to take over. There may have been a bit of a feeling that tea was a British domain. Consumption in India itself wasn't high, like it is today, and whether it was sold here or in London it was generally headed towards Britain.'

'When did that change?'

'It's been happening gradually. The population has risen enormously here, that's one thing. Living standards are up, too. Then there's competition in the world market. Britain gets most of its tea from Africa these days – Kenya and Malawi. On the whole it's cheaper than Indian. Most of it is exported, because Africans don't have a taste for tea themselves. Shipments arrive in London faster, there are fewer barriers. And then there've been problems here, like the 1984 export ban, which was meant to keep prices down here. The Government has to watch the price of tea very carefully.

'That sort of thing causes havoc to a blender's plans. British companies had to buy a lot more from Africa, and they found that they could do fine without us. Of course we've got a lot of traditional contacts with the UK market, and they come back to us. But as far as the company's concerned, we're happy to make money selling internally.

'We do have a problem when the export quantities are unpredictable. Mainly it's because the British housewife buys on liquor – she wants the right taste – while the Indian buys on appearance. He wants teas that look really black, grainy, knobbly. It's lack of sophistication. So we have to make different kinds of tea. One of the side-benefits of the 1984 ban has been that the Indian consumer has begun to develop a taste for liquoring teas. We had to offload a lot onto the internal market, and people liked it.'

'When did the British start moving out? During the troubles here?'

'Not really. Partly it was political: the government more or less ordered the tea industry to Indianise itself or get nationalised. As it is, no company in India is allowed to be majority-owned by foreign stockholders. This company is 26 per-cent British-owned now. Some are more, a lot are less. Then there was the Chinese war in 1962. The Assam gardens were in the firing line. The British planters didn't want to get caught up, and the government didn't really want foreigners in charge of sensitive areas. Devaluation got the rest, mainly. They drew rupee salaries and in 1966 the rupee was devalued – bang went the little home in England, and all their savings. So they cleared out while they were still ahead.'

'But you stayed?'

'Oh, some of us stayed. I couldn't have left, I love it. I've got a lot of friends here, as well as at home, of course. Also I'm lucky: most of my salary's in sterling.' He chuckled. 'And next year I retire. My wife's in London now. We've got a place.'

A few weeks later I met him again, in London, on leave. He took it every September. At his suggestion we had lunch at a carvery in a hotel on Marble Arch. We talked about the old Calcutta races. He'd had shares in a horse or two. The races had been terrific.

'Remember the Two Monsoons?' he said over the horseradish. 'I've just been talking to an old friend of mine, a chap of eighty-six. Eighty-six summers, as they say. Says that coming home's a question of Two Winters. The first winter you've still got the sun in your bones. It's the second you've got to get through.'

167

I looked around the restaurant. It was full of tourists tucking into the Roast Beef of Olde England, as much of that and roast lamb and pork, as they could bear to eat.

8

Darjeeling

Every weekday in the season Calcutta holds the world's biggest tea auction at J. Thomas & Co's, brokers of Mango Lane. Each sale is conducted – in English – by the company involved; bidding used to be against a candle, and now just at top speed. The buyers shout and hoot like parliamentarians. Oh! Oh! Oh! they cry. Ha! With you! With you! Ha! Want some! Oh!

A timely Ha!, an emphatic Want Some! puts you in the running. With you! is what you bellow across the benches when you want to share a lot with whoever is bidding at the moment All this is happening at speed and we have covered half-a-dozen lots before I am aware that one has been sold. Oh! means something, but I am not quite sure what; encouragement, maybe.

The buyers have the privately annotated catalogues which guide their bidding. A sample of each lot has been tasted by interested parties: unlike coffee or sugar, tea is too variable and susceptible to be treated like a commodity. There are, in this market, no spot prices and no futures. The day begins quietly as everyone gauges the strength of the market. Gogol is buying for the Soviet Union, never paying over 100 rupees, always looking for good appearance even at the expense of quality. Perhaps there is a shade of arrogance in the way he is hunched smack before the rostrum, with the other buyers tiered in rows at his back; willy-nilly they accept a sort of leadership from him. India and the USSR enjoy a massive barter trade: Gogol buys tea with power stations. Bengal has a special weakness for the Soviet Union: the day before I had visited an exhibition of Tolstoy memorabilia, and seen the copper and brass samovar he used for making his tea. Nobody quite knows what happens to the tea Gogol buys, but the lower qualities are probably blended with Georgian, rather as Chinese tablet tea for the Tsarist Russian market used to be 'faced' with Indian tea-dust to give it a good appearance. Tetley's and Typhoo have their men from London, and some of the London houses have their local agents. Lipton and Brooke Bond (India) are here, of course.

'Nice tea, lot 24.'

'Ha! Ha!'

'Oh!'

'Oh! Oh!'

'With you!'

'Oh! Oh! Oh!'

'Brookie? Can we hear from you, sir?'

'Oh!'

'With you!'

'Ha!'

'Division unclear . . . Brookie . . . fourteen chips. Lot 25!'

The lights go out. The air-conditioning cuts. The internal generator gets going a few moments later, cranking the overhead fans, but everyone is soon dripping. Ties are loosened, when worn. Jackets are removed, ditto. I feel I am about to melt, but it would be churlish to abandon Abhijit, my host, who must baboon with the best of them.

'Oh! Oh!'

'Ha!'

'Lot 34!'

I'm exhausted after an hour of this. Abhijit tactfully suggests that I visit the Darjeeling Orthodox saleroom along the passage. It is much smaller, just a room with rows of chairs and a dais. Perhaps forty people are bidding. It is more like a country auction: a finger here, a nod there, a call for any more bids, gentlemen, and the gavel. Only it is very hot. No air-conditioning in the Darjeeling room.

The teas are not on display. They may not even be in Calcutta yet if the sample chest was sent on ahead of a large break in transit from the gardens. The tasters are looking for supplies of particular kinds of tea at certain prices to maintain their blends. They talk nervously about The Housewife, their stern mistress. Her tastes are unshakeable. Her nose is keen, her eye all-penetrating, her tendencies very conservative. She is a tough judge. When a brand-name price war broke out in the 1970s the quality of tea began to slide. Then all of a sudden, She stopped picking the packets off the shelves, and a hasty truce had to be patched up to win Her back.

Blenders are engaged in the Sisyphean task of finding the teas to match up the same old blend, year after year. The problem is that no tea is the same year after year; like wine, it responds to variables of climate and skill. Every year there are some teas known as 'self-drinking' which could be drunk unblended, but generally it's a question of putting together different teas to produce the brew with the right combination of colour, briskness, and strength for the blend. The combinations are reduced to rather dismal formulae which are supposed to be secret, although any taster worth his salt could reproduce his rivals' blend in a few minutes, given stock. He has to watch the price, too: no use creating the perfect match if it costs twice as much. It is a restless search, because no garden can be expected to produce the same quality of tea at the same price month in, month out, so new sources are continually being sought, new breaks tasted.

There are commonsense rules: it's easier and in the long run cheaper to buy large lots of a few teas than to try to make up the blend from dozens of small purchases, even if they come cheap. A blender learns to trust his nose and eye: usually he can work out the blend in his head after tasting hundreds of lots, though the skill takes time to acquire, and is partly a born thing. And in blending, the teas should not be mixed too well, or they will blend patchily like cards in an over-shuffled deck.

Black-tea tasting is standard around the world, from Mombasa to Manchester. It's a minor legacy of the British Empire, like driving on the left or the way telephones ring. Hundreds of sample tins are lined up on a bench, and in front of each one goes a lidded mug of white china and a white ceramic bowl. In each mug a weight of tea equal to an old sixpenny bit is brewed for six minutes. The tea assistant goes down the bench draining each mug into the white bowl and trapping the wet leaves on the underside of the lid, which he then exposes on top of the empty mug. From front to back you now have the tin of dry leaf, the wet tea-leaves, called the infusion, on the lid of the mug, and what you might call the infusion, but which is known as the liquor, in a bowl, looking very dark after a six-minute brew.

The tasters move down the line in their white coats like doctors along a crowded ward. A rather revolting spittoon on castors travels with them, although *de-luxe* tasting benches can have a gutter running with fresh water. The tasters pull out spoons. They put a finger into the dry tea and stir it around. They lift the lid and examine the infusion, tamp it into a small volcano and sink their noses into the crater: the aroma of tea is strongest on the infusion. By now they should know enough to skip tasting the liquor. They see its colour, its 'brightness' and the extent to which it can be said to 'cream', suggesting quality: cream is the film that floats upon the surface of a good tea, and the opacity of the liquor itself. Brightness is a sparkling quality opposed to flatness. When eventually the taster slurps noisily off his spoon he rolls the tea around his gums and breathes its aroma to test for briskness, which they call a 'live' quality.

The upshot of all this sniffing and probing is fairly disappointing to an observer. Tea-tasters aren't a flamboyant breed; they lack the bottly loquacity or tipsy *gravitas* of wine masters, and they express themselves shyly in print. The men taking extensive notes are not blenders but brokers, who judge the performance of a garden under their care and offer advice to the planter. Thus the broker's long-winded comment on the first Assam teas: brisk slightly burnt flavour. Blenders, who don't have to bother about communicating their observations to anyone but themselves, are the voles of their trade, who may be prodded into an admission that a tea is 'useful', at best. Many simply push the mug a certain distance from the edge of the bench, according to a private code.

To reach the gardens I had to enlist the help of Calcutta firms. In London I had met 'Kipper' Atal at the Oriental Club just off Oxford Street. He was running a heavy cold, squashed up against the radiator, serving himself tea and doggedly persevering with a cigarette, a big man in a grey wool suit and a plain tie, with a smooth bulge of shirt at the midriff to attest the years spent running an Anglo-Indian tea company. Portrayed in hectic oils overhead the rebel Tippoo Sahib, splendid and bejewelled, lay dying.

'It's a hard life, managing a garden,' said Kipper. 'A long, hard apprenticeship, too, maybe twenty years. Difficult, when you think you know as much as the old bugger who actually runs the place. But if they're going to last they stick it out. Up at six and to bed at two on a good day, all through the season, February till November. I send them up now, y'know, young men, fighting fit, and no joke but I can't bloody recognise them after six months. That's why so many of them leave, just can't stand it. Graduates these days – somebody's got to employ them. Not enough jobs, not nearly. Thousands of applicants for a handful of positions. Still won't stick it. No conversation, no books, six till two, they come back after a month and say "no thanks". Gets worse, too – last year not a fellow saw it through the season.'

Kipper rubbed a stain from a crested saucer. Outside it had begun to rain and the Indian hall porter belted down the road with a free hand dragging his green uniform jacket over his head, to disappear into the throng coursing along Oxford Street.

'It was different when I started out,' Kipper was saying. 'Fellows came straight out of public school, and after too much English weather and not much going for them at home they took what they could and didn't look back. Not very bright but plenty of muscle, and they stood up to a five-year tour of duty in the back of beyond because they weren't worried about books, just holding their whisky and getting soft on a local girl. They had a good time. Nowadays it's these over-educated chaps with clever wives – and the wives can't bear it at all. Nothing for them to do. They want to go shopping in Calcutta, go to parties with their friends. In the end the fellows snap. Good sorts, most of them, despite all the education. It's the women really. If a fellow can stick it out twenty years he deserves to be manager.'

There was an echo of a retired Home Counties colonial, joking that women lost us the Empire – and not really joking, at all.

Assam was strictly out of bounds: the proper procedure involved feeding the IAS (the Indian Administrative Service) dozens of forms over which they ruminated for months; and even then London directors had still failed to get permission to visit. I was most eager to go to Darjeeling. The gardens could not be raised on the phone, but my new friends thought that if I could be at the railway station at Siliguri at a certain time on a particular day they could probably sort something out.

My last trip on an Indian train had been in the company of a Canadian diplomat from the Havana embassy who invited me to burn with him a *lingam* of tobacco worth 100 dollars. This time I shared a compartment with two quiet businessmen and an accountant called Mr Das who was inexplicably prejudiced against climbing the little ladder to the upper bunk. He railed against the injustice of my having been allotted his berth. I invited him to sit on my bunk for as long as he liked, and while I pressed my nose to the glass to wave at friends he grumbled and expostulated and made himself comfortable, kicked off his sandals, tucked his feet under his little thighs, and fell half-swooning to one side like a Veronese Venus with a briefcase.

Rather as though he had eluded creditors, Mr Das cheered up enormously as soon as our carriage was gathered up and carried out of the station. The beggars and hawkers at the far end of the platform had already turned from us as we swept by. Mr Das unbuckled his case and took out a small newspaper parcel which he unwrapped. Inside were several little green packages, and he picked one up and popped it in his mouth. Chewing pan is an acquired taste, but the fillings are elaborate and beautiful: green pastes, red pastes, cardamom seeds, silver leaf, and all the spices of the East, wrapped up in a glossy green leaf. You can have them made to your specifications. They tend to stain mouths red, and public staircases and whitewashed walls all over India are spattered as after a massacre by scarlet spittle. Mr Das grinned like a ghoul, and tucked the remaining leaves back into his briefcase.

He was on his way up to the gardens to examine the books, but however hard I pressed him to discuss the fortunes of tea estates I was marked as an Englishman and he felt we should talk about cricket and the weather. We groped through the popular issue of London pea-soupers (there had been none, I said, since the Clean Air Act; Mr Das, who had watched his Sherlock Holmes on TV, smiled and knew better) and came out onto the cricket pitch, where I was hopelessly fog-bound myself. Mr Das, however, was a voluble inglorious Wisden, and had gleaned a great deal about batting form from the back pages of *The Statesman*. Listening to him reminded me of school hanging about at the edge of a pitch with nothing to do but let the tiny figures in their whites grow smaller and smaller, and their antics less and less distinct, ultimately so distant that the sight of them all gesticulating with miniature arms and crying faintly means nothing at all, until a thud and an ethereal groan nearby means you have to start running.

On the train I had the advantage of being able to pick up a book and excuse myself on the grounds that I had to do some research. I could feel that Mr Das was watching my face, and out of the corner of my eye I saw his leg slowly extend down the bunk. I put a book down beside me, in the path of his foot. Thus checked, he began to bring the other leg down in little fits and starts, taking advantage of the coach rattling over points, until both feet were almost touching the spine of my book.

It is said that the British won an Empire in a fit of absent-mindedness, and lost it in the same way. I didn't mean to repeat the mistake. Mr Das stood up and nonchalantly brought his suitcase down onto my bunk. He pretended to fuss over its contents and then, satisfied, he lounged back and watched me through sleepy eyes. I was compressed into a small niche by the window, overhanging the ashtray. I read on. Mr Das blundered, and went to the loo; as soon as he was gone I put all his cases onto his bunk and stretched out, pretending to be asleep. He grumbled very noisily and hurled his sandals to the floor, but I slept soundly nonetheless.

There was another European at the railway station next morning, engaged in argument with a booking clerk. He wanted, he said, to take the *toy train* to Darjeeling – a faintly facetious way of referring to the two-foot-gauge railway which connects Darjeeling town with the plains 7000 feet below. The booking clerk shook his head. Darjeeling closed. No train. *Gurkha bandh*. No, no bus. No taxi. *Bandh*. He would have to go back to Calcutta. First he must write his name in the station book.

The European looked well-travelled in a mixture of army surplus and ethnic garb. With his pony-tail and bangles and wooden bead necklaces he looked as if he had strayed over from a role as the jittery element in a Vietnam War film. The news of the Darjeeling troubles, and the Gurkha blockade, had been all over Calcutta, and even featured in the world press, so I suspected that he meant to reach Darjeeling by hook or by crook, and would find his own way up. I was in no position to offer him a lift, and I didn't want to get stuck with him; so I slid past unchallenged and out into the glaring compound, where a few Land-Rovers and Ambassadors were drawn up, and a tea hut had been erected. None of the cars had the number plate I was looking for and I was wondering what to do when a white Ambassador scudded on to the gravel. The name of a tea company was emblazoned on its doors. The driver jumped out and saluted. I saluted back, and he grinned.

'Mr Goodwin? Hottle. Runglee. Good?'

'Hottle?' I echoed.

'Breakfast, sah.' He wagged his head from side to side. If it was practice to offer arriving guests breakfast at a 'hottle' I was unwilling to break with tradition, so I thanked him and climbed aboard.

He took the wheel with the unfamiliar air of many Indian drivers, hugging it to his chest, bow-legged on the pedals and his elbows sticking out rigidly at either side as if he feared I might snatch it from him. The upper part of the rim almost brushed his chin, and while he stared tensely ahead he worked furiously on the gear-lever which sprouted from the steering column. He had arrived with the windows down but he suggested I wound them up to benefit from the air-conditioning; I said I'd rather not, and he seemed pleased. His name was Ben Khazi. He was wearing a brown vest, *lunghi* and sandals and he came from 'this place'.

Not much to look at, this place. Very yellow, and low; brick buildings, some concrete, but mostly mud, and single-storey, straggling along thin roads and backing onto empty shallow river beds of earth and gravel where mat huts had been put up. The Spencer Hotel was a burst of lush garden and whitewash which had been erected to serve travellers, for Siliguri had always been a staging-post on the route up to Darjeeling, the summer seat of the Government of Bengal. The Spencer had probably served much the same bacon-and-egg breakfast with tea a century before, when passengers off the new line from the banks of the Ganges had transferred to palanquins for the climb into the hills.

Siliguri itself lies between the borders of Nepal and Bangladesh, barely a hundred miles apart. If you imagine a pistol ballooning smoke, the handle, very much enlarged, would be Bengal, with Calcutta at the bottom. The thin barrel runs towards Assam in the east, the hanging balloon. Beneath the barrel is Bangladesh. The safety catch is Darjeeling, a tiny upraised quiff between Nepal in the west, Bhutan to the East, and a small border with Tibet to the north.

Not surprisingly, Siliguri is also a garrison town. A leafy avenue runs out towards the hills, and behind the trees are barracks and headquarters whose presence is signalled by boards on the roadside: 2nd Rifle Brigade, 3rd Division, Regional HQ: Military Police; 1st Armoured Division, Divisional Headquarters. Green army trucks ran to and fro; the Blue Berets trotted along the roadside; order and formation everywhere, the straight lines that characterise Army districts: straight roads, rectangular buildings, straight-stepping and square-bashing.

Tea-planters began to regiment this area from the 1850s, twenty years after the Raja of Sikkim had ceded Darjeeling to the British in return for protection against Nepal; the British saw it as a sanatorium for troops and a summer retreat for the governors of Bengal. There were only a few Lepcha hill-men (still to be seen with their elvish mongoloid faces and floppy-eared flying-caps), and the first superintendent, Dr Campbell, set about attracting settlers from Nepal, Bhutan and Sikkim. By 1852 Darjeeling town boasted seventy European houses, a bazaar, a jail, a revenue, a 'simple system of administration of justice', no forced labour, experimental tea and coffee plantations and various European fruits and grapes.

The first tea plantations were made with China stock brought from a western district of Himalayan India. By 1852 it had been found that tea did not flourish in Darjeeling itself, where there was 'too much moisture and too little sun', but a thousand feet lower the tea was 'in a highly-thriving condition', and there was some excitement at the thought that it 'might be cultivated at a great profit and be of advantage in furthering a trade with Tibet'.

Early planters followed what they thought was the Chinese model: 'The first idea about Tea was that it should be planted on slopes. Pictures of Chinese, suspended by chains (inasmuch as the locality could not otherwise be reached) picking Tea off bushes growing in the crevices of rocks, somewhat helped this notion; and when stated, as it was, that the Tea produced in such places was the finest and commanded the highest price, which was not true, intending planters in India went crazy in their search for impracticable steeps! This is especially the case in parts of the Darjeeling district,' noted Colonel Money severely, in his prize-winning essay on 'Cultivation of Tea', 1877. Darjeeling had begun with China bushes and what were considered Chinese methods.

We drove between two spurs of mountain. The way had seemed so flat that only a cyclist might have noticed a slight gradient against him. We had come out of the light forest to join the Tista, a tributary of the Ganges, rising in Tibet. The rivers on the Bengal plains are constantly switching and altering their courses, silting up ports, opening new ones, flooding and disappearing. The dried river-bed showed in miniature the same loops and whorls carved in mud and grey stone, and following it we entered between the fingers of a giant sprawled headlong to grasp at the flatlands of Bengal: the giant Himalayas.

Ben Khazi took the mountain road at a Monte Carlo clip. MAKE THIS AN ACCIDENT FREE DAY a sign suggested, while he toggled the car into third and swung wide on a hairpin bend with the river gurgling 200 feet below beneath the trees. Ben Khazi didn't read much English. Trucks came bucketing downhill with their engines off and their horns blaring: COLLAPSING BRIDGE DRIVE SLOWLY flashed by, almost too fast to read, and the collapsing bridge thundered under our tyres, biding its moment. We came to a fork where one road crossed the river and doubled back on the opposite bank: the road to Assam; and by the bridge, where an obelisk commemorated Sir John Anderson, I caught a glimpse of a little girl emerging from a hut in the trees who seemed to be wearing the uniform of a select London seminary.

I don't know how high we had climbed when Ben Khazi throttled down and spun the wheel hard to the left. Perhaps two or three thousand feet. The new road fell from the mountain, and we ascended in an almost comically repetitive series of switchbacks and hairpin corners, too steep even for trees, climbing to the garden, Runglee Rungliot, which means Thus Far and No Further.

The mountain top was folded into small hills and hollows which seemed to be covered in green snow, a thick quilt which overhung the sunken lane. I scarcely believed it was tea. The bushes were tightly packed, so evenly sized and trim on top that it seemed quite possible to take a tray and toboggan down them, or to stomp across their surface on racquet-shaped tea-shoes. It was nothing like the tea I had seen in China, sprouting here and there like gorse on a moor. Instead women waded up to their waists through the bushes, following invisible paths like rabbit-runs beneath the branches. They wore their hair in thick black plaits, and across their foreheads ran straps which supported the pyramidal baskets they held on their backs, full of plucked leaf (you may pick flowers, but you pluck leaf). Four hours or so after leaving Siliguri we turned by a great jacaranda and arrived at the manager's bungalow.

The house was square, with a shallow roof of corrugated iron painted a rusty red. Tea dropped precipitously in front of it, and tea lapped up behind it almost to the walls — it was like a boulder poised on the lip of a waterfall, a sweeping torrent of tea. It had a small lawn to one side, with a verandah entwined with honeysuckle and convulvulus, where the manager — the *burra sahib* — met me.

They couldn't have chosen a better man, aesthetically speaking, to work at the eyrie. Navim was about forty-five, with an expression part wise and part surprised. He looked and acted like a bird. He was restless, nervous and shy; he always stood up to speak, bobbing his head; when he walked he flapped his arms, and wrapped them around himself when he stopped. His bungalow might have been spirited lock and stock from Eastbourne. The sitting room had a fireplace breasted with parti-coloured crazy paving, a tongue-and-groove semicircular bar with stools, a 'wall unit' containing varied niches and boxes designed to hold, as it did exactly, the stereo, a very few *Reader's Digest* books, and tourist purchases like china dogs and bronze Shivas. There was stiff large furniture from the fifties, upholstered in dingy practical red. In the bathroom hung twee posters of semi-naked blond children, peeing, or wearing mummy's shoes, over suitable captions, and elsewhere there were G-Plan coffee-tables and stamped metal ashtrays set on paper doilies. Navim seemed to have trouble settling into it and he was always springing from his chair, or opening the bar as if for the first time, or leaning his hand against the mantelpiece a little too precisely. He worked as hard as Kipper Atal had predicted – hard enough to avoid the bungalow for most of the day.

His wife was afflicted with the same shyness, her voice barely audible, keeping out of sight as much as possible in pursuit of a child carrying a toy machine-gun. He never pointed the gun at anything in particular but merely compressed the trigger without excitement and let off a wheezy rattling.

With 200 acres under tea Runglee was one of the largest Darjeeling gardens, with a higher yield per acre than any garden in the hills. Navim had almost doubled his yield in the last fifteen years: closer planting, tighter plucking rounds, better incentives. And the quality? Well, the price per kilo was rising every year.

The next morning I accompanied Navim on his tour of inspection. He did not stick a pipe under his nose against the miasma (he had no vices), although the miasma rose – more than an early morning mist, because it was partly cloud, too, which hung in skeins across the level surface of the tea. We took a jeep for the short run to the factory, a tombstone of corrugated iron, grey except for the roof painted in company red, with the name of the garden and the company emblazoned across it: in mountainous country a roof was free advertising. Navim said it was traditional – traditional, at any rate, since Tommy Lipton, the tea man and grocer who almost single-handedly – and single-mindedly – introduced massive brand-name advertising to the UK (his mania for advertisement was so acute that on board a sinking ship he was found furiously stencilling his logo on anything that would float).

Navim met his foreman in one of the small offices beneath the factory. The man was a local – a hill-man, at any rate, descended from the Nepalis and Sikkimese lured in by Dr Campbell over a century ago. He had slanting eyes, and a sun-creased face, and stood about five foot three so that on the face of it he had much more in common with the Chinese I had just left than with his *burra sahib*. He wore a burnt-coloured woollen jacket, and he raised the back of his fingers to his forehead in salute. He spoke no English, but Hindi, which Navim translated reluctantly later on. There was a problem in the labour lines, as the workers' village was called. A woman working in the garden had been molested in the night, Navim said. 'The trouble is that the culprit is not an employee himself, only the brother of a man who works here. So it is a matter for the police. Otherwise I might have been able to work a solution.'

'What sort of solution?' I asked.

'In these cases it is best if the couple are getting married. You see, nobody else will wish to marry her after this hue and cry. You must understand they are peasants. They do not think like you.' It sounded like a Victorian tragedy in the making. Navim was more sceptical. 'Actually, marriage may be happening anyway. But if he had been one of my workers I could have persuaded the parties to come to an arrangement.'

'And no police?'

'That can be part of the arrangement,' replied Navim blandly.

The incident threw light on Navim's role. The people Navim called his people looked quite different. They spoke a different language. They were Buddhists and animists; he was Hindu. Navim thought in terms of Calcutta, perhaps a trip to England, and lived in a house that could have been lifted from the South Coast, while his people thought of the next village or the festivals and lived in cabins and huts. But even now he was not simply a functionary with a diploma. Before Independence the planter had often doubled as the District Commissioner, and if officially this was no longer true he was still required to be something between a medieval baron and a college warden. Calcutta was ten or twelve hours away: suddenly the distance seemed irrelevant. It might have been thousands of miles, or decades. The garden was a fief.

We had climbed to the top of a wooden staircase which clung to the side wall, overhanging a precipitous drop, to the withering loft. The first planters in India withered tea in the open air as I'd seen it done in Wuyi, but the vagaries of the weather turned planters' invention towards artificial withering machines using fans and hot air. The loft was full of broad troughs covered in wire netting on which the leaf was spread overnight; warm air was blown through it by a great revolving fan at the end of the trough, and every hour or so the leaf would be tossed and turned by hand. When the edges of the leaf were almost crackling, it had to be shot down chutes to the rollers below.

It came in a cascade of floppy flapping green, straight to the magnificent BRITANNIAS all the way from Birmingham, crouching four-square on iron legs, painted thickly in cream, bowed over two circular plates of brass. The lower plate was fixed, ribbed radially, but the upper plate swung and thumped parallel to it, quite fast, describing the same circuit again and again. They were Dickens' melancholy mad elephants: the monotonous frenzy like a lunatic's tic. The withered leaf dropped from the loft like corn in a mill, gradually building up between the plates, which thumped and rolled and crushed and tore, breaking the cells and enzymes and polyphenols more surely and relentlessly than any man could do. As the twist tightened the pressure of the upper plate increased, until the supervisor decided that the time had come to scoop it out and recharge the plates with fresh leaf.

The leaf looked like spinach until it was shaken down on a jiggering sieve that sorted it roughly into sizes.

The grading of leaf, which is so erratic in China, follows a system in Indian-style teas. It is a sort of bureaucratic system – a palace bureaucracy, a mandarinate, a Ruritania of titles. Whole leaves are called Pekoe. Broken leaves are called Broken Pekoe. Very small broken leaves are called Fannings, and the rest is Dust.

So much for sizes. Qualifications cluster around each size to describe the quality of the grade. In general only the top two leaves and the tiny furled bud leaf are plucked. Young leaf makes finer tea. If the plucking is late the bud-leaf will have almost unfurled; the teas made from these two and a half leaves are called Orange Pekoe. If the bud is still tight the tea is younger and it will be Flowery Orange Pekoe. The tips of really young leaves do not, on the whole, darken like the rest of the leaf during fermentation, and after drying they appear straw-coloured, or golden. A Flowery Orange Pekoe which contains a fair proportion of 'golden tips' is called *Golden* Flowery Orange Pekoe; if every leaf has golden tips it is described as *Tippy* Golden Flowery Orange Pekoe. The grades are initialled for brevity: TGFOP is as good as you can get.

Tips do not themselves add anything to the flavour of tea, but their presence demonstrates that the tea is made of small fine leaves, which give the most delicate flavour. In Money's day the tendency was to pluck three, four or even five leaves on a sprig with the result that teas were seldom very tippy, but good and strong. But the dealers paid more for tippy teas, as they still do. Money despaired of a solution: 'The difficulty will remain until dealers give up asking for Pekoe tips (not a likely thing) or till a machine is invented, to separate quickly and cheaply, the two small leaves from the others after they have been all picked together.' It is still not likely, but the business is easier now that pluckers take fewer coarse leaves.

This isn't the end of grading. As the tea is rolled, depending on the pressure, it is torn, or broken up, into fragments. These are called brokens. Small, broken leaves ferment faster than larger sorts. Orange Pekoe and Flowery Orange Pekoe, when broken, become Broken Orange Pekoe. They may contain tips – Golden Broken Orange Pekoe. They may be made of entirely tippy tea: Tippy Golden Broken Orange Pekoe, TGBOP.

If the tea-leaves are broken very small, the size, say, of a pinhead, the grade is Fannings, for the simple reason that they could be removed from the mass of the dry tea by winnowing. But the smallest grade of all, which has nothing to do with what is swept up off the floor and, according to the modern myth, put into tea-bags, is Dust.

After rolling and rough sorting the tea is spread out on marble or stone to ferment in cool rooms – it is the fermentation that gives the tea its astringency, flavour and aroma. Then the tea is dried on grilles which enter an oven and slowly descend through it, from the hottest to the coolest part at the bottom. You can watch it drying through a glass panel in the side: the leaves hop about like performing fleas. It emerges brittle, brown and dry, great heaps of it, gloriously tippy like bolts of fine tweed. The smell is warm and biscuity. In the sorting and packing room the air is full of gold dust catching sunbeams. Women are sitting on the floor in companionable circles, each with a round basket full of tea from which they pick the rough bits of twig and stalk. Now and then they stir up the tea with quick casts of their baskets, and begin picking again. Navim has a static drum under which the tea passes on a belt, to pick up light impurities like fibre and pekoe hairs. Then the tea is jiggered again along a series of meshed belts which sieve each grade into boxes, and the boxes are taken to the other end of the room where the packers are building chests.

Navim has a new settling machine which can vibrate tea chests so that the leaf settles down and more can be packed in. Paper is folded over the top, an inner lid is put down and the lid proper is nailed into place. Then the painter comes with his stencils and marks the chest with the various details: the weight of leaf, the name of the garden, type of tea (TGFOP) and the batch number. And the chest is carried into storage to await transport down to the railhead, and auction.

We emerged into the open air. In the forecourt scales were rising and falling with the second plucking of the day and the 'women were coming in slowly, in twos and threes, with baskets full of leaves. Congregating around the scales they had begun to sing pop songs from Hindi movies while they slipped the basket bands from their heads and took off the folded cloths they used to cushion the weight. Once their baskets had been weighed they moved back again towards the garden, or sat down together on the grass verges of the lane to eat lunch, using their printed skirts as overlapping tablecloths.

Navim wanted to introduce me to his under-manager, the *chota sahib* or small boss, one of the Ph.D. generation Kipper Atal had told me about in London. Vimal looked terribly serious: he was in love. He scrambled joyously over the garden, all but caressing the bushes and exulting in their mystery.

'Darjeeling is unique,' he said. 'It's the only place in the world where China tea and Assam tea grow together. The Assam bush is larger leaved, more glossy; the China bush has small leaves – here.' He plucked a leaf and bit it. 'Different gardens have a different proportion of China to Assam. Here it is about 85 per cent China. Newer gardens have more Assam. Some of these bushes are more than a century old.'

'You mean they might have come straight from China?'

'Probably, yes.'

I stamped up and down a bit, cheerful to think that I was standing among bushes which Fortune might have dug up himself in the Wuyi mountains. Perhaps I had seen their parents.

'But nobody quite understands what gives Darjeeling tea its special flavour,' said Vimal, and what he said echoed the delighted bafflement of

Professor Zhuang in Fuzhou. 'Is it the mix of China and Assam? Or the height? It can't be reproduced anywhere else. In the research stations they have every detail of its chemistry, but they can't make sense of that.

'A lot of these plants are too old, really. A bush's yield is meant to decline after about seventy years. Look how thick around the stem they are.' He ducked into the snow of tea. 'Watch out for snakes,' he added as I followed him.

'Do you replant with China or Assam?'

'Neither. We use clones, bred for resistance to disease, high yield and so on. They're China or Assam hybrids, a bit of each. I'll show you the nursery after lunch. Would you like tea first?'

His own modest bungalow was a little further up the hill. Inside, the walls were decorated with a scattering of mildly fetishistic posters and a print of the *Cutty Sark*. Two armchairs and a sofa were squared off against a low table, empty except for an ashtray arranged geometrically in its centre. The whole place was professionally bare and neat, like a dentist's waiting-room. But Vimal was married. His wife was away in Delhi, visiting her family. He showed me snapshots of her looking pretty in Toronto. Navim's wife had moaned softly about how dull it was here, all she ever wanted to do was to go to Cal but they got so little leave, she couldn't go alone, there was nothing to do.

'Does your wife like it up here?'

Vimal smiled. 'I think so. Some women grow to hate the gardens, I suppose. Some men, too, but at least the men keep busy. Women want to go down to Calcutta, and they always complain about how little leave we get. Shanti usually visits her family around now, when it's busy on the garden. She'll be back at the end of next week. And we get a proper holiday every other year.'

A servant brought the tea to table; the full equipage of cups and saucers, strainer and pot and tongs and sugar. Vimal didn't sweeten his tea, as Navim did.

'You're busy now?'

'It's the second flush. Darjeeling is famous for it. I'm giving you first flush, the spring flush. Can you taste how green it is? Very young tea, after the winter period of dormancy. *Banji*, we call it, when the leaf can't grow, and we can't pick. The first flush has a slight edge, a little immature, if you like. Most people find it thin, but it sells because the market is thirsty. In fact the first teas to auction in spring get a premium – like the clipper teas.' He gestured to the print. 'The second flush comes in May and June. It's fuller, more balanced, and the quantity is quite good. Our problem in Darjeeling is quantity mainly. We're a small region and we produce much less per acre than Assam, for instance. It's colder and higher, and growth is slow. But the aroma is terrifically concentrated. It's not a big tea, just very fine, very – well, high. Like the upper scales on a piano. The second flush is a busy time for us because we get the best prices now and we have to organise the rounds to get the most efficient plucking. Bushes can be plucked every eight or ten days during a flush.

'When the monsoon comes the tea grows very fast. We're busy then too, but rains tea is really useless. You get a price for it, but it's just bulking quality, no real flavour or aroma worth speaking of. It all has to be picked, though, if only to clear the bushes ready for the autumn flush. The autumn is actually my favourite. It's quite late in the year, September or October, when the weather is good again after the rains. The flavour is more mellow than second-flush, softer. Like a peach to a pomegranate, or like male and female perfumes. Autumn teas are female. The Germans take a lot.'

The Germans, I had discovered, do not drink all that much tea but what they drink is the best. Did autumn teas evoke some Wagnerian *Waldgeist*, some female spirit at the heart of German longing? Vimal laughed.

'I suppose we should know the world's habits here – most Darjeeling goes abroad. The UK buys a lot, but not the best quality. A lot gets re-exported from London. The Germans and the Japanese compete for the top breaks. In a way it's the Russians who are the fussiest buyers, and some of our biggest customers. They go for appearance.'

'Tippy teas?'

'Tippy and even. Anything that looks ragged won't do.'

'But do Russian tea-drinkers – any tea-drinkers anywhere – really notice what teas look like? Brokers are always supposed to be looking for tippy teas, but do the people who buy the stuff in packets know what that means?'

'You'd be surprised. Even if they don't know much, they do expect to see tea looking good, with a nice bloom on the leaf, evenly graded, black and tippy. If it was dusty and messily broken they'd notice.'

Over lunch with Navim I was unable to banish a vision of Mrs Vimal dabbing autumn tea behind her ears while Vimal slapped a second flush across his chest. Afterwards I joined him for a trip to the nursery. We crossed the spur behind the bungalow by a grassy track and rounded a clump of pine. The ground fell away to a winding thread of road and a cluster of tiny houses thousands of feet below, from where each sound rose clearly on the thin air. A radio was playing faintly. The *toc* of an axe came disembodied from one of the pine forests. A child laughed and two black specks shot onto the white ribbon of road and ran towards a bridge. Across the valley another tea-sown hill rose and fell and was succeeded by hills beyond, fainter and fainter until the green and blue became a purple smudge. Northwards our spur curved like a dragon's tail and swelled to a hill-ridge blackened by forest, while in the south the hills parted and sank to reveal the Tista plains, and the river winding towards the Ganges.

Vimal chuckled and leaned back against a pine.

'So you see, we are pretty happy here. And it looks better in moonlight.'

We recrossed to the nursery, where the slope was gentler. In damp hollows and along the edge of streams grew tangles of foxglove and sprouting cardamom, pine and tall stemmed nut-trees ten feet high, exuberant rhododendron in full flower, all animated by the rustle and singing of birds. It was easy to see why tea estates were called gardens in this part of the world. Rooks cawed in the high branches, mynahs and blackbirds and blue jays perched and hopped from twig to trembling twig, and far above, over the valley in a pale blue sky, wheeled the silhouette of an eagle.

'I think it's like this in Scotland?' said Vimal. 'The man who started this garden was Scottish. He dug himself a lake and stocked it with salmon, and he had a rowing-boat brought up. He used to row into the middle of his lake, it wasn't very far, and sit there fishing, and nobody was allowed to disturb him at all.'

'He must have had an extraordinary view – a lake on a mountain top.'

'He must have had an extraordinary transport system,' added Vimal, practically. 'Pack-mules, elephants, coolies. None of the bungalows were glazed for years.'

'Imagine getting the steam engines up here to run all the new machinery.'

'Or just carrying up a toilet bowl.'

'Or ordering a light bulb.'

'A Christmas pudding,' said Vimal.

'Cufflinks.'

'Cufflinks, exactly.'

'Do you think he dressed for dinner?' I wondered.

'In a kilt? Of course, old boy. Never know who might show up. Didn't want to look as though he'd gone native.'

We looked at one another and laughed. It was only then I noticed that Vimal was wearing a tie.

Navim was in a nervous state when I got back. He was standing on the verandah wringing his hands and bobbing his head more rapidly than usual.

'We are,' he announced unhappily, 'expecting another visitor.'

I nodded guiltily. 'Who?'

'Armajeet Singh, the broker. He's tasting at quite a few gardens. In advisory capacity only.'

'That's all right then. He can help you to even better prices.' I said helpfully.

Navim rubbed his hands together and bobbed frenziedly.

'Perhaps. Perhaps.'

I slid past, not knowing what else to say.

An hour later I heard the sound of a car drawing up outside. Looking out I saw the door open and a very tall man descend, grinning. He was very thin, about sixty, with short and faintly receding white hair around a turtle-shaped head, and a very faint trace of moustache. He held out his hand to Navim: his arm was about a yard long. I had been expecting a plump Sikh sensualist. The two men disappeared onto the verandha and the driver brought a plastic suitcase out of the boot. I stood about listening for the crockery sounds of refreshment, and then went into the sitting room.

Armajeet Singh was folded like an 'N' into an armchair, quite at ease with his cup on a tea-table beside him. Navim was standing before the fireplace, leaning one elbow on the mantelpiece and holding his tea in the other hand. I was wondering how he was going to drink when he introduced us with an ill-timed flourish which poured hot tea into his saucer and over his wrist. He set the tea down and winced. Armajeet extended a long thin arm from his chair. We talked about the delay in the monsoon. Mrs Huria put in an appearance and Armajeet had stood up before I was aware she had come in. She was followed by her child, who hung about the doorway not pointing his gun at anyone.

'The soldier!' cried Armajeet enthusiastically, and there was one of those awkward scenes in which the child fails to live up to anyone's expectations. After much cajoling from his parents he let off a half-hearted hail of machine-gun fire at his foot and left the room, slumping against the door-jamb. Mrs Huria left quietly soon after. Navim screwed up his face to attend the taster.

Armajeet's background was royal, army and anglophile. 'Perhaps you'd like to pop along for the tasting,' he suggested. 'I'm sure Navim has some crackerjacks lined up.'

At first I had assumed that Navim was merely shy, but after a while I came to think that it was more a baron's awe before a king. Armajeet's task was to acquaint the Darjeeling planters with the pattern of demand emerging at the Calcutta auctions so that they could meet it before the profitable second flush was over. Inevitably he was drawn in to giving practical advice. I learned that he was king of the high-grown, lord of the liquor, The Nose. Navim ached to prove fealty.

The yield per acre in Darjeeling is low, and prices at auction reflect this: not enough, according to the planters. There are many 'sick gardens', which revert to the government and have to be mothballed or abandoned, because the rewards are insufficient. The region must survive by coaxing the quality from stubborn yields, running a thin red line on the accounts, labouring for a tiny breakthrough in efficiency and always praying for some happy constellation of climate, perfect manufacture and demand to forestall the banks. The breakthrough occurs just often enough somewhere among the sixty or so Darjeeling gardens to keep the others in the game. And behind the breakthrough, as often as not, will be Armajeet Singh.

In Calcutta he doubles as an auctioneer, where he often brings down the gavel on a break produced under his guidance.

Vimal joined us for the tasting and coaxed this story from Armajeet as we walked over to the tasting room.

'Castleton was a good garden,' Armajeet began, 'a good garden by anyone's standard. It got into hot water in the seventies. Sloppy manage-ment. By the time they called me in, its teas were selling at the lower end of the market and Castleton was damn close to being declared sick. It was sick, you could see how much. The sickness had spread from the manager's bungalow. The *burra sahib* had lost his nerve. The reaction is always the same: push for yield if you can't get the quality. It's almost always a flop, but in Darjeeling it's a disaster. Bad Darjeeling is complete

garbage. It won't have colour or briskness and you can't even use much
of it to bulk a blend.

'The pickers were getting away with souchong plucking – that's three
or four leaves and a bud. The manager had lost the authority to stop it. I
said to myself, the garden will either pull through this season or it'll go
under. We began right at the beginning of the process and worked through
– plucking, withering, rolling, fermenting, drying, the works. I pushed
for a hard wither, which hadn't really caught on much, though now it's
general practice. Even the grading was a mess. That year the price seemed
to bottom out; towards the end of the season it gave a few little fillips,
upwards. The quality was much improved but the buyers were still wary.
The following season I made it clear that I was going to do my damnedest
to raise the garden's standing. The buyers responded with confidence and
the price went up again – I think the ghosts were exorcised. I was spending
quite a bit of time at Castleton and the quality improved steadily to a
point where I thought I tasted something special, you know, hints of the
perfect flavour. There was the steadily developing muscatel flavour but
coming up behind these marvellous highlights, a sort of bloom. It was an
exciting time, experimenting with the wither and the fermentation to
bring those highlights forward. It took two years. In 1984 auctions we
got 157 chips a kilo, just about top whack. Then it was phenomenal.

'I got back to Cal very excited, saying I thought we had a 300-chip
tea. Well, everyone thought I was crackers, the market had barely ever
hit 200. "Old Armajeet's cooked his goose this time," they must've said.
We gave the tea VVIP treatment, sent samples round to anyone we thought
likely as soon as the break arrived, rather than wait for them to ask.
Privately I heard some encouraging noises. At auction I gave it a short
puff, told them my opinion, and took a gamble. The highest price to
date was 217 rupees, but I opened the bidding at 200. There was a
great silence. I thought, oh dear. And then the room exploded. Bidding
reached 300 chips and it was still frantic. I kept cool when we got to 500
rupees. The bidders fell back a bit. A few seemed to be out of the running. I just said, this tea is a record-breaker, gentlemen. It set them off
again.

'At 1000 chips the room was packed – the other auction-rooms had
drained when word got round. All other business stopped. It was damned
hot. Brooke Bond hadn't made a bid yet, but when it looked like Lipton
was about to take it Brookie moved in against him. The price was way

up, too far to end well, really. I had to almost choke the bidding off: 1460 rupees a kilo to Brooke Bond. I think they took it for a Japanese client. The place was in uproar. We went off and cracked some champagne.'

Navim blinked and licked his lips. It was such sweet torment.

It was unlikely that Runglee teas would ever score as high, and even Castleton could hardly hope to do it again. Every garden had its limits – Thus Far, No Further. Armajeet worked without absolute standards, like a piano-tuner, aiming to recognise potential and to work up to it with increasingly subtle adjustments until the tea struck like a nicely balanced chord.

His consultations were lordly and arcane. He bent gravely to the tasting table – Navim unconsciously bent with him and pursed his lips. The flavour and aroma of the liquor are more pronounced on the wet leaves, especially as they cool. Armajeet's nose descended on the volcano. It was a historic nose, a Persian nose, passed down from Zoroastrian priests to hawking desert lords; from hawkers to warriors, and from warriors to the invaders who rode into the desert of Rajasthan. It was quite large, but straight and slim; the skin was fine and very pale over a slender bridge, with nostrils that might have been turned in Cremona. It flared over the volcano, burrowed in and re-emerged with a scattering of wet tea-leaves adhering to its tip, which trembled slightly over the verdict. The small moustache was a discreet cushion for the instrument.

Armajeet straightened up. Navim stooped anxiously.

'Very useful,' said The Nose. For a brief moment I thought I saw Navim actually smile.

Navim would move from the tea-table to the bar around seven o'clock. Sometimes it was a bottle with the zealous name of Amazing Grace, or perhaps Tower Gin, with a squeeze of fresh lime, for a gimlet. I drank gimlets because they tasted less awful than Amazing Grace, which you had to palliate with a splash of soda – only the soda tasted worse – and because my grandfather used to. From upstairs came a monotonous wail as the child was parted from his gun.

When darkness fell the isolation of the garden was complete. The villagers burned few lights; the sky was far brighter than the hills. There was no television broadcast in the area. The nearest planter lived an hour or so away by mountain road. I lay in bed listening to the crickets.

I was going back to Calcutta. I took a lift with Armajeet, who was expected at Castleton. The factory there burned to the ground the winter before we came. A new one was going up already, a corrugated skin around a concrete frame, but it wasn't ready for this season's crop. Castleton was manufacturing in a derelict factory nearby, a ramshackle collection of empty brick buildings which no one had got around to demolishing. They might have been constructed on the plan of an East End mission: dour, built of greeny-grey brick and hurriedly re-roofed; a makeshift affair into which the rescued equipment had been dragged and re-assembled. While Armajeet and the manager shut themselves in the office, I wandered through the building. The withering loft was cool and bright: the windows at the farther end were low and square, like bright tablets leaning against the wall. Smooth planking made the floor; the walls were padded with crumbling lime and whitewash and the wooden doors swung silently on grease-smooth loops of rope.

Armajeet stuck his nose round the door.

'Crackerjack,' he whispered 'Damn crackerjack.'

9
Gardens and Estates
Dooars and the South

With big soft hands and bulbous calves, the brush of thick black hair and moustache, Bobby could have passed for a young Sicilian. Like many planters he was a Sikh – undaggered and shorn, certainly, but forever, socially, Sikh; and his wife came from Punjab.

He sent his son to St Paul's in Darjeeling, one of the best Indian public schools up in the mountains. Their lower slopes were just visible from the bungalow at Matelli Murthi, which was raised on a mound over a lake of tea, Matelli land as far as the eye could see, all lotus-eating, Cluniac land – with the tea glossy and level, and the bungalow enormous on its peculiar hillock.

It resembled Runglee as much as Castle Howard resembles Dunroamin. It had a great shallow roof and a glazed skirt on two sides which enclosed the former verandah, full of plants and paved in chequered marble, where stood the breakfast table, cane furniture and those wonderful reclining chairs which have holes in their arms for your drink and the ashtray. The interiors were plastered and wainscoted and moulded; there was a grand dining room, a sitting room, kitchens at the back, and half a dozen bedrooms upstairs with air-conditioning. Bobby trotted about in shorts and a sports shirt and his wife, Raj, dressed in pyjamas. The rules forbade tea talk in the house, but they weren't absolute. We drank whisky from Scotland and beer from India, and talked.

Bobby's faith in Progress was unshakeable. The *Edinburgh Review* once compared the spread of tea to the progress of Truth; and Bobby was a Whig in the grand manner. He was building pukka (stone) housing for the workers. He encouraged sport, especially football, as good for the boys on the garden, meaning teamwork and physical exercise, and his office was encrusted with silver trophies won by the garden's footballers and tug-of-war contestants as well as annual photos of the Matelli scouts and certificates of engineering or medicine awarded to educated villagers. There were scholarships and pensions; free education, clinics, dental treatment, contraceptives. Every two years the workers were issued with brand-new black brollies and they streamed towards the garden on rainy mornings like a phalanx of displaced city gents in bare feet and pyjamas.

Folk legend had it that Matelli Murthi stood over the mouth of a tunnel – it was the meaning of *matelli*: a tunnel – and *murthi*: mouth. It had been dug long before Indian tea (maybe even before China tea) by the Rajas of Bhutan and it led to the cellars of their palace, from where the royal family and its wealth could be borne away to the plain in times of serious danger. The mound on the plain had been made with excavated earth, and upon it a British tea company had elected to build its manager's bungalow.

The butler, barefoot, took me to the bottom of the garden and pointed out a child-sized cleft in the rock as the proof. He had never looked inside himself, because caves hide snakes, but he murmured constantly, reciting the myths of bones and treasure laid underground, and the connection with the secretive Himalayan kingdom.

Bobby said that were it true, the diggers should have contracted for the channel tunnel. Bhutan was seventy miles away.

Matelli straddles the Dooars, a narrow Indian corridor which runs from Bengal to Assam between the mountain kingdoms of Nepal, Bhutan and Sikkim in the north and waterlogged Bangladesh in the south. The corridor is called the Dooars from the Sanskrit which gives us our word 'door' – a door that has opened and closed for the armies of Burma, Assam and Bengal which have marched through the district, skirting the hills and the mud.

Dooars earth is shallow and fertile, strained by innumerable watercourses falling from the mountains, and tea grows fast. The jargon is 'clean', because the made leaf of the Dooars always looks good – clean in appearance, antiseptic in character, tea's dumb brunette.

In tea, as in geography, the Dooars is the approach to Assam. Dooars teas are Assam *jat*; they may, at their very best, outstrip low to middling quality Assams. They aren't a patch on the best Assams: black-brownish teas, large and neat, with such a shoal of golden tips that brokers used to gauge the quality by how easily they could spot a golden rupee tossed against a pile of tea.

Dooars isn't treated in the same way as Darjeeling or grand Assam. Where 'orthodox' manufacture aims to draw out the individual qualities of the tea, Dooars tea is manufactured by a process known as Cut Tear Curl, which promotes the consistent average. CTC manufacture is up-to-date: it makes the kind of tea needed for brewing *chai* and filling tea-bags, which have swallowed the lion's share of the tea market in the UK. The withered leaves are put through a shredder. The emerging slurry is pasted onto a slow-moving conveyer belt which creeps towards the drying trays, giving the tea time to ferment. The colour-change to brown along the belt looks slightly poisonous. The fermented tea drops onto trays to be whisked into ovens where the tea dries into a sort of fine sand, millions of granules of evenly-coloured leaf.

CTC tea is popular with everyone. Planters like it because it's a simpler process; once you've got the hang of adjusting for rainy days, hot weather, or younger leaf, CTC can't go very wrong. You may never be a hero, like the Castleton manager; but you'll never be a failure, either. Buyers and blenders like it because it's reasonably predictable, and can be made in big quantities. The tea drinker likes it because it liquors quickly and looks strong, because the granules are so small; and it snuggles into a paper bag which can be dunked in a mug.

Matelli itself was profitable and employed the population of a small town. There was room for craftsmen and roadbuilders, for drivers and messengers; outside the garden was a village where the shopkeepers, scribes, post-office officials, policemen, tinkers, blacksmiths, tailors and beggars survived on the patronage of tea workers. Darjeeling gardens seemed distant, small and ruggedly independent like mountain kingdoms. Here the atmosphere was as feudal, but settled and rich, as though years of peace and settlement had produced a sort of enlightened estate.

Yet in 1961 the Chinese had invaded Assam over a disputed border, the McMahon line, drawn by the British and maintained by the Indians, and had advanced almost unchecked to within a few miles of Matelli. Bobby showed me the site of an airstrip hurriedly laid out for the Indian air force, and maintained until recently by an estate worker with a roller. Now it was planted with nursery bushes. The planters, who represented the only effective civil authority in the area, had prepared for the inevitable defeat by disabling their machines and retiring to the club, where they set about drinking all the whisky on tick. To their chagrin the Chinese advance was halted, a negotiated settlement was reached and the troops withdrew, leaving the astronomical bar bills ruinously intact.

Beneath the gleaming, mod-con bungalow, the mythic tunnel opened up; bare feet under brollies; the threat of war beneath the calm.

One evening the Commissioner of Police came over for a drink. The basket chair crackled under his weight. He wore a grey safari suit and a Sam Browne. He'd had a good day and caught three murderers. The murderers had borrowed money they couldn't afford to repay from a lender, without family, who was one hundred and three years old. They had defaulted on the repayments until they discovered that the usurer intended to marry. They murdered him in panic.

But one incident over all others impressed me and gave me the measure of Bobby's isolation. There is a kind of snake which likes to sun itself on top of tea bushes, where cool air rises from the ground. Unwary pluckers at Matelli could be bitten, and the venom was considered deadly until Bobby heard of a serum which he made available at the clinic. One morning he was called down to a particular stand where a group of women had found the snake. I vaulted into the back of the jeep and Bobby let out the clutch with a bang.

The snake was lying like a discarded tie across the plucking table. The women stood mute at a distance down the path. There was not much to do except suggest that they move to another stand and start again, and Bobby was about to give the order when an old man came hurrying along the path at the head of a small crowd. Bobby frowned. The old man was dressed in a *lunghi*, and carried a dirty shawl over one shoulder. When he arrived near us he flung up one arm and the crowd became still.

He began to part a way through the stand towards the snake. He moved very slowly. Nobody spoke. He reached out very slowly and suddenly pulled back with the snake wriggling from his fist. He had it in a safe grip, behind the head; the rest of it, about two feet long, wriggled uselessly in the air as he swung round and presented it aloft to the fascinated crowd. Gradually he brought its head towards his left arm; he held it there motionless until with a gasp he jerked the snake back and broke its neck, flinging it to the feet of the crowd, which backed off, as it lay jerking spasmodically. He raised his left arm to show where two brown dots had begun to trickle. Villagers pressed forward through the tea to help him. The women burst into excited chatter. Some young men found a stick and picked up the snake with it. Bobby looked sad. He spoke sharply to the old man as he came past, but the old man shook his head. He didn't want the serum.

'The stupid man will die,' said Bobby. It was the first time I had seen him angry.

Later the old man smeared his arm with a herbal preparation and tied it up with a cloth. In three days his arm was black and swollen. He lay on his bed and scattered leaves over a fire. Bobby insisted he be given the serum; the man refused.

Bobby was always present when the workers queued to receive their wages every week, calculated according to the weight of tea they had brought in. He was ready with encouragement and congratulations; he sought to identify himself very closely with the paymaster.

Breakfast one morning was interrupted by a messenger from a nearby garden whose manager was appealing for help. For the second week running his company had failed to send up the wages. The workers were restless and mistrustful. He had held them off for one week with promises and threats. Now he did not know what to do. The bosses at head office in Calcutta were not answering his calls and letters. Bobby shrugged. He couldn't help. It wasn't his money. His indifference seemed out of character. But he was, I think, appalled. The default was more than a breach of trust, it was a revocation of the pact of progress. Its implications were too appalling to consider.

Bobby was proud of the generating system installed on the garden, which provided electric light to every home and worked all the machinery. It was, he said, very reliable and cost-effective. One evening we heard screams from the kitchen. Dropping our food we raced from the dining room and found the butler, shaking and hollering, with one hand grasping the handle of the fridge. We pulled a table with rubber caps on its legs up behind him, and Bobby stood on it and prised the man off the fridge.

A few days later I noticed a rubber mat on the floor in front of the machine.

He was proud, too, of his garden, and the tea he made. 'It isn't the first quality,' he admitted. 'But it is the best in the Dooars, and better than a lot of sloppy Assam teas.'

I thought of the jungle rising to choke cleared land; forever cut back, forever advancing. Bobby had his established code, and the people around him had theirs. Bobby had the office where he could sit looking at neat rows of scouts in the framed photographs, and the sparkling trophies, and the educational certificates.

No doubt a planter needs optimism. Later I met planters who were so gloomy they reminded me of English farmers; but so far everyone I had met had a belief that what they were doing was right and beneficial. Some tried harder than others. Bobby, I think, was the good imperialist.

Back in London, some weeks later, I had a letter from Matelli. The old man with the snake had not died. On the sixth day he undid the cloth in front of a crowd of villagers, and showed them his arm looking as though nothing had touched him. Now it would be outstretched to collect the fees of patients abandoning the free clinic.

When the Assam Company struggled into profit in the 1850s other people began to consider tea's potential as a money maker. Soon nobody wanted to be left out of what looked like the biggest bonanza since railway stock. Every investor encouraged two more. Land in the empty Assam jungle was cheap. Everyone was drinking tea. If profits were made on the trade in Chinese tea, how much more, they reasoned, could be made by running the whole industry from the ground up, owning the gardens as foreigners were never allowed to do in China?

Companies were founded, capital subscribed, land bought in the unsurveyed jungle of Assam. You had only to clear the land, plant seed, and wait. These were called the Tea-fever days. Lieut.-Col. Money later recalled that 'tea was so entirely a new thing at that time, few could be found who had any knowledge of it . . . Anyone – literally anyone – was taken, and tea-planters in those days were a strange medley of retired or cashiered army and navy officers, medical men, engineers, veterinary surgeons, steamer captains, chemists, shopkeepers of all kinds, stable-keepers, used-up policemen, clerks and goodness knows who besides!'

But the investors were impatient. It took some years for tea bushes to be productive. Instead of waiting the shareholders discovered they could profitably sell land which they had developed for next to nothing – even that they could sell land which they had not developed at all just by calling it a tea-garden – land unsurveyed, inaccessible, right in the heart of unexplored jungle. Every shyster got in, buying and selling, taking on as managers men 'who did not know a Tea plant from a cabbage', until planters took to saying that 'it was very doubtful whether it would ever pay to make tea, but that there was no doubt it paid to make gardens.'

It was only a matter of time before people started to think they'd been had. This sort of thing happens so often in Victorian novels (Venezuelan mining rights, pan-American railway stock, Australian sheep-farm shares, and all the horror of wealthy men waking up paupers) that one wonders how Victorians could have been so persistently gullible. Owners saw that at the prices they'd paid they could never hope to make a profit. There was a stampede to sell, and no buyers. 'Gardens which had cost lakhs were sold for as many hundreds, and the very word "Tea" stank in the nostrils of the commerical public.'

The honest companies, and practical men, rescued the Indian tea industry before it withered. Even during the Fever, output rose. As genuine planters grew experienced they learned how to improve their methods, and the 'Chinese' style of manufacture involving a dozen separate steps was cut to only five: no more tatching in hot woks, rolling three or four times between tatching, no more second firing. The same amount of tea was produced in half the time with less labour. Ever less, because the British were tinkerers and inventors, and began to patent machines which rolled and dried and speeded up the wither, sorting machines and packing machines which could press the tea into the chest. That released more hands to pluck tea, clear land, and weed the gardens.

And the British at home learned to appreciate the empire product. It was coarser, darker and stronger than Chinese tea, as it still is. Tea was initially drunk very weak: Samuel Johnson drank out of a quart cup, and brewed up with tiny quantities. The later spread of tea-drinking to all classes (which Dr Johnson had so disapproved of), and to the working classes in particular, was possible because tea was restorative, hot and cheap. In the 1870s Indian tea was still only used in England for blending with China to give body and strength, and when one or two companies attempted to sell pure Indian to John Bull 'he simply shook his head, the flavour was different to what use had made him familiar, and he would none of it.' Tea brought out the conservative in the late Victorian as in the modern housewife. Yet the ratio in blends began to tilt towards more Indian, less China. By the early 1880s tastes had been remodelled and it was possible to sell the unadulterated article; in 1884 London imported more British Indian than Chinese tea. Green tea was no longer in demand at all, except as ever in America – but America was soon to discover iced tea, and Tommy Lipton.

Lipton was already a millionaire grocer – a new shop opened every week – when he stopped in Colombo on his way to Australia in 1882. The first plantations or estates in Ceylon and South India were of coffee – 'garden' isn't used much in the South, perhaps as a result. But a year before Lipton's arrival a blight destroyed the coffee industry. Those who escaped ruin turned to tea, rubber and chinchona, whose bark makes quinine, but land was going cheap, and Lipton left Ceylon with half a dozen tea estates and an idea which was to make him a millionaire over again. LIPTON'S TEA – DIRECT FROM THE TEA GARDENS TO THE TEA POT. He had realised that the way tea was sold in Britain left the housewife at a disadvantage: she could never be sure that tea scooped from the grocers' bin was not stale, adulterated, or underweight before it was parcelled up. Lipton not only guaranteed the purity and freshness of his tea; he not only sold it for almost half the going price; but he had it pre-packed in quarter-, half- and one-pound packets, emblazoned with his name and logo, and pushed it remorselessly, not only in his own shops. He almost invented national advertising and all its gimmickry single-handed. He did nothing to discourage the idea that all Lipton tea came from the Lipton estates in Ceylon.

While he was making his second pile he anonymously underwrote a flagging appeal launched by Alexandra, the Princess of Wales, to provide 10,000 East End kids with a Jubilee tea. Speculation as to the donor's identity focused on Viscount Astor – whose own grandfather, J. J., had made his fortune in the tea trade. Lipton engineered a leak when speculation was at its height and was soon received and befriended by grateful royalty.

Lipton never bought estates in south India where, as in Ceylon, the estate labour is predominantly Tamil; the climate is comparable. There are two monsoons, and the sea ensures that temperatures neither rise as high nor fall as low in winter as in North India. There is consequently no *banji*, or dormant period, and the bush flushes regularly throughout the year. The advantages are obvious, though they are greater in Ceylon, which is richer land and makes, on the whole, better tea. The Sri Lankans generally do not drink nearly as much as they produce: the island has none of the over-population troubles of its giant neighbour, and most of its tea has always been exported.

To reach the tea-growing regions of southern India I had to fly to Cochin via Madras. Cochin is a port on the Malabar coast in Western India, a few hundred miles south of the old Portuguese resort of Goa. Calcutta is hardly a hive of industry, but Cochin seemed half asleep. The plane overshot the harbour and wheeled round for the approach to the airport in Winham Island so that the tiny porthole framed a picture composed of belts of palm, the white strip of beach and, against the fingers of the quays, cargo ships fermenting rustily like tea in the sun. It was siesta time – 'shut-eye', as planters called it – and the taxi-drivers were dozing on the front seats, feet out of the window, elbows crooked over their eyes, ready to crank themselves upright and ignite their engines, yawning, with a shadow of sweat left on the black plastic seats.

The switch from taxi to the Tata car was to be made at a little up-market hotel in Cochin which catered to foreign seamen. In a freezing timbered bar screened from prying eyes by smoked windows I drank foreign beer with a Norwegian captain waiting for his ship to be unloaded. He was the owner as well as the master of his ship, which was pretty small, and he made his living in cabotage, the coastal trade, running cargoes from Karachi or Bombay to Madras and Calcutta (not Calcutta if he could avoid it, he said: too many perils between unions and shifting channels). Time was, he said, with a vessel like his, when he could have lived just running tea from Travancore to Colombo for the auctions, but that was before the Indians set up their own South Indian auction in Cochin. From time to time he took a tea cargo to Colombo if it could couple up with a consignment of Ceylon tea for London, but not often, because the Sri Lankans didn't like helping the Indian tea men. As often as not, South Indian export tea (for which there is no generic, like Monings) sat in the Cochin godowns, waiting for a ship bound for London or Amsterdam.

'Not so many of those. Your empire's finished, na?' He said without irony. 'Though sometimes . . .' He bent forward until his beard almost touched the far edge of the bar. 'One two three . . .' he counted, cocking his chin at each bottle of Scotch lined up against the mirrored wall. 'Eight different kinds. Not bad for a small port.'

Shipping is one of the disabilities of the Indian export tea trade. The distance between India and London is compounded by red tape, which creates a delay between the identification of a demand in London and its eventual satisfaction. African teas arrive at the blenders in half the time. There is also corruption. The Russians recently complained that they were mysteriously losing 2 kg in every 50 kg chest between packing and loading. Short weight aside, you have the Tea Chest Crisis. Wood is expensive in India – partly accounting for the paucity of furniture in even wealthy homes – and forestry appears to have been handled in the most reckless and short-sighted way possible. Almost every well-born Calcuttan lady I met was involved in the Tree Campaign; there is a real threat of losing Bangladesh altogether unless the flood-retaining forests of the Himalayas are restored. Meanwhile the tea-buyers have to deal with chests made of the thinnest ply which shatter and crack in transit.

The Malabar Coast faces west across the Arabian Sea, towards Africa and the Middle East, backing up to India over the Western Ghats. Northeast India has an Oriental slant towards China and Central Asia so that its influence on the West, and the Western influence upon it, did not begin until the seventeenth century. But for millennia Malabar was the further end of a line of trade and culture which extended into the Mediterranean, pivoting on the Middle East. Pepper, coral, pearls and spices came from here. Malabar received St Thomas in AD 52. Nestorian heretics, condemned at Ephesus in 431, settled and made converts among high-caste Hindus. Christians are called Nazarini, and the name of their churches is legion. The Portuguese brought Catholicism (da Gama died and was buried in Cochin), the Dutch brought reformation, and the English brought Anglicanism. There are Nestorians loyal to the Patriarch of Antioch, and Nestorians in schism; there are Jacobite Syrians and Romo-Syrians; there are Latin rites and vernacular rites; there are some who hold allegiance to the Patriarch of Nineveh, and there are doctrinal Romans who do not recognise the Pope. The cities have Jewish quarters, too, very depleted, and separate synagogues for Black Jews, who settled in 587 BC, and White Jews who came later on. Of course there are any number of Hindus and castes, and, receptive as ever to the latest arrival from the west, the state of Kerala itself is Communist.

Earlier than this, before Malabar teak built the Mesopotamian city of Ur, the coast was home to a race of small dark-skinned people, perhaps a lost tribe of Africa marooned at the toe of India after a prehistoric migration. Later, about the time that the Celts were retreating from the

British lowlands, a farming people from the plains fled the wars of the Pandyan Rajas and escaped into the mountains, carrying their children on their backs: up into the Western Ghats, in the Kanan Devan hills which cluster around the highest mountains below the Himalayas. They called themselves the Mudhuvans, the Back People, and they obeyed a custom of descent to the eldest son of the eldest sister. It is thought that there they married among the remnant of the little black people. They remained aloft and aloof until, almost two thousand years later, they were visited and settled upon by Scots.

The Duke of Wellington, then Colonel Wellesley and in pursuit of the rebel Tippoo Sahib, camped among the Kanan Devan Hills in 1787. Two Murrays explored the area in 1856; a Martin followed, and in 1891 James Finlay of Glasgow bought the concession from the local ruler, the Maharaja of Travancore. From then on it was a Scottish fief.

The Scots in the High Ranges weren't noted for their religious enthusiasm. The high point of their fervour was when they received a cricketing curate who had played for England, but he only stayed a year. What they preferred, practical networkers that they were, clansmen by nature and solicitous of the imperial bonds, was Freemasonry. Funny handshakes spread through the hills. When the Grand Lodge of India was founded in 1962, the High Ranges chapter voted to remain within the Grand Lodge of Scotland.

The Muthuvans had learned to live in the forests on a slash and burn system of agriculture. They had no interest in settling down, let alone to pluck tea: they didn't much care for earning money. But they were not to be allowed to continue their pillage of what forest the tea planters had left standing. Their elders refused to accept school teachers from outside; the government refused suggestions of subsidising them as 'zoological specimens'. In the end their forest was given to them, and they were taught methods of exploiting it without destruction. To the early planters they were invaluable as guides and porters and many were employed as shikari, ghillies. Since hunting has been banned they are employed as game wardens instead.

Ladbroke House was a long bungalow among trees with a croquet lawn and a swimming pool (empty). White-jacketed servants took my bags, fixed my tea, ran my bath . . . Whisky soda? What time eating, sah? It was unnerving. Nobody appeared to live there. I tapped nervously on closed doors, hoping to meet somebody, but eventually I had to accept that a mansion of luxury had been put into service for me alone. Edward Sullivan, who visited Ceylon planters in 1854, had airily observed: 'Hospitality is genuine from any planter's bungalow – you ride up to the bungalow, put your horse in the stable, enter the house, and if the owner be not at home, introduce yourself to his butler, as housekeepers are called, light a cheroot, call for a beer etc, and make yourself at home till his return.'

That was all very well but I had no one to wait for. The invitation to visit had arrived through friends in Calcutta, second or third hand, with only a place to be at a certain time. I was unable to ask the butler anything about my invisible hosts. He was so correct and intimidating anyway that I feared his scorn if he discovered how much I didn't know. I pulled my emperor's new clothes about me and said eight o'clock would do very well – 'if that's all right.' At five to, they called me through to the dining room. At eight I ate soup. At ten past I tucked into a superb beef wellington. At 8.30 I ate queen of puddings, with fresh cream. At 8.45 coffee was served in the drawing room. Port, sah? Yes, please. At nine o'clock I stopped worrying.

The phone rang.

I looked at the butler. The butler looked back impassively.

The heavy receiver disconnected with a *clock!* of bakelite.

'Jason Goodwin? Margaret Sopwood. Everything all right down there? Good journey? Splendid. Are they looking after you? Ask Chelai if there's anything you need. Plenty of hot water. Now, shall we say dinner up at our house tomorrow night? Super, see you then. Goodbye.'

The earpiece gave an amplified clunk and the telephone pinged.

Sopwood. Margaret Sopwood. I drank my port and went to bed, sleeping with my toes pointed towards Cape Cormorin, my head towards the Himalayas.

In the morning I was brought bed tea, with the first good bread I'd tasted in months. The tea smelt good; it came out straw-coloured and thin, the mark of the high-grown. Someone had pulled the curtains already and sun streamed through the Venetian blinds. I watched my cigarette smoke fill one slice of light and then the next, higher and higher until it juddered and dispersed beneath the fan. The precedent was Woosterish. I had a slight headache from the port, but the tea seemed to be buzzing from my ribcage and tickling the ache out of the top of my head. For an odd moment I vibrated all over.

I was nearly dressed when the butler brought in an old man with grizzled white hair in the khaki cotton uniform of an outdoors servant.

'My name is Christy, sir. I am taking you to Munnar station.'

I thought I was being run out of town. Later I found that Munnar isn't served by rail. At the beginning of the century there had been something called a bullock-drawn monorail – a cart guided by the wheels on one side – but it had been washed away in the flood of 1926 and replaced by a cable-car (which ran from Top Station to Bottom Station) and motor roads. The monorail carried a special waggon fitted with curtains after government officials complained of the lack of 'first-class accommodation' on the ascent. Planters got horse allowances, and sometimes ran motor-bikes (married couples still quaintly receive a 'Dearness allowance').

I sat in the front of the Ambassador while Christy, who was indeed Christian, regaled me with Sunday-school homilies which reminded me of Fuzhou John – a succession of aphorisms indicating his popularity.

'I am working in Munnar all my life, sir,' he boasted. 'Everybody knows me. I have no enemies. It is easier to lose a good name than a bad one. You are from Scotland, sir?'

'No, from England. London.'

'Oh,' said Christy, 'London.' He might have said 'I see'. We drove on in silence. If you could get a bad name as quickly as this in the High Ranges, Christy must have been very circumspect all his life. After a while he returned to the subject to give me a second chance. 'Scotland is a very beautiful country, like Kanan Devan. God's country,' he added with challenging emphasis.

'Very beautiful,' I agreed.

'Strong,' countered Christy.

I digested this remark.

'Strong people?'

'Strong country!' Christy argued fiercely.

'God's country,' I murmured feebly. Christy, to my relief, agreed to the wording, which took us back to the beginning of our conversation.

'God's country,' he repeated. 'Strong country.'

I copped out. 'Yes,' I said. Christy grunted.

The Munnar station – or township, or, to quote *Hobson Jobson*, 'the place where the English officials of a district reside. Also the aggregate society of such a place' – lay in a shallow bowl of hills. The offices were housed in a plain whitewashed building set like a mill near a stream, and approached over a plank bridge. From the bridge you could see Munnar's four churches, including the impoverished baroque façade of the Catholic church and the square tower of the Anglican. The other two were much smaller; there was no mistaking where the endowments had gone. There were a mosque and a Hindu temple as well, discrete and unique, showing up the squabbles of Christianity rather shamefully.

After meeting people in the office I spent the day in a jeep, climbing to Top Station. All the tea belonged to Tatas, on the largest estate I'd ever seen – really six or seven separate gardens amalgamated for economy. The hills undulated gradually upward; the road was lined with Australian eucalyptus and much twining morning-glory which arrived in the twenties to screen a tennis court and scattered out to menace the tea stands. Christy was right in a way. The Ranges themselves did look rather like parts of Scotland. From the peak of Annemelai the grassy uplands rolled down to Munnar, broken by rocky crags and streams. There are Nilgiri Tars here, a sort of goat, which are not shy. We visited a seedling nursery, row after row of pale green plants under bamboo awnings, where the company scientists were developing suitable clones. Every garden worth its salt has a nursery like this, to serve a rolling programme of grubbing up old plants and replacing them with good new ones, which then start to produce after two or three years. The clones are supposed to resist diseases, flush more vigorously, and taste better.

Much the same improvement was being made to the children of pluckers and planters when we pulled up around noon in front of a school where children were educated together for a nominal enrolment fee. It was Tamil medium, and taught English; planters' children, who were often not Tamil, thus got to learn the local language, which would be handy if they decided to become planters themselves. (In the old days the Scots assistants were forbidden leave until they had either spent four years on the garden or passed proficiency exams in Tamil.)

The butler had packed me a lunchbox, and I was relieved to see that Bopi, the assistant showing me around, had one too, because the warm wind was making me hungry. On cue we tilted left and rattled down a track which petered out in front of a small yellow cabin with a verandah. It was made of weatherboarding and had a tin roof.

'This is the old Top Station club,' Bopi explained. 'Before the good roads Munnar was too far off for an evening out, so the local planters came here. Pretty informal.' He pointed out the rugger field, which sloped away to the rim of tea spreading darkly up the hill.

In the clubhouse there was a framed poster advertising the Munnar Exhibition of 1901:

Saturday October 13th: Opening Ceremony 2 pm
　　　　　　　　　　　　Button Sewing Competition 2 pm
　　　　　　　　　　　　Book Title Competition 4 pm
　　　　　　　　　　　　Tea – Tennis – Tea
The Exhibition will close at 6 pm to enable visitors to disperse for Dinner and return to the Exhibition in Time for the Dramatic and Variety Entertainment at 8.30 pm. Visitors are respectfully requested to be in their seats before the Curtain rises.
Sunday October 14th: Hat trimming competition 11 am
　　　　　　　　　　　Lunch 12.30 pm
　　　　　　　　　　　Sketching competition 3 pm
　　　　　　　　　　　Anna Auction. 'Auctioneer' M. A. Martin 3.30 pm
　　　　　　　　　　　Presentation of Prizes 4 pm
　　　　　　　　　　　'God Save The Queen'

There were also a few wicker armchairs and a bar which released a couple of beers. 'Not cold, I'm afraid.' We sat on the stoop and munched sandwiches and I asked him to tell me about life on the Ranges.

'It has got easier, and harder. Easier, because in the old days there was more discipline and a man doing my job would be absolutely enslaved to the *burra sahib*. Actually, one of the old planters used to make his assistants come to his bungalow after work with sticks and evening dress and act out the stories he read to his little girl. They couldn't say no. Sometimes he gave them a drink afterwards, and sometimes they just had to ride back to their places in all weather. There was much less leave, and getting married is easier now. You have more time to yourself if you want it and going to the club isn't as tricky as it was, when assistants and managers didn't mix. You can enjoy yourself a bit now.

'But it's harder, also. We worry much more. About the fortunes of the area, especially. Finlays could almost guarantee export sales but all that's dried up and we've had to make our market over from scratch. Right now, you see, we're losing five rupees on every kilo. We always have to think of ways to save money. We even use shears to pick tea.'

I'd seen that on the way up. The pluckers' shears were hung with a cotton bag, shaped like a pelican's beak.

'The shears come from Japan. They mean we get in more tea but the quality suffers. It's easier to pluck too many or few leaves, and after a while the plucking table gets ragged and makes that problem worse.' He bumped his bottle against the palm of his hand. 'There is *so much* talk about mechanical pluckers, the garden of the future, all that, but machines just can't do it. Maybe they'll invent something with an eye and an arm and a mechanical hand, and wheels. And the first thing we'll have to do is move the lines further apart so that the machine can get between them, and we'll lose yield. And then the computer chips will get wet, or knocked about, and they'll cost a fortune to put right. We'll need fewer people, but they'll all have to have degrees in computer science.

'What we may get is higher-yielding bushes. That's possible. It may even make a bit more money, after we've employed extra labour and fed them and housed them. That's a good thing, and I hope it happens. We need to educate people to buy better-quality tea, too. We must establish our name with the public. Right now we just sell our tea and it goes into blends and that keeps the prices down because the blenders can threaten to go elsewhere.'

'So you'd like to sell tea like wine? Garden by garden?'

'I don't think we could afford to go quite that local. Blends will always be important, and if you undermined them where would you be in a bad year? You wouldn't sell anything. But you could produce blends for a district like this one – a light, high-grown tea with character. Perhaps a fairly limited amount could go into a top-class High Ranges blend, if it was packaged properly and so on.'

Bopi warmed to his theme.

'The rest you'd sell as usual, or in a South Indian blend, or whatever. But that isn't happening!' He cried almost despairingly, gesturing with his beer bottle. 'No, we go the other way – shears and now CTC. Anything to get some money back without spending much of it. But I don't think CTC is an answer. It cuts us right out of the international market, because this high-grown tea doesn't make the liquory CTCs people want. The UK wants strong-flavoured tea-bags, which is what CTC is for. So where is this delicate CTC going to go? On the domestic market. The demand for tea in India is so high you can usually sell any kind of tea in the end – but not at a good price. So we'll go on losing five chips a kilo. Maybe it'll get worse.'

'So you worry.'

Bopi smiled.

'Yah, we worry. We worry about our future.'

Bopi backed the jeep up the track and spun onto the road. About half a mile further we parked and walked through tea to the brim of the hills. Thousands of feet below the plain looked scrubby and light. The plain was in Tamil Nadu: every twenty yards a bare pole rose out of the tea, all the way to the bottom – to Bottom Station, in fact. The cables had gone. Until the road up the Western Ghats was built, everything and everybody came up from the east; even after 1932, the tea went east. But about fifteen years ago the Kerala state government decided it didn't want the tea going to Tamil Nadu any more, and the economic grace of the cable was replaced by convoys of trucks racketing down the western hillside to Cochin. The railhead on the plain was abandoned. Once the whole concession had been wired like an old-fashioned department store, and chests swung to and fro and whizzed downwards by magic, but with the main cable gone and better roads installed, the subordinate system had been abandoned.

The plain began to fade and haze; the sun disappeared and it rained suddenly and hard. We yanked up the hood of the jeep and made a quick dash to the nearest shelter, a factory mothballed in a recent rationalisation. But it was coming back on stream because the mountain reservoirs were low and Tatas expected power cuts. This factory possessed its own generator. The tea machines were being dusted and oiled and tightened and adjusted by a gang of greasy workmen; a tarpaulin slid from a great dumb obedient BRITANNIA, another from a SCIROCCO, and the sight was immensely cheering. I thought of the rep I'd met in Calcutta, working for a Midlands firm: a huge bewhiskered Yorkshireman who'd been coming out all his life, knew everyone, and loved India, the Dales and his machines, in that order.

'Bloody marvellous, those creatures,' he boomed. 'Cast iron chassis! Solid brass plates! A twenty-horsepower engine, and the finest calibrations and tolerances all the same. That's engineering for you. You know how much a roller weighs? How much? A ton and a half.' He pinched his moustache. 'And that's our mistake, I'm told. We built them to last too long. You had to have pride. Solid buggers, running for years and years.

I still see machines put in by the chap before me, and maybe by the one before him. And that's going back.

'We had the whole business, and we kept standards. We sold them to the shaving Japanese until they started building their own. They had a home market, didn't they – their government saw that they supplied their home market. That's right. Now they're coming into ours. Not a big deal for them, they've got security. They'll undercut us until we go under and then they'll have it all. Does their stuff last? Not much, but it's cheap, I'll grant them that.'

Now a belt was slipped over a wheel; a plate was notched into position; a chute was swung heavily back and racked beneath the withering loft. I'd seen the same machines in Darjeeling, thumping away, from the days when machinery was machinery and engineers were called Mac.

So it says, anyway, in 'Rings from a Chota Sahib's Pipe', a collection of sketches appearing in *The Englishman* which was published in 1901. Mac, says the author, has a temper and thick double-soled 'tacketty' English boots. Every morning he appears dressed 'Clean and neat . . . Five minutes in the tea house and he is himself again.' He hangs up his coat among the wrenches, 'gives a sigh of contentment and rolls up his shirt sleeves, exposing to view a forearm of massive proportions, hardened by years of "work at the file in the shops at home". He then proceeds to poke his hand into every part of the engine, which he addresses familiarly in this way: "An' hoo are ye feelin' this mornin', ye auld Rechabite, ye?"

He has no fear; he chucks her under the chin here, he tickles her there, he wrestles with the great piston, he climbs over the fly-wheel, he opens and shuts every handle she's got; he dives under her, he slides along her, he slaps her, and after risking every limb he possesses, he emerges from the conflict, smeared with dirt and oil but with the flush of victory on his face . . .

'Yes!' the sketch concludes, 'It's quite worth anyone's while to go round the tea house with Mac.'

After tea at Ladbroke House I sat reading a memoir of 'One Hundred Years' Planting' which the company had printed for its friends a few years previously. In 1892 the *Madras Mail* carried an article by one of the pioneers, who wound up:

Pleasure and profit attend a settler in these altitudes. Where the delicious climate, pure water, and healthy life really make life worth living; where a man can rear his family and make unto himself a home to last for his life and for his sons' lives, where he can grow chinchona and tea, and make 50 per cent on his capital, where he can teach his boys to pull the ibex by the beard, and adorn the walls of his bungalow with tusks and horns; and whereas girls lose not their roses, nor his wife pine away with fever and longing for familiar faces – for as usual it profit a man nothing if he gain the whole world and lose his own health, and what can a man give in exchange for health?

Plenty of gravestones in Calcutta, and those solemn ceremonies up the Pearl River – tea was brought to Europe at a price, and health was a measure of it. The High Ranges were advertised as a sort of imperial *Kurbad*.

Christy arrived to take me to the Sopwoods. He didn't like driving in the dark.

'Too many elephants,' he complained. 'Sometime very dangerous. First elephant, then car is coming, and then only elephant is leaving.'

I watched out excitedly but we arrived unharmed. The Sopwoods thought Christy perhaps exaggerated the dangers, although they had once been surrounded in the night by a herd of elephants in the garden who tore up the garage, smashed windows, and vomited a valuable collection of orchids onto the front steps.

Without the elephants it was imaginable that the Sopwoods lived in a comfortable Cotswold village. The furniture was newly upholstered in a bold Laura Ashley print; there was a pale Wilton carpet scattered with Persian rugs, and an Art Deco fireplace. India had crept in as clearly as it had in my grandmother's cottage: a few hunting trophies, including a snarling panther, hung over the sideboard. The Sopwoods visited England every two years. They had grown-up children there, and a boy at school who came out in the holidays.

'If you've been visiting people in India you're probably fed up with English meat and two veg,' observed Margaret Sopwood shrewdly.

I wanted again to know what had changed. I mentioned the *Madras Mail* letter to Mr Sopwood.

'In planting, you mean? The atmosphere, I think, very much. I think it's true to say that planting used to be a way of life, and now it's more like a career. Take a boy from Scotland, forty or fifty years ago, one who liked to shoot and fish. The sort of fellow who'd want to run about and get mucky rather than study books. Probably was in cadets or the Scouts, maybe even in the army for a spell. Knew something about discipline and management. I'm probably not making him sound very attractive, am I?

'Anyway the fellow had a sneaking yen to spend the rest of his life stalking, marrying, fishing and solving problems. Just what he might do in Scotland, really, if there'd been any job to go with it. He'd have got hold of the sort of idea in your *Madras Mail* article, signed up with Finlays when he was nineteen or something, and come out here. He couldn't believe his luck.

'He had to work hard — very hard. He was pretty well cut off from Indian society — didn't know anybody in Calcutta or Bombay. He'd burned his boats, too — no leave at all until he'd learned Tamil — and that was his advantage over today's fellows. He got to see that he could stick the life — and he got well and truly stuck in. He worked hard, and played hard, as they say. There were high jinks, big drunks, binges, you know, every now and then, parties, shows, all arranged locally. If he got lonely he found a girlfriend here, there wasn't too much prudishness, and he looked after her properly if he knew what was good for him. Nobody minded as long as he saw after her.

'And that's all changed. An Indian is in his own country. He goes home more often, because it's nearer and anyway he can fly. In every way he's a more sophisticated, cultivated man than the British planter ever thought of being. He's got a proper education and a good degree, a lot of friends and relations at home who he keeps up with. He seldom quite settles down in the area, and his efforts with his friends here are, well, half-hearted by comparison. He can't get involved with a local girl even if he wants to, because the locals wouldn't like it.

'I know it seems odd, but in some ways the Scotsman, who should have been distant and aloof, dug into the area and the people more than the Indian. He had his shikari, and they were almost brothers. He knew most of the people working for him, and he'd paid them the compliment of learning their language pretty well. The distance between him and the locals was huge, and that made it somehow easier for everyone.'

'Modern planters seem to worry rather a lot,' I generalised inquisitively.

'Well, it's quite true there's more worry for the industry now than there was. But look, a modern planter is probably paid more than the English griffin — and deserves to be, because he's better qualified. But he's also paid more because he's making more of a sacrifice, he thinks. Higher pay's meant cutting their numbers. So the Indian *chota sahib*, who thinks of it

211

all as a job more than the Englishman anyway, gets doubly worried about promotion, getting on, and so on.'

After supper we drank South Indian coffee and smoked South Indian cigars until Christy brought the car round.

'Mind the elephants!' called Mrs Sopwood as we started off. Christy looked round in alarm.

'What did she say, sir?' he fretted.

'Careful of the elephants.'

'Ha. Mrs Sopwood is very good joking, sir. Always joking.' All the same he leaned forward and peered along the beam of the headlamps, muttering 'elephants' under his breath.

Before I left the south there was one place I wanted to see. When my father, aged ten, was about to go Home to school, my grandmother had brought him to Ootacamund so that he could see what England was going to look like. Most southern planters wanted to see Ooty as often as possible: they went there whenever they were sick, and whenever they had short leave. The government of Madras moved there in the Summer, because Ooty is a hill-station like Darjeeling.

We were having a tasting of Nilgiri high-grown after tramping over the garden. We'd talked about the difference height makes to tea, and whether the height, the climate or the soil made it; we talked about Darjeeling, which the planter blamed for taking all the publicity while nobody paid any attention to establishing Nilgiri teas in the public mind, and when we got into the offices the potboy had a row of white bowls laid out and ready to brew. I suggested out of curiosity that we taste a Darjeeling too, and since my bags were in the bungalow nearby a boy was sent to fetch my packet of Castleton.

Soon with our spoons we went down the short line, slurping and discussing. The teas were very neat to look at, the infusion was bright and the liquors pale. They made me think of Victorian child heroines with flaxen hair and shining blue eyes: charming but frail, too. I said all the nice things I could think of, and he seemed to be pleased.

He took a swig of the last tea in line, and stopped.

'This is Darjeeling?' He asked. But he knew that already.

I gulped a spoonful, and realised what I'd done, which I've regretted ever since. The tea's bloom was magnificent, the muscatel aroma thoroughly pronounced, the background round and full. It all fitted and supported itself exactly. It was tea with comportment.

'It, is, really, superb,' said the planter.

What made it worse was that I hadn't given him an ordinary Darjeeling to taste at all. In my embarrassment I forgot to say I had given him the very best.

A few weeks later I got a letter from Armajeet Singh, the Nose. There was a clipping with it: Castleton had broken its own record once again: 1716 rupees a kilo. The Nilgiris are still lucky to see forty.

10
London

For the Mad Hatter it is always six o'clock, a perpetual tea-time (six o'clock was Alice Liddell's family tea-time; five o'clock was more conventional). There is no time to do the washing up, so the Mad Hatter can only move his little party around the table from setting to setting until – well, Alice's question goes unanswered, and an argument about Time opens instead with the dunking of a watch in tea. In London you can feel as excluded as Alice at the tea party: the city consumes and moves on amid a growing confusion of bricks and mortar instead of cups and saucers, surrounded by the detritus of earlier feasts. The stories London tells in the composition of certain streets, in the splendour of particular buildings, in the Corporation plaques and among the workaday buildings of the river, are tantalisingly fragmentary, like the Dormouse's tale.

London doesn't concern itself with Statements. Rome or Paris, Washington or St Petersburg are all in their various ways bedizened masterworks encapsulating grand designs of state. They are cheerleaders for Empire or Liberty, Democracy or Autocracy, designed to be comprehended at a stroke. London doesn't ask for your comprehension. London is almost wilfully close, impenetrably private, begrudging the calculations of effect and the whiff of interference as suits a city born of trade, busy and practical, where suburbia and joint stock and the commuter railway were invented.

The A4 comes into London through the tea-bag boroughs: the anonymous early Victorian terraces, stuccoed and sadder than Miss Havisham's wedding cake, divided and subdivided, where grey bulging sacs bob at the mug's rim, hedged in with sticky spoons and crinkled sugar bags. You continue towards the museums, passing on either hand the dusty tree-lined avenues and 'gates' below Kensington Gardens, where tea is taken at 5 pm by old ladies who once dined with Lytton Strachey, and who sit in apartments that smell of cats and old newspapers, near the consulates of lost countries like Estonia, and the embassies of countries which survive on remittances from Stanley Gibbons.

If you came into London further north, you would pass Paddington Street, where John Ruskin opened a shop to sell the poor pure tea, done up in little packets of various sizes to suit their purse. The experience exasperated him. 'The poor', he said, shutting up shop, 'only wish to buy tea where it is brightly lit and eloquently ticketed.' You would continue past Marble Arch to Oxford Street, north of which the men who grew rich upon the Eastern trade tended to settle by the early nineteenth century; Harley Street was even nicknamed the 'Tea Caddy', because so many East India Company directors and nabobs lived there – and their equivocal position in English society seems to be preserved in the same streets today, the haunt of the bland anonymous rich, a blur of fox fur and Jaguar, of doctors and their fleeting anxious patients.

But the southern route takes you around Hyde Park Corner and Apsley House – Number One, London: the home of the Duke of Wellington, tea lover, a stone's throw from the walled grounds of Buckingham Palace, where garden parties are held with tea and sandwiches, then up Piccadilly, passing the clubs of St James's, some in descent from coffee-houses, like Boodle's and Whites.

At Fortnum & Mason there is the odd spectacle of Japanese queuing to buy tea – even Chinese tea which they can buy in Tokyo – and Americans and Europeans, too, carrying away the produce of India or China as a souvenir of England. Tea suffers a sea change *en route* to England: it is reborn as English tea, drunk by the visitors in the Fountain, the Ritz, Claridges and Bendick's. There is English tea, too, for the workmen brewing up in a stripy shelter by the roadworks; the sort being advertised on the sides of buses (red double deckers: a meeting of London totems) as Typhoo or 'D'.

Times have changed at Charing Cross: wicker baskets with a full tea set and a slice of cake aren't passed through the train window at one station and returned at the next any more; now you get a bulging wheel on a metallic strip which looks surgical, dunked into a bendy plastic beaker of hot water (an improvement on the heady days of progress in the seventies, when BR brought in instant tea).

Beyond Aldwych on the Strand is the narrow front of Twining's, which inspired the verse:

> It seems in some cases kind Nature has planned
> That names with their callings agree:
> For Twining the tea man, who lives in the Strand,
> Would be Wining deprived of his 'T'.

On the Embankment you pass Sir John Lyon House, for twenty years the focus of the tea trade, where the brokers have their workrooms overlooking the Thames, and the London auctions are held every Monday. Before the move, tea firms had their offices in Mincing Lane, until Mincing Lane became a by-word for the trade. You are entering the Golden Mile, in the thick of the old coffee shop world.

You glimpse the river, which used to be almost tea-bound, solid with tea-laden lighters towed up to Butler's Wharf. Many wharves were built with timber salvaged from East Indiamen broken up on the Company's demise: the ships fetched £7000 apiece because their timbers were sea-seasoned and strong. In this Mad Hatter's city they were picked clean and pushed to the side of the plate, so that by roundabout logic the same timbers protected tea on land and sea. Tea no longer comes to the London wharves and the commerical cacophony of the docks has vanished, stranding tags that recall the eastern trade: Cathay Street, Amoy Place, Cinnamon Street, Mandarin Stairs, Nankin Street, Pekin Close, Teak Close, Poonah Street, Oriental Road and White Chu Lane, among the hundreds of seaborne names of distant states and cities, of celebrated sailors and discoveries, of the trades that flourished along the river until they were beached by the ebb of commerce.

The tea wharves have gone, too; a lot demolished, some converted into homes. Until the sixties the ratcatcher at Butler's Wharf would put in an order with the lightermen to knock off a couple of chests, very precise orders for Assam BOP or TGFOP, and blend them himself. Tea leaf, in rhyming slang, means thief.

Tea's popularity in the British Isles is hard to explain. It was, from the start, a substitute for alcohol; it was tasty (though we would find eighteenth century tea weak and musty) and mildly stimulating.

The earliest references to the drink in England can hardly settle upon a generic name, let alone discriminate between types. Pepys calls it 'tee' and 'tea'; Garraway calls it 'Chia'; Pope 'tea' to rhyme with 'obey'. By 1701 customers were more sophisticated. Bohea, to rhyme with tea or tay, was black tea from Wuyi. Singlo, also from a range of Chinese hills, was green tea; Imperial was a particularly fine grade of green tea. The names grew more elaborate over the next half century. Congou and Pekoe were better sorts of Bohea, and Twankay joined Singlo as a cheaper green, whose better sorts were called Hyson and Young Hyson.

By then tea was being sold in coffee shops like Garraways, which were all-male preserves as much as the taverns. Coffee arrived in England about ten years before tea, and caught on quickly; the shops also sold a range of mineral waters and spirits. There were Whig and Tory shops, literary shops and business shops of every hue. Edward Lloyd's, for instance, was the place for shippers, shipowners and insurers to meet; the Stock Exchange began at Jonathan's; Boodles and White's were coffee shops; Twinings, near the Temple Bar, was the place to find your lawyer. There were supposed to be over 2000 coffee shops in London in 1683, where for a penny you could be supplied with tea and hot water to last you all day: hence the nickname 'penny universities'. A little extra in a box marked To Insure Prompt [Service] supposedly introduced the TIP.

Samuel Johnson could be found drinking tea at the Sultaness' Head. 'He was,' a biographer wrote, 'a lover of tea to an excess hardly credible, for whenever it appeared he was almost raving, and called for the ingredients which he employed to make the liquor palatable. This in a man whose appearance of bodily strength has been likened to Polyphemus.' Johnson responded vigorously to an essay by Joseph Hanway, the inventor of the umbrella, who had just written:

He who should be able to drive three Frenchmen before him, or she who might be a breeder of such a race of men are to be seen sipping their tea!
> Was it the breed of such as these
> That quell'd the proud Hesperides?
Were they the sons of tea-sippers who won the fields of Cressy and Agincourt or dyed the Danube's streams with Gallic blood?

Dr Johnson declared himself to be 'a hardened and shameless tea drinker, who has for twenty years diluted his meals with only the infusion of this fascinating plant, whose kettle was scarcely time to cool, who with tea amuses the evening, with tea solaces the midnight, and with tea welcomes the morning'. Dr Johnson agreed that 'tea is a liquor not proper for the lower classes of the people'. Drinking tea was a privilege, and not yet a necessary part of the image of Englishness.

While tea caught on in the all-male coffee houses, the actual preparation and ceremony – the 'teaing' – was associated with women. If Mr Harris kept house for the Directors of the East India Company, it was Mrs Harris who took delivery of their tea, and brewed it up. In 1662 Pepys sends for a dish of tea at work, but seven years later he finds his wife drinking the stuff which the apothecary, Mr Belling, tells her is good for colds and defluxions. In 1694 Congreve has a character in *The Double Dealer* observe the ladies 'retired to their tea and scandal, according to their ancient custom', and it is Catherine, Charles II's bride, who introduces tea drinking to the royal court. She is Portuguese, and she brings the habit, and Bombay, as her dowry. Tea was a woman's preserve, and men had to conform to sobriety and gentility if they wished to share it.

Queen Anne, dull, fat and tragically childless, was an eager tea drinker like Pope, who wrote;

> Thou, great Anna, whom three realms obey,
> Dost sometimes counsel take – and sometimes tea.

Pope seems to have been the first to make a connection between tea and loneliness, writing of a lady who went to the country 'To part her time 'twixt reading and Bohea,/To muse, and spill her solitary tea.' (A contemporary observed that the waspish poet himself 'could not drink tea without a stratagem'.) Widow Twankey, from the Aladdin pantomime, is named after the second grade of China green; in the nineteenth century, 'tea kettle' was slang for an old maid.

By then the coffee houses, as coffee houses, had dwindled away. London life was never so public again. Their clientele had become too rough and too disparate to make them very attractive to men of substance and like minds. A number became deliberately exclusive, such as White's and Boodles; some just dropped the refreshments and became insurers or broking houses; others became shops, like Twinings, or chop houses, or were wound up. Tea became more than ever a private affair, dominated by women at home; with tea retailing at anything up to 36 shillings a pound it was kept from the servants in caddies to which only the mistress of the house had a key. London itself began to zone and subdivide and spread towards the west and east. The medieval tradition of townsmen living on top of one another and thronging the street began to fade as the city crept in behind the locked front door.

For the wealthy and the merely comfortable, mixing in public was licensed by the new fashion in tea gardens. Vauxhall, towards the end of the eighteenth century, was probably the most fashionable; Thackeray sends Becky Sharp et al to wander there in 1812. The gardens closed, dingy and neglected, in 1859. Other gardens aimed to mimic Vauxhall's success; not only Ranelagh, which was quite classy, but simpler gardens like Bermondsey and Hampstead, catering to the reasonably genteel. All charged an entrance fee, which might entitle you to tea and bread and butter; in contrast to coffee-houses, women were allowed to meet men and one another publicly in the tea gardens. Like cinemas, their decline attracted speculators; not a patch of green in London is in direct descent from the old gardens.

Tea wasn't popular with everyone. There had been the scares, like Hanway's, in which well-to-do tea drinkers clamoured against the people's squandering their own and the nation's resources wholesale upon a foreign herb. For every physician who approved there was one to damn the new drink, which threw some people into vapours, enfeebled the strong and spoiled the will of the labourer. The argument slipped from doctors to drinkers, who derided 'the base Indian practice of calling for tea, instead of pipes and a bottle, after dinner'; thence to the economists who were alarmed by 'men making tea an article of their diet almost as much as the women, labourers losing their time to come and go from the tea table, farmer's servants even demanding tea for their breakfasts!' In the 1740s the topers allied with Edinburgh economists and officials to encourage a campaign against the 'tea menace', pointing to the manlier attractions of domestic beer.

John Wesley thundered against the extravagance of tea, a way of squandering money that was better put to charitable uses. He remembered how his hands shook in his student days until he had given up tea. He had a headache in three days, but he prayed and the headache disappeared, and his hands too shook no longer. His London congregation gave up tea and put the money by, and in under a fortnight £30 was raised for the relief of the poor. But later Josiah Wedgwood made Wesley a five gallon tea pot which he used at Sunday breakfast parties before chapel.

During the eighteenth century tea paid duties of up to 200 per cent and almost half the tea in Britain was smuggled in from the Continent. Smugglers landed tea all along the coast, so that it reached people who might not otherwise have taken to an expensive London drink (coffee hardly figured in the smuggling trade, and its consumption was less widespread). The poor could also drink 'smouch' – British tea, as it was sometimes called – or reconditioned tea leaves. The fake tea business was enormous. There was some adulteration of coffee, too (with dandelion root, acorns, chicory and dried beans); but it was hard to get much out of a third or fourth brew. Smouch drinkers were natural candidates for real tea when the price dropped sufficiently.

With Pitt's Commutation Act of 1784 the duty was reduced to a mere 12½ per cent. The smuggling trade was demolished overnight and the appetite it had whetted was met by legal tea. Pitt's Act vastly increased the volume of the entire trade. Five million pounds were sold legally in 1784; 13 million the following year (though smugglers' agents bid up the auction prices at the first sale). The downside of cheaper tea was the compensatory window tax, which remained in force until 1851, the year of the Great Exhibition.

Tea could now be drunk by a class which had previously stuck to ale and water. Southey recalls in his Commonplace Book (1811) the family who sat down to a dish of tea, and chewed the boiled leaves with salt and butter, and wondered what everyone else saw in it. William Cobbett had a nearly obsessive grouch against tea and continued to rail against its growing popularity. In *Cottage Economy* he analyses the time it takes for a country housewife to make a pot of tea for the family, from lighting the stove at the unaccustomed hour of four, to washing up the crockery afterwards; two hours a day, he reckons, though he allows one for the sake of argument: three hundred and sixty five hours a year, or thirty whole days, a month devoted to the spurious, overpriced, unproductive business of making tea.

But Cobbett was flying in the face of events. The final impetus towards popular tea drinking was given by the temperance lobby.

Alcohol was not a serious problem amongst a predominantly rural population, but as towns grew in the shadow of the mills the problem of urban poverty and disorder grew as well. Early thunderers against Gin Alley had tended to attack tea in the same breath – Gin bottle and slop kettle. 'Slops' was established Georgian and Victorian slang for tea – slop-feeder, a tea-spoon; slop-tubs, tea things. The temperance lobby, by a rapid about turn, promoted tea as the sensible alternative to liquor. Eager reformers sang THE CUP FOR ME:

> Let others sing the praise of wine,
> Let others deem its joys divine,
> Its fleeting bliss shall ne'er be mine,
> Give me a cup of tea!

The OED says that 'teetotal' is derived from 'T-Total', mere emphatic repetition. The point is unproven. What is certain is that it was coined at the same time as the big tea-and-temperance meetings.

Tea continued to be perceived as a luxury which had to be paid for as a luxury for a long time after tea-drinking had become fairly common. In 1830 a Select Committee was told that domestics served the tea trade with their conviction that tea couldn't be good if it was cheap, and so drank 'black tea at 6s and 8s a pound, when you may drink it, in many instances, at a shilling or two less.'

By the 1870s Britons were drinking three pounds a head each – and the poor rather more, according to Mayhew (six or seven pounds). It may be the size and wealth of the booming trade which got the sum of £5000 nicknamed a 'teaspoon' in the 1850s. At first Indian teas were used to bolster Chinas, but the proportion of the mix changed gradually, until by the 1880s the importation of Indian teas outstripped China and Indian teas could be bought unmixed. Green tea, which had been the most popular sort in the eighteenth century, all but vanished as the British quickened their pursuit of strength and briskness.

Tea's naturalisation was assured in the 1850s with the invention by Anna, Duchess of Bedford, of afternoon tea. She complained of a 'sinking feeling' between the gaieties of lunch and dinner, and instituted afternoon tea with pastries at five o'clock as an excuse for entertaining again. You were meant to arrive a little late, and leave by six o'clock after one cup.

We owe much of the stylisation of 'Britishness', from tartan plaid to royal ceremonial, to the Victorians, and tea is no exception. To a people with a passion for ritual, the rites of tea proved irresistible. The Japanese have their *cha no yu*, but the British ceremony is no less elaborate for being unnamed. The number of separate utensils that can be used to make a cup of tea is staggering, each one performing a precise duty in a ritual series. Few of them have any function beyond the tea table. Tea was ceremonial before the Victorians, but it was they who codified it, and presented it, like Mrs Beeton, in its absolute and inviolable form.

The Dutch, who were the first Europeans to appreciate tea, had introduced the tea-room in the early seventeenth century: a part of the house reserved for taking tea rather like the English parlour kept, along with the good china, 'for best'. Seventeenth century Dutch paintings show the *theeraak*, a set of hanging shelves for stowing the tea tackle. Dutch tackle included cups for steeping saffron in boiling water, which was customarily added to green tea.

Until the early eighteenth century, in Holland and England, tea was usually drunk from the saucer with appropriate snuffles and slurps of appreciation; once the Chinese cups were given handles the problem of hot tea was solved and the practice discontinued. The memory of the habit is perpetuated in Victorian taboo. Even my grandmother thought it worthwhile to warn me not to drink from the saucer, although the idea never entered my head. It was common, she said – the same thing went for slurping noises.

Tea cups were initially tiny thanks to the exorbitant price of tea, but as it began falling – from 35s for a pound of bohea in 1709 to 14s in 1775 – tea cups accordingly grew. Dr Johnson's celebrated quart cup was an eccentricity. Breakfast cups, which are larger than tea-time tea cups, were adapted from morning coffee. Teaspoons, which start out the size of coffee-spoons, get bigger too. De Quincey writes of teaspoons the size of the dessert-spoons of his youth (with asperity: it made it hard to regulate his laudanum dose).

By the early nineteenth century the drawing room of a well-to-do British household could be furnished with a lidded table containing the paraphernalia for 'teaing', known as a teapoy, or teapoise. (The word is Hindi for a three-legged table; the false connection was first made in London, where 'teapoy' was introduced to describe a tea chest on legs. A four-legged table in Hindi is called a *charpoy* – and there is no tea

connection there, either.) Out of the teapoy came the teapot and the tea
caddy – a box usually with two compartments lined in lead to seal in the
aroma, which may have originally held a catty or so of tea, and a small
tea shovel or spoon. Such caddies have died out along with the custom of
buying loose tea; now most people who buy their tea pre-packed in a tin
call that a caddy as well.

In Holland and New Amsterdam (New York), both loaf-sugar and
powdered sugar were provided in what was called a 'bite and stir' box (the
loaf sugar was nibbled). Modern sugar lumps are only refined sugar
compressed. The original custom survives in Russia, where tea may be
sipped through a sugar lump held in the mouth. For the lumps, sugar
tongs. There is the milk jug. The tea strainer comes with a shallow rest
to avoid staining the tea cloth; and with the tea cosy, and perhaps a spirit
lamp and a tea stand – and the tea-tray and -table and -trolley there are
enough things to carry the point that tea is ceremonial.

Clearly the mid-Victorians merely set their imprimatur upon a ceremony
which was already established. The proper way to make tea, with some at
least of the required utensils, lays down an inevitable order of service.
Père Couplet as early as 1667 said tea should be allowed to brew 'as long
as it takes to chant the Miserere slowly'. The British had not evolved the
ceremony in isolation: besides the Dutch impetus, Madame de Sévigné is
credited with the idea of putting milk in tea.

A corpus of liturgy and stylised activity had already grown up around
the serving of tea. This is the catechism:
A watched kettle never boils.
Warm the pot.
One for each person and one for the pot.
Take the pot to the kettle, not the kettle to the pot.
Milk in first.
One lump or two? (For the response)

The ceremony is deliberately conversational – 'the gossip of the tea table
is not bad preparatory school for the brothel,' as Cobbett rather hysterically
puts it. Tea is a rite which has gathered its own mysteries, as rites will.
Some of the litany and parts of the equipage are atavistic, with only the
mysteries of tradition to recommend them. No other domestic activity is
so stylised, so encumbered with dead tradition; it could be the tridentine
mass in the hands of Bishop Lefebvre – or the investiture of a British

monarch. Sugar cubes represent the height of stylisation with the minimum of utility. The roots of the milk-in-first argument lie in the false assumption that hot tea would crack thin porcelain. The days are long gone when tea was first served in new-fangled thin china, but the assertion is still made, and has congealed into a hotly disputed point of etiquette. The truth is that the tea should go in first: hot tea poured onto milk becomes greasy. But then the royal family put MIF, which might settle the matter. It is a letters-to-*The Times* debate, on a par with the question of whether trimmings should be removed from a lawn, or not.

The British were attached to tea by the late nineteenth century: they were not yet inseparable. The French spoke of '*thé anglais*' first in 1878. Tea was not fully incorporated into the 'image' of England until that image began to evolve towards the turn of the century. Then tea was found to dovetail very neatly indeed.

By the late nineteenth century an awareness of the British Empire, and of India's position in it, was being actively fostered among the common people of Britain. Disraeli, the conservative who widened the franchise in 1868, had Queen Victoria proclaimed Empress of India in 1882: it was pure showmanship pitched at the innate conservatism and chauvinistic pride of the working classes, and it kept the Tories in power for a generation. Tea was a British Empire product. An advertisement from the 1890s shows Victoria in her familiar black bombazine, trailing lace from her hair to her shoulders, a pinched little man beside her. The legend runs: Mr President, can I offer you a cup of India or Ceylon tea?

The approved set of 'English values', something like bowdlerised Burke, could be summed up as 'common sense'. They were to be found in the British 'sense' of fair play, the British 'sense' of humour, the British 'sense' of proportion. Being sensible had saved Britons from the absurd extremism of foreigners, with their love of abstracts and arbitrariness, kilos and revolutions.

All the same this immoderate faith in their own superior moderation must have teetered on the ridiculous. Self-deprecating humour was perhaps the instrument with which the British tried to preserve the balance. Noel Coward turned it on the empire; P. G. Wodehouse upon the upper middle classes; Sid James on the common man. Eccentricity – rooted defiance of normal behaviour – won the affection of the public. 'We are surely the least quarrelsome of all nations,' wrote a historian as late as 1956, 'and in this the tea-table has undoubtedly played its part.' The British were different.

Tea was one of the totems by which this Englishman could be recognised, along with the brolly, the bowler and the pea-soup fog. Lord Emsworth returns from America having remarked nothing but the eccentricity of people who put their tea in little paper bags. The rest of the world seemed happy to accept this image of an Englishman: the pig-bound outlook of the aristocrat or the rule-book trade unionist claiming his tea-break.

Coward wrote the screenplay for the classic weepie, *Brief Encounter*. The film is about a suburban adultery which never gets within consulting distance of the Hayes Code of Ethics. It's hard to imagine the story standing up in, say, France or even America. Celia Johnson does the sensible thing in the end. The film opens and closes in the tea room of a railway station: the first shot is stirring. It's bathos, English and repressed. It is a storm in a tea-cup.

The Portrait of a Lady opens upon 'the ceremony known as afternoon tea.' The anglomaniacal Henry James calls the tea hour 'an eternity of pleasure.' By constant repetition through generations the ceremony has acquired the power to affirm stability and continuity. A Chinese poem describes tea as a bridge to men of old: in the moment of eternity, the familiar making and serving of tea, the bridge is incessantly remade, strengthened, and carried forward. Hence, too, the 'Blitz Spirit' brewed in innumerable mugs of hot, sweet tea, proclaiming through the chaos and uncertainty and the slippery grasp on 'civilised values', Business As Usual.

The effect of 'a nice cup of tea' (a phrase also coined in the mid-nineteenth century) is to deflate over-excitement. Mawkish attempts are being made to win Youth over with a phony image of tea as a cool and trendy bev, but tea will not be dolled up. While sales of ordinary tea decline the so-called speciality teas, the 'traditional' grands crus like Darjeeling and Earl Grey (Victorians, both), are selling like never before.

Coffee and chocolate have gathered no charms, but the rites of tea suggest by repetition a continuity with the past, and so have learned to foretell the future. Reading the leaves must have begun very soon after the introduction of tea into England, because Charles Churchill in 'The Ghost' in 1725 writes of:

Matrons, who toss the cup, and see
The grounds of fate in grounds of tea.

Other superstitions have grown up around the act. To stir the water in the pot is asking for trouble; bubbles rising in your cup mean kisses are coming; a floating leaf warns of the impending arrival of a stranger, whereupon you fish it out, put it on the back of your hand and count how many times you have to tap the hand before the leaf falls off, to tell how many days he'll take to arrive. You should expect plenty of strangers if you make tea without boiling the water, and a girl who lets a man pour her a second cup is doomed to succumb to his designs.

Restrained abracadabra, all passion in prospect. To take part in the ritual of tea is to enter a moment of control. You could not murder over the tea table. *Arsenic And Old Lace*, after all, is comedy.

Epilogue

At Greenwich (where Charles II welcomed his tea-drinking, Bombay-bringing Queen Catherine) the *Cutty Sark*, the last surviving tea clipper, is in dry dock at the water's edge. Her masts are visible from the river, dominating the little terraces and the plain pilots' houses like a church. The mainmast soars 145 feet, bravely decked with fluttering pennants and rigged in tracery. It is not hard to imagine the dark outline of the topmost spar seeming to brush the stars at night, moonlit on the South China Sea while running down the Indo-China strait with a load of fragrant tea. Like a church, too, the *Cutty Sark* is a place of pilgrimage and worship, and a rough and gaudy wooden congregation is assembled in the hold, a collection of figureheads rescued from gardens on the South Coast and from Sales of Goods at washed-up shipbreakers' yards, here to pay homage to the survivor: a long-sleeved Chinaman from the Mandarin, Jolly Jack Tar with parrot and eye-patch, and juicy wenches in numb coquetry with one massive Negro who rolls his eyes in eternal appreciation.

The figurehead of the *Cutty Sark* is the witch of the Burns ballad. She is luminous and her teeth are bared; in her outstretched fist she holds the mare's tail. It's a sinister carving: the witch hangs where the dry black bulk of the graceful cutter is brought to a knifepoint; one frozen outflung arm towards the river, and blind eyes searching the water.

I had found traces of the tea trade all through *Lord Jim*. Even the ill-fated pilgrim ship, the scene of the white men's corruption, was called

Patna, like the opium that tea traders ran up the China coast. The inquiry into the events aboard the *Patna* is chaired by a Captain Brierly – a thinly veiled portrait of the real Captain Wallace. Wallace skippered the *Cutty Sark*, and he may well have been on the Min estuary to load teas, keeping an eye on the pagoda, cutting up to Fuzhou in a jolly-boat, in the 1870s. Conrad never met Wallace, but he read about him in the papers, and followed up the eventual inquiry in the records. He used him as Captain Brierly in *Lord Jim*, and in a short story, *The Secret Sharer*.

Both Wallace and the *Cutty Sark*, skipper and ship, met with tragic ends. The witch strains towards the water she can never reach: ironies had dogged the vessel from her launch and ominous naming in 1869. She was built to compete with the fastest ship afloat, the *Thermopylae*, and she raced tea twice. The first year her rudder broke; the second, when she was running almost neck and neck with *Thermopylae* across the Indian Ocean, her mainmast sheered off. Before she had a third chance steam had destroyed the point of her. She was hived off onto the Australian wool and tea run, where she clocked up dozens of speed records, unobserved. She had been a whisker from success, just like her namesake, when her prospects of glory were petrified by history. She was too late.

When Captain Wallace took command of the *Cutty Sark* in 1880, she was carrying coal. His first mate – 'a notorious Yankee bucko' – struck and killed a malingering sailor. The mate was clapped in irons to be returned to England and the courts; but Captain Wallace allowed him to jump ship in an Eastern port. Whether the mate had killed in self-defence was never established, for not even Captain Wallace returned for the inquest.

Whether he became alarmed at the possibility of his own disgrace, or recognised an affront to justice, will never be clear. One night he set a long course, did the rounds of the ship, had his dog locked up and walked off the side of the ship into the sea at four bells.

Glossary

amah wet-nurse, nanny
babu native clerk who writes English
bandh strike, boycott
banji dormant period
burra sahib big boss
cash low-value coin
catty a weight (1.33 lb avoirdupois)
cha no yu Japanese tea ceremony
chin, chin-chin salutations, adieu
chokidar watchman
chop 1. seal; trademark; brand of goods; 2. batch of chests; 3. lighter
chota sahib small boss
chow-chow mixed goods, assortment
comprador native agent employed by European house, butler, victualler
cumshaw gratuity, baksheesh
da cha large-leaf tea
fanqui foreign devil
gerao a surrounding
griffin newcomer to India
Hong corporation of Chinese merchants *or* foreign factory or business in China/Japan
Hoppo The Chinese Superintendent of Customs at Canton

jaozes dumplings
jat strain of tea
jelabah/djellaba Arab headdress
kakemono Japanese wall painting on silk
kang bed built of brick or earth, heated with a fire underneath
kung-fu Chinese form of unarmed combat; hard work or mastery of skill
kurtha loose shirt worn outside trousers
kutharee dagger
lakh, lac 100,000 rupees
lingo linguist
lunghi length of cloth worn around waist
mimi secrets
'oula Custom' old custom, established practice
pan-leaves betel leaves
peon messenger
poey drying
renminbi people's money
sampan boat of Chinese pattern
samshoo Chinese rice spirit
shikari guide to European sportsmen
shroff examiner of coin
singsongs automata
smouch adulterated tea
smug boats boats in contraband trade
supercargo superintendent of cargo on merchant ship
tai-chi Chinese martial arts
taipan head of company
tatching rolling and roasting of tea-leaves
topee sunhat
yen cha rock tea